Interactive Language Teaching

CAMBRIDGE LANGUAGE TEACHING LIBRARY
A series of authoritative books on subjects of central importance for all
language teachers.

In this series:

Teaching and Learning Languages *by Earl W. Stevick*

Communicating Naturally in a Second Language – Theory and practice in
language teaching *by Wilga M. Rivers*

Speaking in Many Tongues – Essays in foreign language teaching
by Wilga M. Rivers

Teaching the Spoken Language – An approach based on the analysis of
conversational English *by Gillian Brown and George Yule*

A Foundation Course for Language Teachers *by Tom McArthur*

Foreign and Second Language Learning – Language-acquisition research
and its implications for the classroom *by William Littlewood*

Communicative Methodology in Language Teaching – The roles of fluency
and accuracy *by Christopher Brumfit*

The Context of Language Teaching *by Jack C. Richards*

English for Science and Technology – A discourse approach
by Louis Trimble

Approaches and Methods in Language Teaching – A description and
analysis *by Jack C. Richards and Theodore S. Rodgers*

Images and Options in the Language Classroom *by Earl W. Stevick*

Culture Bound – Bridging the cultural gap in language teaching
edited by Joyce Merrill Valdes

Interactive Language Teaching *edited by Wilga M. Rivers*

Interactive
Language Teaching

Edited by
Wilga M. Rivers
Harvard University

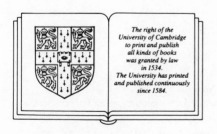

The right of the
University of Cambridge
to print and publish
all kinds of books
was granted by law
in 1534.
The University has printed
and published continuously
since 1584.

Cambridge University Press
Cambridge
London   New York   New Rochelle
Melbourne   Sydney

Published by the Press Syndicate of the University of Cambridge
The Pitt Building, Trumpington Street, Cambridge CB2 1RP
32 East 57th Street, New York, NY 10022, USA
10 Stamford Road, Oakleigh, Melbourne 3166, Australia

First published 1987

Printed in the United States of America

Library of Congress Cataloging-in-Publication Data
Interactive language teaching.
(Cambridge language teaching library)
Bibliography: p.
Includes index.
1. Language and languages – Study and teaching.
2. Social interaction.   I. Rivers, Wilga M.   II. Series.
P53.I517   1987   407'.1   86–13716
ISBN 0 521 32216 2 hardcover
ISBN 0 521 31108 X paperback

"Scaffolding" from *Poems 1965–1975* by Seamus Heaney. © 1966, 1969,
1972, 1975, 1980 by Seamus Heaney. Reprinted by permission of Farrar, Straus
& Giroux, Inc., and Faber & Faber Ltd.

"Fatigue" by Peggy Bacon reprinted by permission; © 1932, 1960 by The New
Yorker Magazine, Inc.

"Solomon Grundy" by Martin Bell reprinted by permission of John Milne.

Portions of "What has happened to Lulu?" from *Collected Poems* by Charles
Causley (Macmillan) reprinted by permission of David Higham Associates Ltd.

Contents

Section I   What is interactive language teaching?

Section II   Language in the classroom

Contents

Contributors

Robert Ariew, Associate Professor of French and Director of the Center for Computer Assisted Instruction, College of the Liberal Arts, The Pennsylvania State University, has published on computer-assisted instruction and the use of media in teaching foreign languages. His publications include works on pedagogy, textbooks, and software for teaching French and Spanish.

Raymond F. Comeau, Assistant Dean and Coordinator of Romance Languages at the Harvard University Extension School, is co-author of *Ensemble*, an intermediate French program consisting of three integrated textbooks, and *Echanges*, a beginning French textbook using the Direct Method. He has taught a variety of French language and literature courses at the Harvard University Extension School, Boston University, Wayne State University, and the University of Kansas.

Anne R. Dow has been Director of ESL Programs at Harvard University since 1972 and has twelve years' experience teaching academically oriented adults. She has developed extensive home-study programs for Japan: *Pro-English Learning System* (audio) and *In America* (video) for adults, and *Disney's World of English* (multimedia) for children.

Judith G. Frommer, Senior Preceptor in Romance Languages and Literatures at Harvard University, has developed audiovisual materials and, most recently, an authoring system for computer-assisted language learning on the Macintosh. Her publications include French textbooks (*Face à Face*, *La France et la francophonie*) and articles on language teaching. She has given numerous workshops on methodology, curricula, and computer-assisted instruction.

Claire J. Kramsch, Professor of Foreign Language Acquisition and Head of Foreign Languages and Literatures at the Massachusetts Institute of Technology, has published extensively on the teaching and learning of foreign languages in classroom settings. Her publications, which address specifically the dimensions of discourse in language learning, include two books on methodology and one textbook.

Alan Maley, currently responsible for coordinating British Council programs in India, and formerly English Language Officer in Yugoslavia, Ghana, Italy, France, and China, has published widely in the field of creative methodology and materials. His books include *Drama Tech-*

niques in Language Learning, Poem into Poem, The Mind's Eye, and *The Inward Ear* – a resource book for the teaching of poetry.

Bernice S. Melvin is the Margaret Root Brown Associate Professor of Foreign Languages and Literatures at Austin College in Sherman, Texas. She has published articles on the implications of memory models for foreign-language acquisition and has also worked on projects to adapt authentic video material for use in first-year French classes.

Marlies Mueller, Director of Teacher Training for French at Harvard University since 1975, has developed curricula of language courses at various levels, researched foreign-language teaching in American high schools for the American Academy of Arts and Sciences, and evaluated tests used by the U.S. Armed Forces. Her publications include a textbook for elementary French (*A Propos*), articles on teaching language and literature, and a socio-historical criticism of seventeenth-century French literature.

Anthony Papalia, former Chairman of the Department of Instruction at the State University of New York at Buffalo, published extensively on the teaching of a second language. His publications include works on learner-centered language teaching, learning styles and learning strategies, interactive behaviors in the classroom, and modern languages for communication. He was also the director of masters and doctoral programs in foreign- and second-language education at SUNY Buffalo.

Karen Price is Associate Director for Research and Program Development in ESL at Harvard University. Teacher, consultant, researcher, and international lecturer on visuals and technology in foreign-language learning since 1974, she patented an audiovisual device in 1976 and is a Steering Committee member of the TESOL Computer-Assisted Language Learning Group.

Wilga M. Rivers, Professor of Romance Languages and Literatures and Coordinator of Language Instruction at Harvard University, has published numerous books and articles on the theory and practice of language teaching, drawing insights from psychology and linguistics. Specific books deal with the teaching of English as a second or foreign language, French, German, Spanish, and Hebrew. She has lectured in twenty-eight countries and her publications have been translated into nine languages.

Gail L. N. Robinson, Executive Director of the Center for Language and Crosscultural Skills in San Francisco, has served as Language Teaching Research Specialist, SONY Language Laboratory, Tokyo; and Senior Research Officer, N.S.W. Department of Education, Sydney. She has also taught modern languages, ESL, and cross-cultural education. Her most recent publications are *Crosscultural Understanding, Computer-*

Assisted Instruction in Foreign Languages, and *Issues in Second Language and Crosscultural Education.*

Gloria M. Russo, formerly coordinator of the multilevel language sequence of the French Department at the University of Virginia, has published works on language teaching, teacher training, and eighteenth-century French literature, as well as textbooks.

Joseph T. Ryan, Jr., has taught a variety of English for Specific Purposes programs in eight different countries since 1970. He is currently coordinator of a Business Case Study Program for international students at Harvard Summer School and coordinator of a program for International Teaching Associates at Northeastern University in Boston.

Stephen A. Sadow is Associate Professor of Modern Languages at Northeastern University in Boston, where he teaches Spanish and where, in 1982, he was awarded the university's Excellence in Teaching Award. His writings in foreign-language pedagogy have centered on ways of provoking student creativity, utilizing group process, and increasing cross-cultural awareness. He is the author of *Idea Bank,* a resource book for teachers. He also has extensive experience teaching English as a second language.

David F. Stout is Associate Professor of German and Chair of the Department of Foreign Languages at Austin College in Sherman, Texas. Since 1979 he has worked with colleagues in various language organizations and in seminars sponsored by the National Endowment for the Humanities and the Goethe Institut to produce and distribute authentic language materials. He has produced several video programs for language instruction as well.

Peter Strevens, Director-General of the Bell Education Trust, Cambridge, is also Chairman of the International Association of Teachers of English as a Foreign Language. He has published extensively in the fields of applied linguistics, language teaching, teacher training, and English as a foreign language.

Richard Via is currently an Educational Specialist at the Institute of Culture and Communication, East-West Center, Honolulu, Hawaii. His interest in using drama for language teaching began while in Japan on a Fulbright Grant after twenty-three years as actor-stage manager for Broadway Theatre. He is author of *English in Three Acts,* a book about using drama in the language classroom.

Preface

A group of school children in Thailand responds to the stranger's question, "Do you like English?" with a firm, clear "Yes, we do." On the Bund in Shanghai, a two-year-old in his father's arms sees the fair-haired, round-eyed lady and immediately pipes up: "Hello! Hello! How are you? How are you? How do you do! How do you do!" In Japan, signs in English proliferate, both public and private. In London and Paris, business people rush off to proprietary schools for foreign-language lessons with their next assignment in mind. In the United States, interest in foreign languages is on the rise in the community and in colleges, and international students pour in to study English before undertaking advanced studies. The problems of second-language learners in India, Singapore, and Hong Kong are the subject of much research, as practical ways of improving the learners' use of the language are sought. Will we miss, through conservatism or inertia, this new wave of enthusiasm for what has always enthused us? In this atmosphere of opportunity, *what shall we do in class today*? This is the teacher's urgent question – a question that we, the authors of this book, have tried to answer.

Classroom teachers are close to students. As they watch their students learning languages, they note perennial problems of language learners – some specific to learners from particular language communities and others common to learners of a particular level of maturity or social experience. Hoping to find solutions, they turn to books or meetings for ideas on how to develop an environment and techniques conducive to confident and effective language use.

Over the last few years, however, teachers have been dragged "every which way," as competing notions about language learning have been hammered out in public debate. Sometimes ideas based on informal learning by immigrant children (in situations where the new language is used all about them, but nobody understands their first language) have been enthusiastically, and sometimes unreflectively, extrapolated to formal language learning by adolescents who feel no immediate need for another language (except perhaps to pass an imminent examination). At other times, what has been effective in developing early communication skills with an experimental group in a psychologist's office is promoted as the answer for language learners in classes of fifty with a teacher whose own knowledge of the language is very limited. Some of the ideas put forward have been based on well-documented research, some on experimental classes that could not be shown to have achieved significantly better results than a more traditional class (or whose poor progress has been explained away as resulting from faults in experimental design).

The goals of approaches that are proposed also change. This frequently parallels a normal shift as times change, reflecting community perceptions of the place of language in the education a certain society desires for its children. (Language-teaching goals are usually situation- and place-bound.[1]) Sometimes, however, these shifts result from arbitrary decisions of protagonists in intellectual debate and have little relationship to needs in particular countries, districts, or schools.

In recent years we have moved from the listening, speaking, reading, writing goals of audiolingualism, with its inductive approach and structured learning, to the deductive, rule-learning cognitive code approach, where listening, reading, and speaking come after learning grammar rules.[2] Then the stress moved to communicative competence (of the structured kind with discourse functions or the unstructured kind with an emphasis on pragmatic functions and much talking[3]), and for a while there was little reference to reading or writing. Next came the structured Silent Way, with attentive listening to a reduced input, the emphasis being on inductive thinking, problem solving, and production of utterances by the student in carefully circumscribed circumstances. In the unstructured, inductive Total Physical Response there was plenty of "comprehensible input," visually accompanied, but with deeds, not words, as response. In Counseling-Learning/Community Language Learning the input was the interlanguage of other students, not the authentic materials from native speakers and writers that were also being actively promoted at the same time.[4] With Suggestopaedia, the learning of much vocabulary was back, in long dialogues that are first studied and translated in printed form, then in lengthy sessions of listening preceding the communicative activities that provide opportunities for students to use what they have absorbed rather than memorized.[5] In the Natural Approach the mother tongue is banned (as previously in the

1 "Educational Goals: The Foreign Language Teacher's Response," in Rivers (1983b), reports language-teaching goals from fifty countries.
2 Audiolingualism is described fully in Rivers (1981: 38–48). For a brief description of cognitive code learning see Rivers (1981: 49–51) and Chastain (1976).
3 On communicative competence see Finocchiaro and Brumfit (1983); on pragmatic functions see Savignon (1983).
4 On Silent Way see Gattegno (1972); on Total Physical Response see Asher (1966). *Comprehensible input* is defined in Krashen and Terrell (1983: 36). On Counseling-Learning/Community Language Learning see Curran (1976); *interlanguage* is defined in Selinker (1972).
5 Lozanov (1978).

direct method) and there is much comprehensible input, in the form of simplified teacher talk, again with much vocabulary; speaking is delayed but the reading of what one is hearing is advanced; and affective, humanistic activities eventually encourage the productive use of inductively acquired language.[6]

In the past, students have memorized dialogues and spent long hours substituting items in pattern drills, in accordance with audiolingual edicts. They have tried to express their own meaning from the beginning without studying forms, as in Counseling-Learning/Community Language Learning. They have studied rules and paradigms and endeavored to construct grammatically well-formed utterances at the teacher's behest. They have jumped up and down, carried books on their heads, and hidden the chalk behind the door. But have they learned to communicate their own meaning with each other? we may ask.

And so we dance around the act of communication that is still our central goal, whether we mean communication between speakers or through the written text, as in many Language for Specific Purposes and Language through Literature classes. Should we listen a great deal? Should we read a great deal? Should we write? (Some people point out that knowledge of the culture of the other parties is an important feature of communication.) Is it not possible that language use is such a multifaceted process that there are many ways to approach its acquisition (or the learning of it)? Yet it is a process, and we need experience in the process.

Controversies that arise in the language-teaching profession are interesting, even exciting, as ideas and proposals are thrashed out in journals and workshops. Language teachers need these new ideas to refresh their minds and revitalize their teaching. Frequently, however, they come back from their search confused and befuddled by a plethora of conflicting assertions and recommendations. The next day they must go straight back into the classroom to teach. Their students, with their lives before them, cannot wait until conclusive answers have been found for the problems of language learning and teaching. Teachers must make the most of what they have learned from others, sift it, sort it, and select from it according to their own experiences in a particular situation.

What can we sift from these conflicting claims, assertions, and proposals from leaders in the profession? As we have seen, *communication, whether in speech or writing, remains our central goal* as language teachers. Communication derives essentially from *interaction*. Someone has something to share with someone else, who is interested and attentive while the interest (and therewith the interaction) lasts. If communication of message (spoken or written) in another language is our objective,

6 Krashen and Terrell (1983).

then interaction must be present from the first encounter with the language. (Interaction implies both reception and expression of messages.[7]) But, note, interaction takes place when interest (attention to the communicative act) is present. Where there is no interest, there may be a perfunctory exchange of words, but communication of personal messages does not take place. To promote interaction in another language, we must maintain a lively attention and active participation among our students. Interest and desire to participate have deeper roots than mere surface reactions would indicate. Emotions, the impulse to guard oneself from hurt, fear of peers or authority figures, desire to excel, to please, to be successful, anxieties based on factors of which the teacher is ignorant – all of these militate for or against a comfortable participation.

For interaction, then, more is necessary than a set of techniques or devotion to a particular approach. There must be cultivated relationships that encourage initiation of interactive activities from either side, because interaction is not just a matter of words. Words express or camouflage the interactive intent. Students need to participate in activities that engage their interest and attention, so that the interaction becomes natural[8] and desirable and words slip out, or pour out, to accompany it. Establishing such a situation requires of the teacher the greatest pedagogical skill and keeps his or her own interest high as well. Dynamic, exciting classes are within the grasp of all teachers if they learn to involve the imagination and activity of all. (This approach, *interactive language teaching*, is discussed more fully in chap. 1, this volume.) Interactive techniques are available to all because they are invented by all, as the writers of the various chapters in this book demonstrate. Consequently, each teacher becomes the architect of his or her own success in the classroom.

Fortunately, there are many excellent classes all over the world. As language teachers we are a group with mutual interests and concerns. We need to share experiences and experimentation. Researchers and scholars can explain many facts of language to us; they can open our eyes to many facets of how languages are learned and used; they can explain to us the dynamics of groups – but what are we to do about all this? It is for us as teachers to decide. We know *our* students; we know *their* needs; we know what *we* can do confidently. What is appropriate for an adult immigrant learning a second language in order to live and work in a new land, or for a college student studying abroad, is not necessarily going to help a young boy or girl learning a foreign language in an isolated village. In fact, we must recognize that *foreign-language learning* (that is, in situations where the language is rarely heard, except

7 See skill-getting and skill-using model in Rivers (1983a: 43).
8 See "The Natural and the Normal in Language Learning" in Rivers (1983a: 104–13).

in recorded or broadcast form) is quite different from *second-language learning* (where the learner is surrounded by a community that uses the language for its daily purposes). The former is limited to what the teacher can give or arrange for the student to receive; in the latter case, the class contribution can be immediately supplemented at the will of the student who enters a shop, talks to a fellow-passenger on a bus, turns a switch on a radio or television, or picks up a newspaper or magazine. (The exception, of course, is the group of "second-language" learners who are restricted in their access to association with the majority-language community, through prejudice, hostility, or governmental decree – an unfortunate situation that still exists in some areas.)

Nor are these the only differences in our situations. Some are teaching students who wish to know how to use the language as fast as possible in a specific work situation. Others are preparing students to read particular kinds of material in the new language. Yet others are providing students with a mind-expanding experience of the way another people thinks, feels, and expresses itself, as an element of the students' general education. Still others, perhaps reluctantly, are overtly preparing students for some particular proficiency hurdle that will determine their career options. We hope that all, no matter what their type of course, will find some ideas in what we have written to enrich and enliven their teaching and that our ideas will stimulate theirs.

All the authors in this book are experienced practicing teachers, as well as writers of books, articles, and teaching materials. They are well aware of the latest trends and specific needs. They themselves have been incorporating into their own teaching, in an imaginative fashion, insights into the ways in which languages are learned, while experimenting with teaching approaches that promote communication in speech and writing. They are sharing with you here what they themselves do, in the hope that this will stimulate you in your individual thinking and planning. Write to us; share with us. We, in our turn, will be happy to share further with you. We enjoy interaction too.

This book, for the most part, is geared toward the practical, everyday concerns of our professional life. The first two articles set out more theoretical ideas that have shaped our thinking: the first deals with cognitive psychology and what we can learn about the interaction of perception and expression in oral or graphic communication; the second discusses the dynamics of interaction in the classroom. These may be read and discussed at the beginning or at the end of the course, depending on the sophistication and previous experience of the group. In fact, all the articles are self-contained and may be approached in any order that suits the purposes of the course or the individual reader. The suggested activities appended to each chapter are designed to help you incorporate into your own teaching adaptations of the ideas expressed, in ways that are appropriate to the objectives of your students in the particular situation in which you find yourself. We have personally selected what we consider to be the most immediately useful readings, should you wish to explore any area in greater depth, and we have annotated these. We have chosen only books and articles that you should be able to find without undue difficulty; full bibliographical references to sources from which we have drawn may be found in the bibliography. For teacher-training programs, the references in the annotated reading lists will supply a shelf of basic readings as the nucleus for a more fully developed library.

To all who have influenced us and helped shape our thinking we are grateful, especially to the many teachers who have asked questions and shared their experiences with us at meetings, in workshops, and in teacher-training seminars. We are still learning; so too, we hope, are you.

A special thank you is due to Claire Riley, Thérèse Chevallier-Stril-Rever, and Deanne Lundin-Manson, whose energetic endeavors kept us all in touch and enabled us to put a joint manuscript together, despite long distances and busy schedules.

Wilga M. Rivers,
for all the
co-authors of this book

Abbreviations

used in annotated readings lists, footnotes, and bibliography

ACTFL	American Council on the Teaching of Foreign Languages (Hastings-on-Hudson, New York)
AL	*Applied Linguistics* (Oxford: Oxford University Press)
CMLR	*Canadian Modern Language Review* (Welland, Ontario)
EFL	English as a foreign language
ELA	*Etudes de Linguistique Appliquée* (Paris: Didier Erudition)
ESL	English as a second language
ETS	Educational Testing Services (Princeton, New Jersey)
FL	Foreign language
FLA	*Foreign Language Annals* (ACTFL)
FR	*French Review* (American Association of Teachers of French)
IRAL	*International Review of Applied Linguistics in Language Teaching* (Heidelberg: Julius Gross Verlag)
LL	*Language Learning* (Ann Arbor, Michigan)
MLJ	*Modern Language Journal* (Madison, Wisconsin)
NEC	Northeast Conference on the Teaching of Foreign Languages (Middlebury, Vermont)
TESOL	Teachers of English to Speakers of Other Languages (Washington, D.C.)
TQ	*TESOL Quarterly* (TESOL, Washington, D.C.)

Section I What is interactive language teaching?

1 Interaction as the key to teaching language for communication

Wilga M. Rivers

I remember my first language class. I was eleven at the time, living in a country where the language was never heard, except in a small expatriate club lost in a big city. We were many thousands of miles from any place where the language was spoken and our teacher had certainly never been there. Along with some thirty-five other eager almost-teens I had the time of my life. We all remember our young teacher with great affection.

We performed actions; we handled objects; we drew large pictures and labeled them; we sang; we danced; we learned poems; we read little stories, which we acted out and improvised upon. I rushed home after the first lesson, on a scorching February day, sat on the step of a wooden washhouse, and read aloud in French to my monolingual mother as she stirred our clothes in a wood-fired copper. The French was probably execrable, but I couldn't wait to share with her the exciting information that our flag was red, white, and blue, whereas the French flag was blue, white, and red. Of course, that night I diligently drew, colored, and labeled the flags in my new language.

How did this young teacher arouse such enthusiasm for her esoteric subject? First of all, she loved young people and she loved teaching. She used her imagination as she shared with us the knowledge, perhaps imperfect, she possessed. She had us doing things and living them in a vicarious way. She wove us into a group who worked together, talked together, played together, and were interdependent in our progress. Her methodology was some form of modified direct method, probably best labeled as eclectic (Rivers 1981: 35, 54–5). It was active, imaginative, and innovative, and clearly reflected our teacher's individual personality – all ingredients for effective language teaching (or for any teaching, for that matter). She developed a rapport with us that made us want to communicate with her and with each other in situations that stimulated our interest and involvement.[1]

---

1 The author pays tribute to Kathleen Meldrum of Essendon High School in Victoria, Australia.

Wilga M. Rivers

The centrality of interaction

Students achieve facility in *using* a language when their attention is focused on conveying and receiving authentic messages (that is, messages that contain information of interest to speaker and listener in a situation of importance to both). This is *interaction*. As Wells has expressed it: "Exchange is the basic unit of discourse.... Linguistic interaction is a collaborative activity" involving "the establishment of a triangular relationship between the sender, the receiver and the context of situation" (Wells 1981: 29, 46–7), whether the communication be in speech or writing. (For Wells the content of the message is part of the "situation.")

Interaction involves not just expression of one's own ideas but comprehension of those of others. One listens to others; one responds (directly or indirectly); others listen and respond. The participants work out interpretations of meaning through this interaction, which is always understood in a context, physical or experiential, with nonverbal cues adding aspects of meaning beyond the verbal. All of these factors should be present as students learn to communicate: listening to others, talking with others, negotiating meaning in a shared context. A structured sequence or structured activities we may or may not have; we may promote inductive or deductive learning,[2] or a mixture of the two; but communication there must be – interaction between people who have something to share.

Collaborative activity of this type should be the norm *from the beginning of language study*. Part of the teacher's art is to create, or stimulate student creation of, the types of situations in which interaction naturally blossoms and in which students can use for actual communication what they have been learning in a more formal fashion. In this way, they are already engaging in the central activity for which language is used in human relations.

Why is interaction so important in language-learning situations? Through interaction, students can increase their language store as they listen to or read authentic linguistic material, or even the output of their fellow students in discussions, skits, joint problem-solving tasks, or dialogue journals. (As teachers, we frequently overlook how much students learn from their peers.) In interaction, students can use all they possess of the language – all they have learned or casually absorbed – in real-life exchanges where expressing their real meaning is important to them. They thus have experience in creating messages from what they hear, since comprehension is a process of creation (Rivers 1981: 160–2), and

---

2 In this chapter, and throughout this book, the words *acquisition* and *learning* are used interchangeably, not as Krashen (1981: 1–3) uses them to distinguish between "subconscious *acquisition*" and "conscious *learning*," except when specific reference is being made to Krashen's Monitor model.

4

in creating discourse that conveys their intentions. Even at an elementary stage they learn, in this way, to exploit the elasticity of language, to make the little they know go a long way. The brain is *dynamic*, constantly interrelating what we have learned with what we are learning, and the give-and-take of message exchanges enables students to retrieve and interrelate a great deal of what they have encountered – material that, in a foreign-language situation, might otherwise lie dormant until the teacher thought to reintroduce it. In a second-language situation, interaction becomes essential to survival in the new language and culture, and students need help with styles of interaction (as discussed by Robinson, this volume, chap. 11).

Student needs; course design; classroom procedures

How interaction is achieved in formal situations is a matter of technique or of classroom approach; in less formal situations it involves imaginative planning with student input. In either case, the teacher has a number of options drawn from the experiences of predecessors and contemporaries. (For some, see Rivers 1981: 28–90.) How can teachers select judiciously from this great variety of proposed approaches and techniques? What kinds of guidelines can they follow?

First, in all teaching, comes the *student* – the raison d'être of teaching. The teacher needs to consider the age of the students, their scholastic background, their culturally absorbed ways of learning, and their objectives in studying the language (to communicate orally, for instance; to read specialized texts; to learn about other peoples and cultures; or to prepare for study abroad) without ignoring the political and social pressures (including career opportunities) that are largely determining their motivation. Only after such matters have been taken into account and decisions made about *the kind of course* that will meet the students' needs in their particular situation will teachers begin to reflect on appropriate ways of *selecting and presenting material*, so that the objectives of the students may be achieved. At this point, approach, design, and procedure become of interest (Richards and Rodgers 1986: 16–28).

Furthermore, each teacher has *a personality to express*. Teachers are individuals who teach and interact most effectively when what they are doing conforms to what they feel most comfortable doing. Some teachers love play-acting and leading students out into expressive performance; others are indirect leaders, providing almost imperceptible encouragement for self-expression; still others can orchestrate assured and vigorous activity. We have all seen extremely successful language classes taught by teachers favoring most diverse approaches, where very different activities were taking place; yet interaction was stimulated, even if in quite unexpected ways.

Teachers should not be looking for the one best method for teaching languages (or helping students learn languages), but rather *the most appropriate approach, design of materials, or set of procedures in a particular case*. Teachers need to be flexible, with a repertoire of techniques they can employ as circumstances dictate, while *keeping interaction central* – interaction between teacher and student, student and teacher, student and student, student and authors of texts, and student and the community that speaks the language (and, in the future, student and computer program, as Ariew and Frommer show in chap. 14, this volume). Many ideas for focusing on interaction are elaborated in successive chapters of this book, both for oral and written language. Teachers of very different personalities will find much from which to choose.

Comprehension and expression as an interactive duo

Whether in oral or graphic form, comprehension and expression of meaning are in constant interaction in real-life communication. Some scholars maintain that all that is needed for students to acquire language is plenty of comprehensible input, and "the ability to speak (or write) fluently in a second language will come on its own with time" (Krashen and Terrell 1983: 32); in other words, after a great deal of listening, speech will emerge spontaneously in a natural order.[3] In fact, Straight goes so far as to say that "communicative proficiency is most effectively and efficiently achieved by means of instruction that emphasizes the development of comprehension skills (listening and reading) to the virtual exclusion of training in production.... The best way to acquire a language," he continues, "is to acquire the skills needed to comprehend it fluently, and ... everything else will follow, if not automatically, at least far more easily and effectively" (Straight 1985: 19, 27). This approach to language learning is called "natural" because it endeavors to replicate the situation of the child learning a first language or a second language in informal situations.

However, first-language acquisition studies do not reveal the listening, noncommunicating child this theory assumes to exist. First-language studies are identifying earlier and earlier attempts to communicate in the infant's babbling, as well as in its kinesics and physical behavior.

3 The "natural order" refers to the acquisition of a small number of grammatical morphemes by first- and second-language acquirers of English, which Krashen refers to as a "difficulty order" (1981: 52). He has interpreted the presence of a "natural order" in the adult performer "as a manifestation of the acquired system without substantial interruption or contribution from the conscious grammar, or Monitor" (p. 52).

Trevarthen observed, for instance, that two-month-old babies were already using their lips and tongue and waving their hands as people do in conversation. He considers that "the foundation for interpersonal communication between humans is 'there' at birth, and is remarkably useful by eight weeks when cognitive and memory processes are beginning" (1974: 230–5). At twelve months babies are uttering single words and at fifteen months are putting two words together, although at this stage they have clearly not yet developed the "*very* advanced comprehension skills" Straight considers necessary "before one starts producing output" (Straight 1985: 34). Some of these very early utterances are imitative (memorized) prefabricated utterances or formulaic speech, as Hakuta and Wong Fillmore have demonstrated, with analyzed productive speech, where material they have heard is put together in new ways, developing later (Hakuta 1986: 126–30).

Moreover, research by such scholars as Carroll, Tanenhaus, and Bever (1978) and Schlesinger (1977) brings out differences between listening and speaking that make it unlikely that intensive listening alone will lead to fluent and effective production of utterances (although much is, of course, learned from listening, as from reading). Listening draws on *knowledge of the world and expectations* aroused by the situation and by the persons involved in it. Listeners have little control over the elaboration of speech to which they are listening, although they may signal their need for more simplified input by facial expression, gesture, or oral request. In interpreting what they are hearing, listeners are guided primarily by the rhythmic segmentation of the speech by the speaker and the sequence of *semantic elements* that permits them to construct a plausible message from what they are hearing. *Inference* plays a large part in this process. Listeners resort to surface-structure cues, such as salient morphology for plurals and tensed endings to verbs, only when meaning needs to be clarified or disambiguated (Carroll et al. 1978: 187–218). What is extracted in listening as semantic meaning is not stored in memory in its original syntactic form and, past the echoic interval of several seconds, cannot usually be restated in that original form (Rivers 1983b: 78–90). If we are cultivating effective listening skills, we teach students to *rely on semantic cues and NOT to focus on the syntax.* (What is said here about listening can be applied equally to reading. Fluent readers draw on semantic cues and by inference create meanings. Concentration on analysis of the syntax impedes the extraction of meaning, except at points of special difficulty.)

On the other hand, speaking begins with the intention of the speaker. Unlike the listener, the speaker controls by his or her selection of lexical and syntactic items the level of language and the elaborated or simplified form that will be used. Consequently language learners, when speaking, can keep within a simplified syntax and reduced vocabulary to express their meaning, and this is what they should be learning to do: paraphrasing, circumlocuting, and simplifying when they are unsure of the exact words or structures to express their meaning.

Speakers need grammar to express their meaning with any precision and to retain the listener's respect and attention. Listeners, on the other hand, may bypass much of the grammar by resorting to semantic strategies, since many formal features concern them only when the interpretation becomes complex. This is the *fundamental difference between listening and speaking*. Because of this difference, neither alone can lead to the other in some incidental, subconscious, unfocused way. Even with attentive, focused listening, the listener is paying close attention to details of the content and the development of thought rather than to specific elements of syntax, except where there is ambiguity or unclear meaning. (The same thing happens with attentive reading, which is why proofreading is so difficult.) Moreover, the grammar we draw on for effective, real-time comprehension is different from the grammar we need to express our ideas explicitly. Unless the listener is focusing very attentively on the syntax with the intent of inductive analysis, it is not clear how listening can lead automatically to the internalization of a grammar that will be useful for expressing one's own ideas. In other words, by teaching learners to concentrate on elements of production grammar while listening (or reading), we are teaching them to be inefficient listeners (and readers); yet, unless they do so, it is not plausible that they will acquire the elements they will need for speech (or writing). Both comprehension and production are demanding processes that require time and increasing knowledge of the language to develop, and much practice in real communication to perfect.

Unfortunately, despite all we know about the differences between listening (and reading) for comprehension and speaking (and writing) to be comprehended, few materials teach the type of *recognition grammar* and *recognition vocabulary* that listening and reading require, and even fewer initiate students into the different strategies we employ in receiving and communicating messages. Students are not even made aware of the need for developing different strategies for these two aspects of communication. They do not learn how to piece together meaning from semantic elements and draw on context and previous knowledge for listening and reading, and how to develop inferencing skills through intelligent, fact-based guessing and supplementing where the signal is not clear (see Papalia, this volume, chap. 6). Nor do they learn that for speaking (and writing) we make the most of what we have, making infinite use of finite means (to use Humboldt's phrase), daring to create new utterances and, in oral communication, judging by the reaction whether we need to paraphrase, expand, or use visual prompts to fill out our meaning. In listening, the syntax may be beyond our previous experience, but this does not faze us because we draw on inference and, in normal conversation, we can ask for clarification when problems arise. In speaking, we are in control, and with practice in the right strategies we can make a little go a long way. But we must possess that little! Let us not deceive our students into thinking control of a new language will come easily and effortlessly. There is, however, pleasure in meeting the challenge, and the rewards of being able to interact confidently in another language make the effort worthwhile.

Promoting interaction

In interactive language teaching, comprehension and production retrieve their normal relationship as an interactive duo. To achieve this, we need an ambiance and relations among individuals that promote a desire for interaction. Individual strategies, temperaments, and preferred modes of operation on the part of students and teacher make each class session a unique experience and each succession of classes a variation on the basic chemistry. Theory can suggest ideas to teachers and to learners, but not impose them. Students continue to learn second and third languages, in all kinds of ways – with teachers, without teachers, and despite teachers or theoreticians.

For the genuine interaction language learning requires, however, individuals (teachers as well as students) must appreciate the uniqueness of other individuals with their special needs – not manipulating or directing them or deciding *how* they can or will learn, but encouraging them and drawing them out (educating), and building up their confidence and enjoyment in what they are doing. Teacher-directed and -dominated classrooms cannot, by their nature, be interactive classrooms, and this is what language teachers need to learn. Interaction can be two-way, three-way, or four-way, but never one-way.

Why is it that students in so many classes do not seem to pass a certain point in achievement: They know much but they cannot use it to express their own meaning. In many such classes, the teacher teeters on the brink of interactive practice and students withdraw, hesitant and cautious. For both teacher and students, this is an experience new to them and they are not sure how to handle it. Real interaction in the classroom requires the teacher to step out of the limelight, to cede a full role to the student in developing and carrying through activities, to accept all kinds of opinions, and be tolerant of errors the student makes while attempting to communicate. This many teachers are reluctant to do. Never having experienced an interactive classroom, they are afraid it will be chaotic and hesitate to try. Some students, too, because of rigid formal training, have no experience in exercising initiative and participating imaginatively in task-oriented, purposeful learning, or cooperative learning. Co-operative learning means sharing, encouraging, and accepting responsibility for one's own learning and that of others (Rivers 1983a: 77–8), not leaving all responsibility to the teacher. Interaction is also an affective, temperamental matter, not merely a question of someone saying something to someone. Without mutual respect, the building of confidence, and the creating of many opportunities for experimentation in communication without undue direction, classrooms will remain quiet places with inhibited students who dare not try to express what really matters to them. Once teachers have tried to carry through a well-prepared interactive class session and find it can be done, they lose their hesitancy.

Because interactive language teaching means elicitation of willing student participation and initiative, it requires a high degree of indirect leadership, along with emotional maturity, perceptiveness, and sensitivity to the feelings of others. When a teacher demonstrates these qualities, students lose their fear of embarrassment and are willing to try to express themselves. Kramsch speaks of "saving one's own and other's face" (this volume, p. 20). Once students feel appreciated and valued, they are anxious to show what they can do, to propose and participate in activities.

Whatever promotes student participation in a relaxed and enthusiastic atmosphere stimulates the interaction that is essential to successful language learning. The interaction may be quiet; it may be noisy; it may be alert and dynamic; it may take place in large groups, small groups, or pairs (see Kramsch, this volume, chap. 2); but it will be there, with students deeply involved in tasks and activities that draw on their creativity and stimulate that of the teacher.

What happens in an interactive classroom?

1. In an interactive classroom there will be, first of all, *much listening to authentic materials*, with no prohibition or discouragement of spoken response or student-initiated contribution. The listening will be purposeful as students prepare to use what they have heard in some way. "Authentic materials" include teacher talk when the teacher is fluent in the language. When teachers cannot provide this kind of input, they will rely heavily on audio- and videotapes or, for reading, on newspapers, magazines, cartoon books, letters, instructions for products, menus, maps, and so on (see Melvin and Stout, chap. 4; and Price, chap. 12; this volume). Where available, native speakers will be brought into the classroom to interact informally with the students, even at an early stage. They can often be persuaded to allow videotaping or audiotaping of

their discussion for use with other classes. Authentic materials need not be difficult materials. With careful selection and preparation they can be fine-tuned to a level accessible to particular groups of students. These materials will always be used in some productive activity: as background for a research project to be discussed with others; for reenactment in a role-playing situation with a problem-solving component; as a dramatization or skit; or as input for a small-group discussion or debate about controversial or unexpected elements, perhaps cultural, that need study in order to be understood and accepted in their context.

2. Students from the beginning *listen and speak* in reacting to pictures and objects, in role plays, through acting out, and in discussion; they create radio talk shows; they conduct class flea markets with personally selected artifacts (buying, selling, negotiating, explaining, persuading, retracting). Students simulate cocktail parties or job interviews. They report on newscasts, providing their personal commentary from their own cultural and national viewpoint; they argue about events and positions taken and share points of view. (Many useful activities are proposed by Sadow, this volume, chap. 3).

3. Students are involved in *joint tasks*: *purposeful activity* where they work together doing or making things, making arrangements, entertaining others, preparing materials for cross-cultural presentations and discussions, arranging international festivals or open days for parents – all the time using the language as they concentrate on the task.

4. Students watch *films and videotapes of native speakers interacting.* They observe nonverbal behavior and the types of exclamations and fill-in expressions that are used, how people initiate and sustain a conversational exchange, how they negotiate meaning, and how they terminate an interactive episode (Keller and Warner 1979). Useful for this type of observation are soap operas or television serials, which students can use as starter material for developing their own episodes, taking on roles of characters in the original series and interacting as they do. If these episodes are developed in groups, the members of each group must listen carefully to the presentations of other groups in order to be prepared for their own. Videotaping is useful. Peer critiques are often sufficient to draw attention to problems of comprehension due to weaknesses in pronunciation or syntax. Varieties of language, stress, and intonation can also be acquired and practiced in this type of activity.

5. Pronunciation may be improved interactively not only while listening and speaking conversationally, but also in *poetry reading and creation* (see Maley, this volume, chap. 8) or while preparing dialogues, *plays*, or skits where reading the material over and over with each other is the learning procedure (see Via, this volume, chap. 9). In identifying with a role, students approximate the pronunciation one would expect

from a certain character without the psychological trauma of appearing to be other than one's accustomed self.[4]

6. *Cross-cultural interaction* is important in language use in the real world. Students *share* their values and viewpoints, ways of acting and reacting, and their speech styles. They recognize the stereotypes they hold of speakers of the target language and of each other's culture. This learning experience can be in a direct exchange of opinions or through initiation into the activities of another culture. Guided activities and projects that gradually lead students to successful cross-cultural encounters, rather than misunderstandings, give students confidence for future cross-cultural interactions (Robinson 1985: 85–97). Observing interaction between people from different cultures, becoming aware of one's own reactions to other people, monitoring one's own speech style, and practicing diverse interaction skills help students learn to cope successfully in another culture (see Robinson, this volume, chap. 11). In foreign-language situations, students act out problem-solving scenarios where cultural misunderstandings are confronted (Di Pietro 1982; Scarcella 1978) and, where possible, discuss with available native speakers the appropriateness of the decisions they have made from the point of view of a person brought up in the culture. *Songs, music, and dance* also help the student appreciate the cultural ethos of the other group (see Maley, this volume, chap. 8).

7. If *reading* is the activity, there should be lively *interaction of reader and text* – interpretation, expansion, discussing alternative possibilities or other conclusions. Often reading leads to creative production in speech or writing, as students are inspired to write stories, poems, plays, radio programs, or film scenarios, or their own dénouements for stories and plays they have been reading.

8. What is written should be something that will be read by somebody, as with a group composition (see Russo, this volume, chap. 7) or an item in a *class newspaper* or on a bulletin board. *Dialogue journals* are an excellent example of interactive writing. Students write to the teacher or to each other, and the reader responds with a further message, thus combining reading and writing in a purposeful activity. Instead of "correcting," the teacher respondent rephrases awkward expressions while commenting on the content.[5] As with phone conversations with an instructor or target-language friend, students become bolder and bolder in expressing their real feelings in journals, where the interaction is not face-to-face. A similar reduction of inhibitions takes place when students

---

4 For useful readings on the psychological problems of pronunciation, see Guiora and Acton (1979), Guiora et al. (1972), and Guiora, Brannon, and Dull (1972); for intonation and gesture see Bolinger (1983) and Wylie (1985).

5 Empirical support for the claim that "commenting" is more effective than "correcting" is found in Robinson et al. (1985).

correspond with a native speaker of their own age or a stranger selected from a telephone book from a country where the language is spoken.

9. Interaction does not preclude the learning of the grammatical system of the language. We interact better if we can understand and express nuances of meaning that require careful syntactic choices. Learning grammar, however, is not listening to expositions of rules but rather inductively developing rules from living language material and then *performing rules* (Rivers 1981: 194–6). This process can and should be interactive, with students internalizing rules through experience of their effectiveness in expressing essential meanings. Many activities can be developed where students use particular structures without feeling they are "learning grammar." Simple examples at the elementary level are "Simon Says" for imperatives; "Twenty Questions" for yes/no question forms; "My uncle went to market and bought me a fan" (*some melons, a pair of shoes...*) for count and noncount nouns; "If I Were President" for hypothetical expressions and conditionals. Many other activities will come to mind for practice in using expressions of time and aspect (see Comeau, this volume, chap. 5).

10. Testing too should be interactive and proficiency-oriented, rather than a sterile, taxonomic process. Students should be put in situations where they hear and react to real uses of language or where what they read is to be incorporated into some further language-using activity. Multiple-choice and fill-in-the-blank tests are *about* language; they are not normal language-using activities. *Tests should replicate normal uses of language* as much as is feasible. A first step is to make traditional tests reflect the reality with which the student is surrounded. The next step is to develop tests where there is genuine interaction as part of the test, not just in an oral interview but in other areas as well (see Mueller, this volume, chap. 10). As soon as the test becomes an interesting and absorbing activity, the student is mentally interacting with the test writer or administrator or with other students, and the test becomes an organic process of construction of meaning in comprehension and expression. (For the test as part of the learning process, see Rivers 1983b: 141–53.)

11. *We must not forget interacting with the community* that speaks the language. So many opportunities are missed when students are not sent out into the community (where such a possibility exists) with a clearly defined project that involves talking with native speakers – finding out information; helping with some project; joining some group (photography, bird watching, or whatever interests them); joining in festivals, festivities, and leisure activities; talking with or working with children; explaining their culture to the other community and listening to what members of that community have to say about theirs; offering help to and accepting help from the community. Where there is no neighboring group of native speakers, the community may still be reached and tapped

through its newspapers, its magazines, its shortwave radio programs, its films, its cartoons and jokes, and the occasional visiting native speaker. Consulates may be approached for travel brochures to add reality to the project of planning a trip through the country. Correspondence becomes important. Classes may write an account of their school, their town, and their ways of spending leisure hours to exchange with a school in a country where the language is spoken. This written account may be illustrated and enlivened with photographs, tapes of personal reminiscences, songs, and even small artifacts of the region. In this way, a "twinned classroom" situation is established that can blossom into an exciting partnership on a continuing basis.

A diet of grammar exercises and drills cannot give the feeling for other living, breathing human beings that exploring the things they enjoy can do. (Strevens, this volume, chap. 13, lists many such possibilities.)

12. Special-purpose language classes can also be interactive. Students preparing for careers or already in careers for which they need access to sources in another language can *supply much of the content*, which may be unfamiliar to the language teacher. They can discuss and explain technical information in articles and books they are reading; they can propose activities that simulate the types of problems they will face in business, commerce, international banking, journalism, or foreign affairs. Dow and Ryan (this volume, chap. 15) demonstrate how useful the *case study method* is in preparing people for careers.

Language learning and teaching can be an exciting and refreshing interval in the day for students and teacher. There are so many possible ways of stimulating communicative interaction, yet, all over the world, one still finds classrooms where language learning is a tedious, dry-as-dust process, devoid of any contact with the real world in which language use is as natural as breathing. Grammar rules are explained and practiced; vocabulary and paradigms are learned by heart and tested out of context; the "book" is "covered" and students move on.

Fortunately, there are other classrooms where students are comprehending, communicating, and creating language that is meaningful, even original and stimulating (if occasionally odd). In these classrooms students are interacting in the language – perhaps painfully and painstakingly at first, but with greater abandon as they acquire confidence. To move from one type of classroom (as boring for the teacher as the student) to the other, all that is needed is a decision to try – to overcome a certain timidity, even nervousness, for at least one segment of one lesson and try something new. (Any one of the many suggestions in this book will do.) With one new activity tomorrow and another next week (or perhaps even next day), an unimaginative, conventional classroom can gradually be transformed. An atmosphere of excitement and trust can be created where confident students initiate and cooperate in imaginative activities, sharing with each other real messages in authentic and exhilarating interaction.

Let's act on it

1. Think back to the first language course in which you participated as a student. How was it conducted? How did you react to this approach? What problems did you yourself experience? What advice would you give your teacher now from your perspective as a student or practitioner of language teaching?
2. List ten activities in which you commonly engage in the classroom (or which are recommended in the Teacher's Manual of a textbook for the level you will teach). How could each of these be made more interactive?
3. Discuss which elements of the grammar of the language you teach are essential for the listener. In establishing your list, consider semantic and syntactic redundancies,[6] the question of perceptual saliency of morphology (that is, what can and cannot be heard clearly), and what can be supplied by inference. Would a recognition grammar for reading contain the same elements?
4. Discuss the differences between vocabulary as it is commonly taught and the demands of aural recognition vocabulary for listeners. What suggestions would you make for improving the teaching of vocabulary for listeners?
5. If the sequence *student needs – course design – classroom procedures* (see p. 5) were to be adopted in your school (or the school where you studied a language), what changes would have to be made in the present instructional program?
6. Listen, as an observer, to your friends over lunch. Which factors in the expression and comprehension of messages particularly struck you as you observed? Which of these are provided for in teaching materials with which you are familiar? How could the others be incorporated?

Annotated reading list

Hakuta, K. 1986. *Mirror of Language: The Debate on Bilingualism.* New York: Basic Books. A thorough, up-to-date discussion of how children and adults learn a second language, with careful consideration of political and social as well as learning factors.

6 For an explanation of redundancy in the linguistic sense, see Rivers and Temperley (1978: 7, 59).

Richards, J. C. 1985. *The Context of Language Teaching*. New York: Cambridge University Press. See especially chap. 6, "Communicative Needs in Second- and Foreign-Language Learning," and chap. 9, "Cross-cultural Aspects of Conversational Competence." Discusses meaning-based, conventional, appropriateness, interactional, and structured aspects of communication.

Richards, J. C., and Rodgers, T. S. "Method: Approach, Design, and Procedure," in Richards (1985), pp. 16–31. Explains the meaning of these terms, with implications for teachers and materials writers. Also in Richards and Rodgers (1986), chap. 2.

Rivers, W. M. 1981. *Teaching Foreign-Language Skills*, 2d ed. Chicago: University of Chicago Press. See chap. 6, "Listening Comprehension," and chap. 8, "The Speaking Skill: Expressing Personal Meaning." Gives a more detailed analysis of these two aspects of interaction, with many proposed activities.

Rivers, W. M., and Temperley, M. S. 1978. *A Practical Guide to the Teaching of English as a Second or Foreign Language*. New York: Oxford University Press. See chap. 2, "Autonomous Interaction," and chap. 3, "Listening." Also in parallel *Guides* for *Hebrew* (in press), and the second editions of *French*, *German*, and *Spanish* (1988). Gives many suggestions for interactional activities.

Wells, G., et al. 1981. *Learning Through Interaction: The Study of Language Development*. Cambridge: Cambridge University Press. A readable, theoretical account of the characteristics of conversation as a collaborative activity, considering both the role of the listener and that of the speaker. Discusses turn-taking in the negotiation of meaning, devices for maintaining continuity of topic, ways of linking exchanges, types of speech acts, the indirect relationship between form and function, and the importance of nonlinguistic cues in the situational context.

2 Interactive discourse in small and large groups

Claire J. Kramsch

As students sign up for a foreign-language class, their expectations and their fears are often similar to those they bring to the study of any other subject. They look forward to acquiring a new skill and they fear personal failure. They are rarely aware that learning the forms of a language and using them appropriately is quite different from learning math or history. By entering a foreign-language classroom, students leave behind the social reality created by their native tongue and start constructing a new reality, which is potentially very different from the one they just left.

Indeed, the foreign language is not only a tool for future encounters in the outside world; it is the instrument that creates and shapes the social meaning of the class itself. "Speaking a language means more than *referring* to the world, it also means *relating* to one's interlocutor" (Kasper 1979: 395). Learning takes place in a double context: On the one hand, students learn words and grammatical structures that refer to an established distant culture, the external context of language. On the other hand, they use these words and structures to communicate with others in the classroom. This internal context of language brings about an interaction that is created anew by every group of teacher and learners. It is through the interaction with this social group that the language is used and learned. In turn, it is through the use of the language that the group is given a social identity and social reality (Berger and Luckman 1966). Learning a language is a socially mediated process (Vygotsky 1978: 126).

The microworld of classroom interaction

The dual nature of the language-learning task – learning the forms and learning how to use them – creates tension between individual work and group work, between teacher-controlled and group-managed learning. This tension characterizes the microworld of the foreign-language classroom.

The interaction continuum

The interaction among group members in a classroom moves between the two poles of a continuum consisting of what Stern calls "instructional

17

TABLE I. THE INTERACTION CONTINUUM

	Instructional discourse	*"Convivial" discourse*	*Natural discourse*
Roles:	Fixed statuses		Negotiated roles
Tasks:	Teacher-oriented Position-centered		Group-oriented Person-centered
Types of knowledge:	Focus on content, accuracy of facts		Focus on process, fluency of interaction

options" (1983: 506). These concern the roles of participants, the tasks they accomplish, and the type of knowledge that is exchanged (Table 1). At the one end are the fixed, institutionalized statuses (Cicourel 1972: 231) of teacher and student, with their expected and predictable behavior patterns, acquired through years of schooling. At the other end are a variety of roles and tasks, negotiated by speakers and hearers brought together by the common foreign language and engaged in natural conversation. Neither extreme ever exists in its pure form exclusively. Between the instructional and the natural, we should aim at establishing a "convivial" form of discourse, which, to use Ivan Illich's definition, is "the autonomous and creative discourse among persons and the intercourse of persons with their environment, . . . in contrast with the conditioned response of persons to the demands made upon them by others, and by a man-made environment" (Illich 1973: 11). In other words, social roles have to be, to a greater or lesser extent, negotiated between teacher and learners for the successful completion of learning and teaching tasks.

Tasks also vary along the interaction continuum: On the one hand, we have "position-centered" teaching and learning (Applegate and Delia 1980: 277), in which information is conveyed and received. Focus is on the content of the lesson or what is learned. Position-centered teaching stresses accuracy in the use of the language and the individual acquisition of linguistic skills. On the other hand, we have "person-centered" communication, in which information is exchanged and a speaker's utterances must be adjusted and readjusted to fit the hearer's ability and willingness to understand the meaning intended. Emphasis is on the interactional process itself: that is, the way in which each learner interacts with the material and negotiates intended meanings with the other members of the group (see Rivers, this volume, p. 4). Toward this end of the continuum, learning *how* to learn, or how to acquire control over the discourse of the classroom, is at least as important as what is said and learned (Allwright 1984; Breen and Candlin 1980: 90). Here, the accent is placed on ease and fluency of language use and the acquisition of interactive skills.

The way in which students learn how to use the language thus depends largely on what information is exchanged, how and by whom, and where the three parameters of classroom communication we have discussed are placed on the interaction continuum. But it is also determined by the way in which members of the group present themselves in relation to the others, and how they deal with the uncertainty and insecurity of the language-learning situation. We will address these issues in the next two sections.

Presentation of self in the foreign-language classroom

We can distinguish three factors affecting the way in which teacher and learners present themselves to one another in the classroom (Brown and Levinson 1978).

RELATIVE POWER

Notwithstanding the institutionalized authority of the teacher, power in the foreign-language classroom can have various origins and be unevenly distributed. It often stems from a greater knowledge of vocabulary and grammar, but is usually due to a better control over the interaction. It seems that after a certain level of proficiency is attained, control of group or dyadic interaction is largely due to the mastery of discourse or communication strategies. In whole-class exchanges, some students know how to monopolize the teacher's attention (Allwright 1980); in small-group discussion, some retain this control by making others talk or by eliciting help, or by the skillful use of short and long turns (Brown and Yule 1983; Porter 1983). Teachers know how to keep control of classroom discourse by managing the dialogue away from trouble sources.

SOCIAL DISTANCE

The closeness or distance learners wish to establish with one another has to do with how well they know each other, how it will affect their self-image (e.g., the socially expected behavior of males and females, or whites and blacks in each other's presence), and what benefits they hope to gain from it (Bourdieu 1982). The concept of social distance is, moreover, culturally determined. In multicultural classes, differences in the value attached to verbal versus nonverbal communication can affect the distance learners wish to maintain in the foreign language. Hall (1976) has shown, for example, that students from cultures in which behaviors are highly predictable because of the homogeneous normative structure of their society (e.g., Japanese or Korean) tend to underestimate in Eng-

19

lish the importance of rhetorical skills and of the communicative dimensions of discourse. By contrast, these are essential in a society such as the North American, where, on the whole, individuality is prized and where social relationships have to be more or less negotiated in every communicative situation. Japanese students' lack of verbal involvement in class interaction may be perceived by a North American ESL teacher as the maintenance of an inappropriate social distance toward the group and thus lead to misunderstanding.

SOCIOCULTURAL IMPOSITION

Each language has its own rules of usage as to when, how, and to what degree a speaker may impose a given verbal behavior on his or her conversational partner. For instance, in North American culture, paying a compliment to someone obligates that person to answer "Thank you," whereas in another culture such a response might be both inappropriate and embarrassing. Norms of imposition vary also according to the social and personal habits of the speakers. Silence or withdrawal on the part of some students may make others feel imposed upon to speak more than they normally would. The directness of North American questioning patterns may threaten ESL students and in turn affect negatively the way they use classroom interaction to learn the language. Female group members may feel obligated to adopt a male style of participation in group discussion, and vice-versa (Treichler and Kramarae 1983).

The degree of imposition exerted by the various members of a group on one another in the language classroom requires a great deal of what Goffman (1967) calls "face-work," which we will now examine.

Saving one's own and other's face

"Life may not be much of a gamble, but interaction is." This statement by Goffman (1959: 243) underscores one of the major concerns of language learners – not to lose face when using the language incorrectly or inappropriately. As members of a group, they want to maintain both their positive face, that is, their need to be appreciated by others, and their negative face, that is, their freedom from interference by others. Not being able to continue speaking because of a lack of vocabulary is a threat to one's positive face, but asking for help may be perceived as a threat to one's negative face. In their native tongue, speakers have a host of strategies to avoid a difficulty, to self-correct, or to ask for help in case of linguistic trouble. They also know how to show others that they acknowledge and appreciate them, without unduly imposing on them. In short, they know how to save both their own and the other speaker's positive and negative face.

The problem for learners is to save face in a classroom situation where possibilities of avoidance and escape are more limited than in natural settings. Arguably, the need for face-work in teacher-controlled classrooms is greatly reduced by the "fool's impunity" that accompanies the institutionalized status of learner and by the institutional authority granted the teacher. However, where turns-at-talk are up for grabs, where the actions and reactions of others have to be anticipated and intentions correctly interpreted, where the risks and consequences of speaking up have to be weighed, students need strategies of indirectness in discourse.

To save their own face, they can be taught how to gain time while talking ("As I was saying before," "This is a rather difficult question to answer"), how to hedge ("Well, it's hard to say ... "), how to acknowledge their limitations and ask for help ("I'm sorry, I don't know how to say ...," "How do you say ... ?"), and how to participate in a group conversation even if they have nothing new to say, by commenting, paraphrasing or expanding on what others have said. To avoid putting a conversational partner directly on the spot, a student can learn how to save the other's face by using, for example, prefacing markers ("Could you please ... ?", "May I ask you a question?", "Excuse me, but ... "), mitigators ("Would you mind repeating ... "), echoing statements ("You mean to say ... "), or feedback techniques ("Yeah/right/quite/good point") (Edmondson and House 1981).

As we have seen, there are two types of language used in the classroom: (1) the lesson content that is taught and learned, for example, grammar, vocabulary, cultural facts; and (2) the interactional language that is used by teacher and student to deal with the lesson content, for example, "Please speak louder.", "What do you mean?", "Now let's turn to ... ". Traditionally, the second type of language has been under the control of the teacher. In a group-oriented classroom, students have the chance to use it within a variety of group formats. Whether these groups are large or small, whether they include the teacher (whole-class activities) or not, they are socially held together by the joint efforts of the participants, who are in turn speakers, listeners, addressees, or bystanders. Speakers achieve a desired interactional climate by the way they take or avoid, sustain or yield turns-at-talk; by the way they initiate, build, and steer topics; and by performing the repairs required by actual or potential breakdowns in communication.

The interactive discourse of groups

Turns-at-talk

Observers of language classrooms have noted the power that comes from controlling the turns-at-talk in the classroom (Mehan 1979). In teacher-oriented interaction, the teacher selects the next speaker and automatically selects him- or herself for the succeeding turn. There is little motivation for students to listen to one another, and the only motivation to listen to the teacher is the fear of being caught short on an answer.

Teaching students how to take turns, as easy as this might seem, requires teaching a number of skills that are not automatically transferred from the mother tongue. Students must learn to listen to the utterance of the previous speaker across its delivery, process it as it is spoken, interpret it, create and formulate a reply as they listen, find a natural completion point in the speaker's discourse, and take the floor at the appropriate moment. This requires a concentration and combination of listening and speaking skills that need to be practiced.

In group-oriented interaction, the teacher should systematically encourage the students to take control of the turn-taking mechanism by adopting some of the features of natural discourse:

- Tolerate silences; refrain from filling the gaps between turns. This will put pressure on students to initiate turns.
- Direct your gaze to any potential addressee of a student's utterance; do not assume that you are the next speaker and the student's exclusive addressee.
- Teach the students floor-taking gambits; do not grant the floor.
- Encourage students to sustain their speech beyond one or two sentences and to take longer turns; do not use a student's short utterance as a springboard for your own lengthy turn.
- Extend your exchanges with individual students to include clarification of the speaker's intentions and your understanding of them; do not cut off an exchange too soon to pass on to another student.

By moving toward more group-controlled forms of turn-taking, classroom interaction also gives the group more practice in the management of topics.

Topic management

Control of the turn-taking mechanism generally gives the teacher control of the topic. At one end of the continuum, the information exchanged between teacher and students and among students is predictable and most of the time ritualized. Questions are mostly display questions: questions in which the student is requested to display a knowledge that the teacher already knows. At the other end of the continuum, the questions of the teacher show the information gap characteristic of natural discourse, in which speakers ask questions only when they need information they do not have. Answers are not judged according to whether they correspond to what the questioner had in mind, but are assessed according to how well they contribute to the topic. Perceptions and intentions are the object of negotiation and constant readjustments between speakers.

If students are to take an active part in interactions, they must be shown how to control the way topics are established, built, and sustained, and how to participate in the teaching and learning of lessons. The following suggestions for teacher behavior can be useful here:

– Use the target language not only to deal with the subject matter, but also to regulate the interaction in the classroom. You will thus offer a model of how to use interactional gambits in natural discourse.
– Keep the number of display questions to a minimum. The more genuine the requests for information, the more natural the discourse.
– Build the topic at hand together with the students; assume that whatever they say contributes to this topic. Do not cut off arbitrarily a student's utterance because you perceive it to be irrelevant; it may be very relevant to the student's perception of the topic.

Repair tasks

Linguistic errors and other sources of trouble, such as procedural problems or problems of transmission, are addressed at one end of the continuum mostly on the initiative of the teacher. The teacher alone points out linguistic errors, and requests speakers to correct their own or fellow students' mistakes. To show that there is a problem (grammatical error or inaudible speech, for example), the teacher usually withholds evaluation, ignores the answer given, and repeats the question, repeats the trouble source as a query, or changes addressee. Procedural problems, such as misunderstandings in the activity rules (e.g., individual response instead of choral response), are also taken to be an "error" on the part of the students and are redressed by the teacher.

In a group-oriented class, errors are considered to be natural accidents on the way to interpersonal communication. Natural forms of interaction in the classroom would therefore require that the teacher frequently adopt the following communicative behavior:

– Pay attention to the message of students' utterances rather than to the form in which the utterances are cast (unless you are engaged in a structural drill, where only the form is important). Keep comments and repairs for later.
– Treat the correction of linguistic errors as a "pragmatic" or interactional adjustment, not as a normative form of redress, for example, by restating the incorrect utterance in a correct manner rather than pointing explicitly to the error.

23

- Leave students a choice in the linguistic form of their utterance. For example, if they are not sure of their subjunctive, allow them to avoid this form and to find alternatives.
- Make extensive use of natural feedback ("Hmm, interesting, I thought so too"), rather than evaluating and judging every student's utterance following its delivery ("Fine/good"). Do not overpraise.
- Give students explicit credit by quoting them ("Just as X said"); do not take credit for what students have contributed by using what they said only to further your point.

Diversifying interaction formats

The versatility of interaction formats through which the language is used and acquisition can take place in the classroom should reflect the multiple communicative needs and purposes of the social group engaged in the learning process. Restricting classroom interaction to the public, teacher-monitored, and teacher-controlled discourse of twenty-five students answering display questions is not only an unnecessary reduction of the interaction potential of the classroom, but it ignores the social dimensions of language learning. The fear that errors will be transferred from one student to the other if they are not immediately corrected by the teacher is an unwarranted behaviorist view of language. A study by Porter (1983) shows that in small-group work only 3% of the errors are incorporated into the speech of peers. Moreover, if language learning is an "innovation and experimentation" process (Rivers 1983a: 53), making mistakes is part of the hypothesis testing and negotiation of intended meanings necessary for communication. Learning to recognize one's mistakes on one's own from the interactional context in which they are made, and having the freedom to act upon this awareness, can be developed within a variety of interactional contexts and group formats.

Although much has been argued in favor of pair and small-group work (Brumfit 1984: 76–82; Gaies 1985; Kramsch 1981a, 1983; Long et al. 1976), many teachers are still reluctant to have students do in small groups what they feel they can do more conveniently, quickly, and accurately in a teacher-controlled, whole-class situation. They fear the potential chaos and conflicts arising within groups and, in classrooms where students share a common native language, the schismatic use of the mother tongue.

The argument made here is that *group behavior in the foreign language can be taught* and that the various forms of discourse must be demonstrated and practiced for different interaction formats. The following will illustrate some of these options (for further activities, see Kramsch

24

1981ab, 1983, 1984). They have all been used successfully in foreign-
and second-language classes. They all present a very specific task that
requires deliberation and negotiation among members of a group. This
task is to be achieved within a strict time limit. Introduction of interactional constraints reduces the uncertainty and potential anxiety inherent in any group-controlled situation and lowers the level of
communicative stress (Brown and Yule 1983: 107).

Large group work

GROUP DECODING OF A TEXT

A reading has been assigned overnight as individual homework. Students
sit in a circle; the teacher acts as recording secretary. The group brainstorms lexical items they find important toward understanding the story
(time limit: four minutes). Students can take the floor if and when they
wish; the teacher writes all contributions on the board in their correct
form, without evaluating them. During the time allotted, the students
are in total control of the discourse. After the brainstorming, the teacher
suggests linking the separate items to make coherent "islands of understanding." The students again take over and suggest which items can
be linked in which way. The teacher draws the links on the board and
recapitulates at the end the suggestions made.

TEACHING FACE-SAVING GAMBITS

The teacher explicitly sensitizes the students to the routine of group
conversation and the mechanics of perceived fluency: appropriate ways
of opening and closing conversation, and polite ways of interrupting,
making a request, or making a negative comment. Three or four alternative gambits are written on the board, such as "I have a question.",
"May I ask a question?", "May I interrupt for a second?", "I would
like to ask something." The group repeats these to practice appropriate
intonation. The students then practice them individually by addressing
the teacher or a fellow student as opportunity arises within the limits
of the lesson.

INTERPRETING A STORY

The teacher chooses one open-ended question that allows many possible
answers, all of which illuminate various meanings of the story. For
example, for James Thurber's "The Catbird Seat," the question might
be: "Why does Mr. Martin want to 'rub out' Mrs. Barrows?". The
teacher writes the question on the board and the group brainstorms
different responses. The teacher neither prompts students by name, nor

25

monitors or evaluates the responses. The teacher merely records on the board in its correct form what the students say. Students' contributions are freely initiated, and one idea often prompts another, as in natural discourse, especially if the teacher does not intervene in any way. In less spontaneous classes, students can be given two minutes to write their answers; the papers are then collected and read aloud anonymously by a student. Since students focus their response according to their perception and personal experience, the list written on the board offers multiple perspectives on the subject, which can then be discussed as a group. As a result of this discussion, the teacher suggests grouping items, using such logical links as analogy, contrast, or inference. Interpretation is arrived at through common exploration and discovery by teacher and students.

Small-group work

GATHERING INFORMATION

Having been assigned a particular grammar unit to learn or review individually, students in groups of three or four then discuss in the foreign language "the three or four most important points to remember in this unit" or "some unresolved questions" (time limit: ten minutes). The teacher goes from group to group without intervening, but taking mental or written notes of confusions, errors, or interesting insights. One student per group takes notes and reports to the class as a whole. Groups with similar findings feel acknowledged; others are provoked into disagreeing. When the opportunity for using face-saving strategies presents itself during the small-group discussions, and when lexical and grammatical needs arise, the teacher makes comments and suggestions directly related to the observed needs of the learners.

The same format can be used to (1) gather lexical resources before the discussion of a topic (What words do we need to talk about X ?: List as many words as you can in four minutes); (2) prepare three or four arguments for or against a topic to be debated with another small group; (3) solve a given problem that requires a group decision.

GATEKEEPING

Whenever discussions must be conducted according to culturally appropriate rules of turn-taking or certain forms of topic management, one student per group is assigned the role of gatekeeper. This student makes sure everyone has a say, helps others elaborate their turns, keeps track of time, and performs similar tasks.

PEER OBSERVATION OF DISCOURSE

Three or four students lead a five-minute debate on a topic of their choice in front of the class. One-third of the class observes the turn-taking routine, one-third the way the topic is steered from speaker to speaker, and the other third the way in which errors or misunderstandings are repaired and how. Instructor and students then conduct a fifteen- to twenty-minute debriefing.

Pair work

FINDING KEY SENTENCE

Pairs of students are assigned the same paragraph of a given text. They have to read it silently, check each other's understanding, and agree on and underline one key sentence that best conveys the intent of the passage. Comparison and justification of the underlined sentences among the groups serve as a basis for a whole-class interpretation of the paragraph.

DISCURSIVE ROLE PLAY

After the teacher has introduced a given discourse strategy to the whole group (by modeling it or by playing a recording of native speakers), pairs of students are given two minutes to act out a situation requiring the use of this strategy. One example is a fictitious telephone conversation, in which the connection is so bad that the two speakers repeatedly have to ask for clarification, check understanding, and request and offer rephrasings, repetitions, or paraphrases. Another example is giving listener's feedback to a fellow student who is recounting the most frightening experience he or she ever had ("My God!" "Really?" "How awful!" "At night?").

One peer observer notes how the pairs manage the conversation and the gambits they use. The observers then report to the class. This elicits a general discussion on the role of the listener and brings the interaction process into explicit focus.

THE HELPING ENCOUNTER

Each student has four minutes to get to know a fellow student well enough to be able to write a paragraph on that person. The interviewer may ask only four direct questions. The rest of the conversation must be steered through interpretive statements ("Oh, so you don't live in the United States."), paraphrases ("You mean, you don't like to travel?"), or comments ("That's interesting.") that show empathy and understanding. A peer observer notes the strategies used and makes a report to the class.

Conclusion

Despite their good intentions of increasing the amount of communication in the classroom, students and teachers often fall short of their goal because their style of interaction remains at the instructional end of the continuum. Furthermore, by maintaining patterns of institutionalized interaction and, in monocultural classrooms, a social reality typical of the native culture, teachers of a new language reinforce ethnocentric attitudes rather than help to dispel them. On the other hand, pretending that the classroom is similar to the natural environment of the other culture and relinquishing the control of the interaction entirely to the students is both deceiving and threatening to all parties involved.

Traditional forms of classroom interaction need to be reassessed in the light of the new language to help learners move from "institutional productivity" to "productive conviviality" (Illich 1973: 26). Only by broadening their discourse options in the classroom can learners stop being foreign-language consumers and become the active architects of interpersonal and intercultural understanding.

Let's act on it

1. You would like to have a student peer observer note the way students interact in a small-group discussion. What features would you want him or her to observe? Make a list of three features of turn-taking, topic management, and repair work.
2. As soon as you approach students engaged in small-group work, they stop talking to one another and turn to you for help and advice. What can you do to prevent this?
3. Record yourself in the classroom and note your responses to your students' utterances. How predictable are your responses? How varied? When you say "good," do you mean to (a) judge the quality of the form of the utterance, (b) judge the quality of the content of the utterance, (c) congratulate the student for having responded, (d) frame the exchange and mark a pause before your next question? How could you diversify your responses so as to make them more reflective of your meaning?
4. Watch the way you use the foreign language to control what goes on in the classroom: use of hedges when you don't have a ready

answer; gambits to secure the attention of a student; starters to introduce a new idea; rhetorical devices to go back to a previous point; expressions to summarize, to announce several points, or to gain time to think and formulate your thought. Observe these for yourself or assign a student to note them down while you conduct your class. Which strategies could you teach your students? How could you structure classroom interaction so that the students would have the opportunity to use these interactional strategies?

5. Goffman (1967: 116) wrote: "These two tendencies, that of the speaker to scale down his expressions and that of the listeners to scale up their interests, each in the light of the other's capacities and demands, form the bridge that people build to one another, allowing them to meet for a moment of talk in a communion of reciprocally sustained involvement. It is this spark, not the more obvious kinds of love, that lights up the world." Do you agree with this statement? Develop your view with reference to interaction in the foreign-language classroom.

Annotated reading list

Allwright, Richard L. 1980. "Turns, Topics and Tasks: Patterns of Participation in Language Learning and Teaching," in Larsen-Freeman, D., ed., *Discourse Analysis in Second Language Research*, pp. 165–87. Rowley, Mass.: Newbury House. A fine case study of the way learners contribute to their own and to each other's learning in the classroom. Detailed analysis of an ESL class segment, focusing on the way one particular learner "navigates" and negotiates meanings in his interaction with the teacher.

Breen, Michael, and Candlin, Christopher N. 1980. "The Essentials of a Communicative Curriculum in Language Teaching." *AL* 1: 89–112. This seminal article defines communicative competence as the interpretation, expression, and negotiation of intended meanings between speakers. Emphasis is less on the product than on the teaching–learning process – that is, on the way learners interact with each other and with the material.

Brown, Gillian, and Yule, George. 1983. *Teaching the Spoken Language*. Cambridge: Cambridge University Press. Extremely useful analysis of conversational English. Implications for teaching spoken production and listening comprehension and for assessing spoken language.

Brumfit, Christopher J. 1984. *Communicative Methodology in Language Teaching: The Roles of Accuracy and Fluency*. Cambridge: Cambridge University Press. Discusses the nature of language-teaching methodology and integrates considerations on small-group work (chap. 5) into the larger issues of process versus product teaching and accuracy versus fluency.

Goffman, Erving. 1967. *Interaction Ritual: Essays on Face-to-Face Behavior*. Garden City, N.Y.: Doubleday. A fascinating commentary on how we enact ourselves by our responses to and our readings of other people in social encounters.

Kramsch, Claire J. 1981. *Discourse Analysis and Second Language Teaching.* Language in Education, Vol. 37. Washington, D.C.: Center for Applied Linguistics. Practical applications for teaching the conversational strategies of natural discourse in the classroom.

Stern, H. H. 1983. *Fundamental Concepts of Language Teaching.* Oxford: Oxford University Press. Comprehensive survey of the historical, linguistic, psychological, and sociological dimensions of language teaching and learning. Part four, "Concepts of Society," is of particular importance for understanding the social implications of learning a foreign language.

Section II Language in the classroom

3 Speaking and listening: imaginative activities for the language class

Stephen A. Sadow

Small-group activities that stimulate students to use their imagination and challenge them to think make them want to speak as well. Listening becomes more vital – students care about understanding what others have said. *Imaginative activities provide a crucial connection between skill-getting and full-fledged autonomous interaction or skill-using* (Rivers 1983a: 41–4).

In the past decade, student-directed small-group work has gradually made its way into the foreign-language curriculum. By now, most teachers have at least some familiarity with pair work, group work, and role play. Activities range from structured interviews to "happenings" and from dyads to whole-class simulations. The content of the activity may be taken from a textbook or from real life; for example, students simulate a restaurant scene (probably complicated by some difficulty) or try to find out if someone shares their birthday. Realistic activities have the advantage that they are relatively easy to formulate and can more or less replicate true-to-life experiences that the students might encounter in the target culture (shopping, asking directions, mailing books home). Depending on class level, these exercises can be prompted, written out beforehand, or ad-libbed. The effectiveness of these types of activities is limited, however, by the very realism that they try to promote. The repertoire of exchanges between a restaurant patron and a customer is quickly exhausted even when a series of minor crises complicates matters. When birthdays are matched, conversation ceases.

Imaginative activities work in a different way. Fantasy becomes more important, reality less. *Students are asked to solve a problem they would not normally have to face*, concoct a plan they would never have dreamt of on their own, reconstruct the missing parts of stories, and act in outlandish ways. In groups they must communicate to make things happen.

Although imaginative activities vary widely in theme and organization, they share a number of underlying qualities:

1. Students work from the known to the unknown.
2. The problem is deliberately ambiguous.
3. Any logical response to the problem is acceptable.
4. Role play is commonly used.

5. Listening skills are crucial at several points in the activity.
6. The teacher sets up the activity and then withdraws.
7. There is a summing up or debriefing following student discussions.

Imaginative activities work best when they are an integral part of a course. They are not intended to supplant skill-getting segments. Rather, there is an interplay between the two types of learning. They can be employed at all levels. Often, the difficulty of an activity can be adjusted by changing vocabulary or by adding or subtracting complications. To cite one example, the task of creating a beautiful face given to a group at a low level of proficiency becomes the "invention" of a movie star at a somewhat higher level and the promotion of a new line of makeup at a yet higher one. Although some activities, like finding the uses of an object, can be used at all levels, others, like reenacting a meeting of parliament in an unknown republic, clearly require more developed linguistic skills. Teachers should use their judgment but be free to experiment; they should not underestimate their students' ability to cope.

Beginnings: activities for the elementary level

Imaginative activities can be introduced very early in the foreign-language curriculum. After only a few weeks of language study, students can begin to interact within a structure. Before they attempt a group activity, *students should first become accustomed to working in pairs.* A simple way to accomplish this is for them to practice with two-line question–answer exchanges. In these, part of the question and part of the answer are supplied. Students fill in the missing sections in any way that makes sense. As an example, students may discuss food (or anything else that comes to mind):

What kind of _____ do you like?
I prefer _____ but I also _____ _____ .

Whimsy and humor (if not disruptive) *are encouraged.*

In a more widely used version of this exercise, students employ lengthy lists of questions to guide their interviewing of one another. Or, in a simple group activity, two or more students question one. Following their lists, the students probe personal histories, establish similarities and differences, and compare experiences. The questions generally do not call for imaginative replies, but may be laced with not-so-serious queries like "What is an Ork and what does it eat?"

Students may also work together on a grammar or vocabulary problem. Given a dialogue or very short story, students are told that the cast of characters has been altered. Males and females will switch gender; age and status will be changed radically. Working in pairs, students rewrite the material and make the necessary adjustments of gender, forms of address, clothing, and place in the community.

Once students begin to handle structured pair or group work with some confidence, they are ready to tackle imaginative activities. At the elementary level, the activities are usually tied closely to the material being presented in the course, the emphasis being on using the material in unexpected ways. After students have learned the parts of the face, for example, they may be asked to work together in groups to draw a beautiful face or a suspicious one or a very old one. Alternatively, they can design masks. With automobile vocabulary, students can design used cars that just cannot be sold, or oversized limousines. A unit on housing can prompt an exercise in which students must complete half-built houses. Even a unit on getting a job can lead students to invent the job interviewer they would most like to encounter. With only slightly more fluency, students can file missing-person reports, sell the furniture in the classroom, and compose simple news bulletins, or they can be asked to give directions for finding one's way through subterranean caverns where dragons dwell.

In these activities, the procedures are straightforward, and student interaction takes place on a rudimentary level. Normally, students are divided into groups of three or four. The instructions, given verbally, can be as simple as "Design the perfect student apartment" or "We have to sell all of this stuff quickly!" or "Draw a billboard to advertise _____, but don't use any words on it!" Where necessary, you can give the students drawing paper. Once they know the problem and have a list of relevant vocabulary (most likely from the text), students can proceed, discussing among themselves what they will do. Some teachers may prefer to hand out lists of questions to guide the discussion. After ten minutes, the conversation ends. The groups show what they have drawn, or they read aloud their descriptions. The teacher may correct a few glaring errors and then return to another part of the lesson, preferably one related in some way to the activity.

In *Caring and Sharing in the Foreign Language Class*, Moskowitz (1978) suggests another type of small-group activity that is applicable to the elementary class: humanistic exercises. These encourage students to explore their feelings, memories, values, and fantasies. In one, students are shown a series of shapes and are asked to draw the one they like best. Each explains to the group why this particular shape was chosen. Then the students redivide according to the shapes picked and compare their reasons for making these choices (Moskowitz 1978: 62–3).

Stephen A. Sadow

Think it over! Activities based on problem-solving

With intermediate and advanced students, *intellectually challenging problem-solving activities can be used on a regular basis to promote interaction and divergent thinking.* Role play is commonly part of the procedure. Listening skills become very important, for if students cannot understand a task they cannot perform it. To come up with a group answer, students must fully comprehend each other. In *Discussions that Work*, Ur (1981) suggests a variety of problem-solving exercises. In one, the teacher tells the class that they are extraterrestrials who, for the first time, are coming into contact with earthly objects, such as toothbrushes, watches, lightbulbs, and keys. Without reference to human civilization, the participants must draw conclusions about the objects' functions (Ur 1981: 45). Other activities in this collection deal with ranking lists of food, colors, or heroes according to preference, or choosing candidates for Man or Woman of the Year.

The activities in Maley and Duff's (1982) *Drama Techniques in Language Learning* differ from those proposed by Ur in that they often call for pantomime or acting. In one, students are told to invent a ball game with its own rules, which are then written down. One pair or group demonstrates its game to the others, who try to work out the rules by watching the game. The players can answer questions only with their bodies – not verbally. Different groups can try to play each other's games (Maley and Duff 1982: 148–9). Maley and Duff also have students create a new language, invent a machine, or dream up new meanings for well-known acronyms.

Imaginative activities based on problem solving can be built around almost any theme. The wheel can be reinvented again and again. Students can dream up new pets; design new money; develop a name, trademark, and slogan for a new organization; plan a banquet for a prince; renovate (or sell) a transit system; sell a local river, monument, hill, or desert; plan voyages of discovery; or control the fog. In *Idea Bank*, Sadow (1982) suggests that students be told to describe the people in a very old family portrait, decipher the information locked in a woven cloth, invent a new animal or hobby, or publicize the study of a nonexistent language. In one activity, the teacher, haggard from overwork, asks the class to plan a vacation.

Other activities may focus on listening skills. Using a tape recorder, the teacher can develop a problem around part of a news broadcast, an ad in the target language, a bit of folk music, or a snatch of dialogue. The students must add to what they have heard with what they have not – that is, they must elucidate the story behind the segment.

For the time span of the activity, *the students become experts of some sort*, for how otherwise could they solve the problem being posed? Their expertise may be somewhat nonsensical, as in the cases of the "fog director" or "ferry-riding expert." The activities themselves often involve fictitious countries or outlandish coincidences.

In all such activities, *the teacher begins by telling the class of the problem that faces them*. Presented as a script, the problem-posing is, in effect, a listening-comprehension exercise. The script should be adapted to class level. The teacher may say:

I just received a message from the government of Fisherland. It seems that during the months of October and November, which is Spring there, there are no holidays. Each year the people become bored and restless. The Fisherlandic leaders ask that you, experts in celebrating holidays, invent a new holiday. You should be sure to describe the customs that will be practiced.

The teacher may need to state the problem twice. For an activity of this type, speaking directly to the class is more effective than reading aloud from the script. With a few short questions, comprehension is checked. Relevant vocabulary can be introduced at this point. The teacher may want to mention phrases that students can use to manage their discussion. For instance, students of English can practice using phrases such as "Yes, but..." or "That's a good idea, but..." to express a reservation without being insulting, or ask for a clarification with "I'm sorry, I didn't understand that."

Sufficiently prepared, the students break up into groups of from three to six; each group chooses one member to be a recording secretary. The group knows that it will have to report its conclusions. The groups work together for about 20 minutes. The teacher may act as a "walking dictionary" but otherwise allows the groups to proceed at their own pace. Groups may become quiet, especially at the beginning of an activity, but they usually begin again spontaneously. Teachers should interrupt a group only when it is clearly doing something other than the assigned task. When the allotted time is over, the teacher calls the class together, all the while maintaining the pretense that the students are the experts. The secretaries report their group's responses. The teacher corrects only when comprehension is threatened.

Problem-solving activities lend themselves to follow-up. First, the activity may be repeated in the same or a slightly altered form. Second, a sequence of activities can be developed. After inventing new kinds of pets, for example, students may design the layout of a pet store or run a competition for best pet. Third, the activities can lead to writing assignments, such as making up laws for a new country or composing newspaper accounts of a recent archeological discovery.

Stephen A. Sadow

Fictions: narrative forms that provoke interaction

When working in groups, *students can "build" stories and other literary forms from the constituent parts of each type.* Most students will recognize that genres like mysteries, romances, children's stories, or TV situation comedies always contain certain elements that may vary in detail but are clearly present. Gothic horror stories, for example, tend to contain, among other things, a decaying mansion, an elderly caretaker, a ghost or other such mysterious force, an innocent visitor, and a surprise ending. A class aware of these components can write horror stories.

This type of activity works best when the class has just read a story of the type to be practiced, though this is not absolutely necessary. The class, as a whole and with the teacher's guidance, establishes the "story skeleton." The teacher may first ask, "How does a mystery story usually begin?" About eight elements are required. They should be generic – "an old man" rather than the specific "Peter Jones." In groups, the students fill in the details. The versions are then compared.

Similarly, other types of narrative can stimulate interaction. Fables, folktales, fairy tales, legends can all be recreated by language students. If the class were to compose a biography for the founder of a make-believe nation, they might have to resolve whether the leader, in childhood, lived in a hut or a palace.

The myth of the hero or heroine is an ideal model to use in this sort of activity. This myth, known in some form to many cultures and familiar to younger students through adventure movies, has the advantage of being inherently interesting and capable of being expanded or contracted as the situation requires. In one version the hero or heroine is born in mysterious circumstances. Left as an orphan, the child is brought up by uncaring relatives. The adolescent runs away from this "home" and for years wanders and completes difficult tasks. The youth encounters evil enemies as well as true love. The hero or heroine learns of his or her royal birth and returns to the place of origin to be welcomed as leader and protector. Elements can of course be added or deleted. A less advanced class can deal with a shorter list. An effective way of dealing with an extended literary form is for the students to begin developing the story while they are in small groups and then complete it individually outside of class. At the next class meeting, the students compare their endings. These myths will have several beginnings and as many conclusions as there are students in the class. Members of the original groups will be curious to find out how "their" stories diverged.

Rewrite! Activities based on incomplete narratives

In another variation of the story-writing activity, *students add to incomplete portions of stories, simple plays, or even newspaper accounts*. At the advanced level, the seed material used should be taken from anthologies or recent newspapers. With less proficient groups, teacher-produced materials work well. Many activities that would be appropriate for writing practice may be adapted to small-group work. Not only can students be supplied with the beginning of a story and told to complete it, they can also be given the end and told to compose a story that would lead to this point. Or, they may receive both the start and finish and be asked to dream up the "long-lost" middle section. The story section that is presented can be as long as five hundred words or as short as: "The rain had finally stopped. The young man, well-dressed as he was, paced nervously." or "Exhausted, filthy, but feeling proud, they began the long trip home."

Readings from a text or anthology known to the students can also lead to interactive activities. First, students can look for unexplained but potentially significant details in the narrative being studied. A locked door, an unnamed messenger, a missed appointment, a letter on the table in the vestibule will do. In groups, students explain the "real" meaning of these details. Second, students make up prologues, epilogues, and sequels to the stories being studied. Third, they can illustrate scenes from the stories or design book covers or advertising flyers.

"The gang's all here!" Activities involving the whole class

Activities in which all class members participate at once provide for a constant and varied interaction. They are appropriate at the intermediate level and above. *Activities of this type mimic real-life events while maintaining the protection of role play*. Students can practice language that is close to what they might actually use. These activities can lead naturally to discussions of forms of address and politeness or ways of managing a discussion. In one type of activity, the class provides an audience as each class member proposes a toast, gives a mock eulogy, or makes a patriotic or rabble-rousing speech. The teacher might say:

Beloved Mr. Filmore, chemistry teacher at our school for forty years, is retiring. A banquet is being given in his honor. All of you were his favorite students. Therefore, it is fitting that each of you has been asked to give at the banquet a short speech in his honor. In your talk, please tell how Mr. Filmore influenced your life.

Similar activities can be built around the reminiscences of internationally known philanthropists or champion athletes.

After the script has been read aloud, the teacher checks comprehension and suggests vocabulary words or forms needed in speech-making. Then the class members prepare their speeches. This may be done in class or, more efficiently, they can compose their talks for the next class meeting. They can write notes or the whole speech. Where possible, the chairs should be arranged to resemble a banquet hall or auditorium. One of the students acts as master or mistress of ceremonies. With more mature students the situation can be complicated by having one student, as an interloper, revolutionary, or someone with a complaint, give a talk that contradicts what the others have said. The class members listen to one another and, where appropriate, they applaud. When the last student has finished, the teacher sums up and may correct errors made by some of the students.

In another type of activity, students move around the room and try to make deals with one another. The whole class is involved, with students interacting in a series of pair arrangements. They trade antiques or cars, arrange trips, or seek unusual means of employment. In one activity, the teacher begins:

As some of you know, *Would-Be Television Studies* is looking for a number of little-known actors and actresses to feature in its new series "Beyond Beauty." Half of you here today are agents for the studio; each is looking for an actor or an actress for a specific role in the series. The others here are agents for aspiring actors and actresses who are seeking stardom and fortune. After you have taken a few moments to think about the part you want filled or the artist you represent, the agents for the studio will have a chance to meet with the agents for the performers. Speak to one and try to make a deal; if you can't make a deal, move from one to another until you've found what you are looking for. If time remains, try to agree on a contract.

In another example, students bring to class the most outlandish object they own – large feathers, wood carvings, wicker room dividers, or any unusual object. In class, they write a description of a gift they need to buy. A flea market is set up. Students take turns buying and selling. If buyers cannot find what they are looking for, they must compromise. The sellers, of course, will try to convince the buyers that their articles are suitable substitutes.

During the dealing session, the teacher can monitor the activity by walking among the students, answering their questions and, where necessary, suggesting that they move on to other partners. These activities work best in a room with furniture that can be moved to suggest a market or car dealership; however, they can be managed in more rigid arrangements by having students repeatedly change places. After the deals have been made, the pairs report them to the class.

In a third style of all-class activity, students attend mock birthday parties, garden parties, reunions, inaugural balls, political caucuses and rallies, picnics, graduations, and international conferences. Activities of this type have limited structure. Students are given or choose new identities; often these identities border on the absurd. Depending on the situation, students can be sea captains, millionaires, candidates for political office, famous sculptors, chewing gum manufacturers, or sky divers. Before proceeding, the class members spend a few minutes thinking about their new identity.

In these activities, the situation itself leads to conversation. At times, it is necessary for the teacher to remind students to talk with a number of others. In some scenes, it is possible for one participant to act as the catalyst, making introductions and spreading rumors. Requiring that the students ask set questions like "How do you feel about the new city center?" to at least four classmates is a more artificial way of making sure that the conversation flows.

You are there! Reenactments of history

In advanced classes, students can recreate scenes from history. These scenes may be selected from world history, but are more effective when they come from the target culture. Treaty negotiations, summit meetings, political party meetings (at a particular moment in history), state visits can all provide the structure for an activity. Events in which debate and controversy play a role work well, but outright hostilities can be difficult. Before doing an activity of this sort, students should be very familiar with the moment, period, and personages involved. Students can prepare themselves through textbook readings, pamphlets (where available), and documentary films. An intensive study of clothing, mannerisms, or dialect is not necessary. Historical reenactments are neither dramatic productions nor full-fledged simulations. (See Jones 1982: 55–63 on simulations.) At most the teacher may give a few pointers about the rhetoric of the period or about formalities (or insults) used at political meetings.

For the reenactment, each student should have a new identity. A student can impersonate a specific historical figure such as Bolívar, Cartier, Nehru, Queen Elizabeth I, or Truman, but the scenes are simpler to stage if students simply assume a generic role, such as the leader or ideologue of a political party who advocates terrorism, a leader who urges cooperation with the colonial power, or a representative of the party in power. Reenacting a conference on multiculturalism held in Ottawa, for instance, the students are representatives of the Ministry of State, the Canadian Conference on the Arts, Radio-Canada, Université

41

de Montréal, and Hudson Bay Oil and Gas. More than one student can play each role.

After preparing their roles, the students improvise discussion and debate and may even shout at one another. If called for by the situation, one student can act as moderator. A large class can be subdivided. In an activity of this type, a debriefing is helpful. With teacher direction, the class recapitulates what went on and where they strayed from the historical model.

Conclusion

Imaginative activities do not dominate any foreign-language curriculum. In themselves, they do not constitute a methodology. For that reason, *they can be used alongside many other techniques and in conjunction with many styles of language teaching and at all levels.* As has been shown, a willingness to suspend disbelief, the ability to associate freely and easily, and a good sense of humor help in carrying out these activities. Not all students have large doses of these qualities, but in a relaxed and confident classroom most students can be inspired to use what they do have. The injection of more standard drills, readings, and tapes can quiet the objections of those seeking "serious study." A few students will use their native language from time to time, but this will fade away as they become accustomed to the activities. With practice, interaction and imagination increase. Fluency outruns exactness, but communication grows.

Let's act on it

1. How can imaginative activities be integrated into a more traditional course? Where do they fit? Using a familiar textbook, find the points at which imaginative activities could be developed.
2. Make up a script for a problem-solving activity. Be sure to include an ambiguous situation and a role play. Rewrite this activity to make it appropriate for a more elementary level. Then rewrite it again to make it appropriate for an advanced level. Practice one version with a group of teachers.
3. What nonliterary forms (newspaper articles, for example) can be melted down to their "skeleton" features? What literary ones? Pick one form and identify at least eight components. Based on these, try composing your own version. Then make up a sequel to what you have written.

4. List ten situations (not mentioned in the text) where people give short speeches. Develop an activity around one of these situations.
5. List types of parties, get-togethers, and meetings not mentioned in the text. Pick one that would provide an inviting forum for communication at the intermediate level. Invent numerous roles. Prepare ways to adjust the situation if conversation flags.
6. Prime your own creativity by writing down all the activity concepts you can think of in twenty minutes. (You may borrow ideas from textbooks or the references in the Annotated Reading List.)

Annotated reading list

Birckbichler, D. W. 1982. *Creative Activities for the Second Language Classroom*. Washington, D.C.: Center for Applied Linguistics. A collection of activities taken from many sources, including popular textbooks in French, Spanish, and German.

Jones, K. 1982. *Simulations in Language Learning*. Cambridge: Cambridge University Press. A comprehensive guide to adapting complex situations to language classes; it provides one complete simulation. Best suited for advanced classes.

Keller, E., and Warner, S. T. 1979. *Gambits 1: Openers; Gambits 2: Links; Gambits 3: Responders, Closers and Inventory*. Hull, P.Q.: Public Service Commission of Canada. A three-volume set of exercises for the teaching of phrases useful in opening, directing, interrupting, and closing a conversation. For French and German, see C. J. Kramsch, 1981, *Discourse Analysis and Second Language Teaching*, Language in Education, Vol. 37, Washington, D.C.: Center for Applied Linguistics; and 1981, "Teaching Discussion Skills: A Pragmatic Approach," *FLA* 14: 93–104.

Maley, A., and Duff, A. 1982. *Drama Techniques in Language Learning*. New ed. Cambridge: Cambridge University Press. Very varied communication activities, many based on mime and other nonverbal techniques.

Moskowitz, G. 1978. *Caring and Sharing in the Foreign Language Class*. Rowley, Mass.: Newbury House. A guide to the application of humanistic education to foreign language teaching. Contains many exercises intended to provoke affective as well as linguistic responses. Appendixes give lengthy lists of words and expressions indicating feelings, emotions, and qualities in English, German, Latin, Spanish, French, Italian, and Hebrew.

Sadow, S. A. 1982. *Idea Bank: Creative Activities for the Language Class*. Rowley, Mass.: Newbury House. Activities intended to provoke divergent thinking as well as language use; each is presented in a lesson-plan format. Examples in English with translation of key sections into Spanish, French, and German.

Ur, P. 1981. *Discussions that Work: Task-Centred Fluency Practice*. Cambridge: Cambridge University Press. A set of relatively simple small-group activities; includes guessing games, picture interpretations, detecting differences, and putting things in order.

4 Motivating language learners through authentic materials

Bernice S. Melvin and David F. Stout

As language teachers, we have all used some authentic materials (poems, advertisements, menus, or songs) that bring students into contact with language as it is used in the culture to meet actual communication needs. Many of us, at some time, have organized successful "culture days" or taught "culture capsules," where we have introduced authentic texts and been thrilled by the enthusiasm of our students. These interludes revive flagging spirits and renew interest in the subject matter. We can do more than this, however. Fully exploited, authentic texts give students direct access to the culture and help them use the new language authentically themselves, to communicate meaning in meaningful situations rather than for demonstrating knowledge of a grammar point or a lexical item.

Taking full advantage of the potential benefits of authentic materials may, however, require both a change of perspective and the adoption of some new approaches. Teachers, like the texts they use to teach a language and introduce a culture, tend to tell students about a country and its people instead of letting them find out for themselves. By being too eager to share their knowledge, teachers deny their students the thrill of discovery. Because their experience of the culture is mediated by the teacher, students do not interact directly with authentic materials but rather with someone else's summary or analysis of them.

What then would be a more effective way of using authentic materials in class? Let us begin by giving students units of authentic material with exercises and activities that we design. Let us then allow the students to decide on which of the texts they wish to concentrate. After students have worked with the material, let us give them time to communicate their findings to others. The conclusions they reach are of secondary importance. What matters is their ability to reach conclusions based on work with authentic sources and the opportunity to communicate these conclusions in the new language. The procedure we propose can best be illustrated by the following model unit called "Discover a City," which can be used effectively with beginning, intermediate, or advanced students in any language.

"Discover a City"

Imagine being able to culminate each semester of language instruction by sending students to a city in the target culture for about four days, telling them that their final examination will consist of going to that city for a long weekend (in French going to Paris, in English going to New York, or in German going to Heidelberg), keeping track of everything they do, and reporting back to the teacher or the class. Although beginners would not be capable of the same kinds of interactions with native speakers as advanced students, they would survive and benefit from the experience.

Regularly providing students at all levels with this kind of opportunity as a supplement to the usual class routine would be an incredible motivator. Students who taste success in the use of a foreign language realize the benefits of knowing the other language and culture and seek to repeat the experience.

Authentic materials as a substitute for a trip to the culture

Unfortunately the foregoing scenario is just a fantasy for most of us and our students, but what if we could capitalize on the benefits of such a program without actually sending our students on a journey? Although the actual experience of visiting the city cannot be transferred to the classroom, virtually all the sources of information students visiting the city would use can be made available in a classroom setting. What kinds of materials would enable students to simulate such a visit? What would make it possible for them to "discover a city"? Here are some suggestions:

- city street map;
- public transportation guide;
- relief map of the city and surrounding countryside;
- list of hotels;
- guide to the city's restaurants with descriptions and rankings;
- menus from local restaurants;
- tourist brochures;
- cultural publications announcing opening times of museums, theaters, and galleries in the city;
- catalogues from exhibitions at local museums;
- entertainment sections of local papers;
- student guides to the city with information on educational institutions;
- guide to sports and recreation opportunities;
- movie listings;
- shopping guides and sales advertising;
- business telephone listings (like the Yellow Pages);
- samples of currency in use;

- newspaper or magazine articles describing various aspects of life in the city;
- songs about the city;
- films, television shows, or literature about or set in the city;
- pictures or videotapes of the city's best-known points of interest;
- audio or video interviews with natives and other visitors getting advice on what to see and do;
- radio and television ads for points of interest in the city.

Using these materials productively in class

What kinds of meaningful activities might students be asked to carry out with these materials? The "Discover a City" model asks students to work with the authentic materials for one week. The movement is always from comprehension to production. Students begin by familiarizing themselves through reading and listening with the kinds of materials at their disposal. They are then asked to choose the specific sources with which they would like to work intensively. After concentrated work with these sources, the week concludes with either a written or an oral presentation of how each student plans to spend a four-day period in the city. Students are asked to justify each decision they make and to explain their sources of information.

Perhaps the most important feature of student work in "Discover a City" is the suspension of usual classroom procedures. Students are told from the beginning that their project will be evaluated on their ability to receive and convey information in the language. Accuracy will affect their performance only if errors interfere with communication. Students are constantly reminded that we are simulating what they would experience in the actual city. Time spent worrying about the things they do not understand is simply time wasted. What counts are those things whose meaning they can discover. Just as students do not need to understand every word of a TV guide to decide which program they would like to watch, students can glean a great deal of information from sources containing vocabulary and structures they have not yet mastered. The first exercises, therefore, help students identify what they have understood in a new text. Subsequent exercises send them back to the text a second or third time to refine their comprehension.

Exercises for "Discover a City"

The first type of interaction, regardless of level, is between students and the authentic materials. The kinds of exercises assigned to students depend in large part on their language level; they are, however, always ordered so that they lead the student from comprehension to production. Beginning students are given simpler, more directed activities. Students may be asked to

- locate on a map the sights of interest in the introductory slide show;
- make an inventory of available sources – what types of information can be found where;
- make a list of loan words encountered in the sources;
- identify businesses or activities with counterparts in their home town, for instance, the zoo or a fast-food center;
- find places or activities that are mentioned in more than one source;
- produce, based on a prescribed budget, a detailed itinerary for a four-day visit to the city.

For this last activity, students are asked to

1. pick a time of year for the visit based on seasonal activities available in the area;
2. select lodging for four days and figure out how much it will cost;
3. select from advertisements, restaurant guides, and menus places to eat for four days' worth of meals and estimate the cost of each meal;
4. select at least two places of interest to be visited each day;
5. locate all the places to be visited on the map and figure out how to get from one place to the next, estimating transportation costs.

These activities are all designed to help students work productively with the materials without having to account for each grammatical structure and lexical item. They are intended to maximize the chances that students will encounter items in a variety of different contexts. The emphasis is on successfully processing information from as many sources as possible. Beginners tend to work most productively with sources requiring little linguistic sophistication, such as charts, tables, and lists. More complex sources would of necessity be dealt with superficially at this level, although they would be of considerable interest to more advanced students.

Production exercises grow naturally out of these comprehension activities and might ask students to

- present their itineraries to the teacher or the other members of the class;
- justify each of the selections they have made and describe which sources of information they used in reaching their decision;
- find other students in the class who will be staying where they will be staying or visiting places they will visit;
- figure out how to visit other students in the class while they are both visiting the city;

47

- compare itineraries to determine whose plan is most expensive, whose the cheapest, and share ideas for making the visit more enjoyable;
- carry out role plays with the teacher and other students in which they order food from the menu of a restaurant they have selected;
- fill out a registration form for the hotel they have chosen;
- act out scenes where they ask for extra blankets at the hotel or change travelers' checks at the bank.

In the production stage students move from interaction with the materials to interaction with each other and with the teacher. The more often students refer back to their sources during the production phase the better, since this is where their familiarity with the sources really pays off. The students with the more interesting itineraries will be those who have taken the trouble to look closely at the available sources. The more they are familiar with their sources, the more they will have learned, and the more easily they will be able to communicate what they have learned to others.

Although more advanced students can begin with the activities designed for beginners, they will be called on to do much more:

- find places listed in more than one source and analyze the differences in information provided: for example, a restaurant that advertises authentic atmosphere but is described in a review as a tourist trap;
- find out as much as possible about each item on the itinerary;
- work intensively with tapes of natives and other visitors, analyzing their recommendations and comparing them with other sources of information;
- divide available options into categories, then plan at least one activity in each category on the itinerary, such as culture, nightlife, sports, shopping.

Advanced production activities are correspondingly more sophisticated. Students might

- act as tour guides or experts and explain to the class what they have learned about the various points of interest;
- write diary entries or a letter home describing their experiences;
- interview other students, compare itineraries, and find out why the others made the choices they did;
- evaluate the different sources and explain which were most helpful, most subjective, too vague, and so on.

At this level students concentrate less on survival skills and focus instead on getting to know the city in greater detail. They will also be required to back up their contentions about the city with reference to sources, but they will be asked to look critically at those sources and discover how and why they differ.

The final production exercise at any level consists simply of producing a detailed schedule for each of the four days. Students provide entries in the following categories: time, place, type of activity, information sources used, and why they chose this place or activity. Asking students to justify their choices provides them with the opportunity to show just how much they have learned.

Practical considerations

We turn now to the practical questions involved in the use of authentic materials.

1. Where do I find authentic materials?
2. How do I choose topics and select materials for a unit?
3. How do I assemble the units?
4. What kinds of exercises and activities can I design?
5. How do I get help in working on units?

Where to find authentic materials

Creating a unit as extensive as "Discover a City" takes time and effort. It is most easily accomplished by visiting the city in question and devoting several days or longer to collecting the material. The best way to start is by reading tourist guides to the city. Most cities have tourist information centers with booklets and brochures providing excellent material on where to stay and things to see and do. They may also provide information about local transportation, day trips from the city, major industries, addresses of clubs and organizations, and a brief history of the city. The next step is to visit all the places of interest, taking pictures and gathering relevant printed material. To this can be added magazines; newspapers; postcards; records; videotapes; information brochures from banks, post offices, railway stations, and airports; interviews with native speakers taped on your own cassette recorder; and anything else that seems even remotely usable.

If a teacher does not have the opportunity to travel to the appropriate city to gather materials personally, there are other means of acquiring the necessary items. Friends who are traveling may be willing to collect materials for you, or you may establish contact with a foreign-language teacher in the city and exchange materials about the place where you live. Such a contact may also be able to provide you with videotaped television programs on the city. Students traveling in the summers can often be prevailed upon to bring back materials. Writing to companies, tourist information centers in the city in question, tourist agencies in your own city, or consulates frequently brings in a wealth of material. Area businesses with international connections can also be a source of interesting items. If native speakers are available in or passing through your community, they may be asked to look over the materials and record their suggestions for things to do and see.

Collecting vast amounts of authentic material can be enjoyable, but large units such as "Discover a City" are not the only way to bring authenticity to the classroom. Quite small amounts of material can be used creatively. For example, a quick perusal of almost any newspaper will yield sufficient material to construct a small unit on buying or renting a house or apartment. A collage of owner and realtor advertisements, a headline, and an article dealing with housing shortages or the diminishing population in the area will give students sufficient material for a day's work. More important than the amount of available material is its interest level for the students and the teacher's or students' choice of a theme that draws the materials together in some organized fashion.

How to choose topics and select materials for a unit

The level of the students will influence the selection of materials, but this is not decisive; many good materials can be used with students at different levels. Often the success or failure of a text depends not on its apparent difficulty but on the exercises accompanying it. Some decisions, however, must be made on the basis of length and complexity. A play by Ibsen, a recent study by a Norwegian sociologist on the mother's role in the family, and a television documentary about battered wives would probably best be used with more advanced students. Beginning students would probably deal more effectively with statistics on working women, an excerpt from an article on children's attitudes toward working mothers, and a television advertisement warning parents not to leave their children unattended. The wide array of language used is not the only factor in making material difficult for the student. Culturally unexpected behavior or attitudes can increase its inaccessibility.

Although length, linguistic complexity, interest for the student, and overlap all play significant roles in the selection of materials, *the single most important criterion for selection is content*. Many syntactic and lexical problems can be overcome by the intelligent selection and ordering of exercises; nothing can overcome the obstacle of uninteresting topics or boring activities.

Teachers should not allow abstract notions of student interests to limit their selection. When students in a third-semester college German class in the United States were asked if they were interested in studying sex-role stereotypes, they responded with a resounding "Nein!" When they were asked, however, to work with some popular songs, excerpts from children's theater, and dating-service questionnaires, they became enthusiastic. Their work with these materials brought the topic to life for them. Teachers need to guard against making hasty decisions about what is or is not of interest to their students. Materials that seem to have little or no interest can be used in provocative and productive ways.

How to assemble a unit

It is best to include in each unit items in a variety of mediums that examine the topic from different perspectives. When enough interesting raw material relating to a common topic has been found, it is time to begin turning the material into a unit. If individual texts are too long for our purposes, we can maintain their authenticity without simplifying them by working with excerpts that are relevant to the topic and that tie in well with other materials to be used.

One particularly popular technique is to create collages from a variety of sources. Differences in print size and style catch the eye and underscore more significant differences between the kinds of texts being used. This juxtaposition of several small items relating to one topic can be more inviting to students than a page filled with dense prose, especially if the collage is not overly cluttered.

While assembling a unit, remember that students will be making their own selections from the materials made available to them, so do not limit their choices too severely. Statistical tables may be of no interest to you, but they may interest some of your students, especially if the tables show the topic under consideration from a unique perspective. Since we are providing our students with a variety of sources, it is not necessary to eliminate certain materials because they do not present the culture in a favorable light or because we do not agree with them. In fact, discovering conflicting views in different sources is one of the most productive and interesting student exercises.

Using audio and video materials

Recorded material can go a long way toward bringing a unit to life, but it presents special challenges for both the teacher and the student. It is crucial that recordings be of the highest technical quality. Students have enough trouble understanding native speech in face-to-face situations. A poor-quality recording, regardless of the interest level of its material, is of little use to students. Length of recorded material is particularly important. Students will be more likely to succeed if they work with spoken language in one- to two-minute segments. If a longer program must be used, then one of the first exercises should be to identify short segments to be analyzed in detail.

Videotapes can add a new dimension to the students' experience of other places, capturing sounds, sights, and the nonverbal behavior of the speakers of the language for repeated viewing and analysis. Popular songs can also be used with a unit if they deal with the appropriate topic. A unit on computer anxiety in West Germany, for example, may center on the Georg Danzer song "Zerschlagt die Computer" ("Smash the Computers"). Given the opportunity to work with lyrics that relate to a topic they have been studying, students usually learn the song on their own. The words make sense not only in the song itself but also in the larger context of the unit and can become a part of their active vocabulary.

With both video and audio recordings, students must be able to work with the material more than once, just as they would with a printed text. Sometimes this can be done in the library or a language-learning laboratory. Even when the only option is to play the tape in the classroom, students must be given the opportunity to hear sections of the tape many times. Full comprehension comes only with much hearing, and students will need to check details as they work.

What kinds of exercises and activities to design

Since students talk best in another language if they have something to say, exercises should be designed in sequence to lead from comprehension of the material to student production. Students will be better prepared to talk or write about a topic after they have worked with texts, acquired some vocabulary, and identified some important issues surrounding the topic. Production activities must grow naturally out of comprehension activities. Comprehension activities should never be ends in themselves, as they so often are in textbooks and tests, but rather means to an end, namely, the basis for production, in speech or writing.

COMPREHENSION EXERCISES

What kinds of comprehension exercises are most effective? The most successful exercises are those that help students make sense of new texts they are interested in, yet are flexible enough to encourage them to move on to other interesting texts before they have mastered every word and structure encountered. There will be some students who find it difficult to focus their attention on any given text for longer than a few minutes and others who will find it difficult to tear themselves away from the first text they face. Yet lure them away we must, for we are doing them a tremendous disservice if we encourage word-for-word reading and memorization.

The first step is to help students realize that they can interact productively with a text that appears at first to be too difficult. Our exercises must enable students to overcome this initial feeling of being overwhelmed by new material. The best way to reduce this initial anxiety is to design exercises that draw the students' attention to things in the text they will have understood. These activities might include the identification of number and gender of singers of a popular song or of persons referred to in the lyrics, characterization of the type of text (e.g., poem, advertisement, love letter), or the names of central characters. Identifying loan words and cognates is also a useful preliminary exercise, which frequently leads directly to the central theme.

Students often understand more than they realize, and the first exercises need to make explicit what students know intuitively or by analogy. If, for example, they recognize that the text is a fable, they will expect the characters to be animals with human characteristics. Since exercises at the early stage are quite simple, they give students the opportunity to succeed in their first contact with the text. Given an initial success, they are more likely to approach the text a second or third time. If, on the other hand, initial questions are too difficult, student frustration will increase, thus reducing the chances that they will continue to work at all willingly with the text.

Exercises at the next stage ask students to reorder words or phrases they have encountered in the text. This exercise is based on the notion that even if students do not know the precise meaning of a word, they can often tell from context what function the word serves and what type of information the word conveys. Let us say, for example, that students studying housing problems in an American city are working with the real estate section of a newspaper. Although they might not know the precise meaning of each word, they could probably extract words referring to styles of houses – words such as *Georgian, Victorian,* or *townhouse.* They could also identify words describing attractive features of a house, like wall-to-wall carpeting or a new kitchen, even if they were not sure what was meant by each. Once students have identified the type of information conveyed by a word or phrase, they can then make informed decisions about whether or not they want to go to the trouble of finding out its specific meaning.

Spoken texts present special problems, since students may have difficulty identifying individual words in the flow of native speech. Here a helpful preliminary exercise is to give students an alphabetized list of key words and ask them to number the words as they hear them on the tape. This exercise is particularly useful in helping students to bridge the gap between oral and written language. At the same time it provides them with a list of words they will need to master if they are to communicate clearly on the topic at hand. Their numbered wordlist is also a shorthand version of the text and may make the original easier to understand.

Of course, sooner or later students will need help in making precise sense of new words and structures. This usually means turning to the dictionary – a less than popular activity with most students. If the dictionary work follows preliminary exercises like the ones outlined previously, then looking up words will have become more than simply a finger exercise. The students will have decided that a particular word is important and will want to know its meaning. Since they have encountered the word in a meaningful context, they are also more likely to remember it.

Once students have a general understanding of the text, they will decide whether they want to continue working with it. If the text relates directly to their final production project, students will want to look at it more closely; if not, they will move on to the next text. The emphasis here is on students making enlightened decisions about work with a particular text and on helping them to work with it as efficiently as possible.

PRODUCTION EXERCISES

The design of production activities can decide the success or failure of a unit. Since the emphasis is on communication, questions of accuracy need to be treated with great care. We believe that it is best in working with authentic materials to suspend the normal rules of classroom operation. Students should be told from the start that they will be graded on accuracy only if errors make communication impossible. They should then be put into meaningful situations where they can use what they have learned and demonstrate their communicative skill. Simple role plays set in a restaurant, airport, or hotel work well in beginning classes. More advanced students may be asked to interpret and to look critically at their sources.

Production should not be limited to interaction between student and teacher. We need to put students in a variety of situations where they communicate with one another. Tedium can be avoided in these interactions by varying the individual assignments. In "Discover a City," for example, assigning students different budgets for their stay will prevent everyone from picking the same hotel and restaurants. They can then talk about the relative merits of their particular choice and enter into vigorous discussion about the benefits of their stay.

How to work cooperatively on unit preparation

Since much time and energy can go into the creation of an authentic materials unit, sharing units with other teachers is an excellent way to maximize their benefit. Working collectively on their creation significantly reduces preparation time. For years the Goethe Institute has been sponsoring week-long "Didaktisierungsseminare," during which high school and college teachers come together to sift through available materials and create units complete with exercises. Other teachers use in-service days to create units. Teachers in the same or neighboring school districts can establish networks for collecting materials, refining exercises, sharing finished units, and developing ideas for new ones. Regional meetings of professional organizations provide ideal opportunities for workshops and discussions of results. It is also possible to establish an open-file system by housing master copies of units at one school. Teachers can then be sent copies of units on request. Under this system, every time a unit is used the teacher fills in a critique sheet that becomes a part of the file on that unit. This gives teachers who ask to use the units helpful information on what other teachers have done with the materials, especially what worked and what did not. The open-file system encourages teachers to add new items to the units they have borrowed. Even a small school district can accumulate an extensive set of authentic materials by such cooperation.

Conclusion

Studying a foreign language should be a means to a greater end, namely, communicating with another culture and its representatives. Using authentic materials in the ways we have described allows students to experience early in their study the rewards of learning a language. Students who work with authentic materials have an interest in the language that is based on what they know it can do for them. Students who were previously unwilling to master the forms of the language come to realize the benefits of further language acquisition. Benefits also accrue to teachers who find that they have motivated and goal-oriented students and a curriculum that is stimulating to students and teachers alike.

Let's act on it

1. Discuss experiences you have had using authentic materials in class.
2. Make a list of authentic materials at your disposal. How could you add to your files? What is most readily available to you? What would be the most difficult to obtain?
3. Choose a text from the authentic materials available to you and outline two series of exercises that lead progressively from comprehension to production, one for beginning students and one

for advanced students. In what ways do the two series differ and for what reasons?

4. Describe in detail materials you could gather from your own city for a "Discover a City" unit, and discuss how they might be used productively in a language course.

5. What advantages and disadvantages do you see in the introduction of authentic-material units into the foreign-language classroom? What kinds of materials would interest your students most?

5 Interactive oral grammar exercises

Raymond F. Comeau

Baudelaire in *Les paradis artificiels* referred to grammar as "l'aride grammaire." Many instructors and students would probably agree with Baudelaire, for grammar study, especially in review grammars, is often associated with the dry memorization of rules and the equally dry prospect of applying these rules in fill-in-the-blank, pattern practice, substitution, transformation, and translation exercises. This stereotypical view of grammar study, fortunately, is only partially true. Most modern language textbooks, especially at the elementary level, include at least some grammar exercises designed to allow students to use grammar in interactive situations.

What is an interactive oral grammar exercise?

The word *interactive* is derived from the Latin verb *agere*, which means *to do*, and the Latin preposition *inter*, meaning *among*. An interactive grammar exercise, therefore, stresses the teaching of grammar through mutual participation, usually in small groups. It is active rather than passive, student-centered rather than language-centered, cognitive rather than behavioristic, indirect rather than direct, and personal rather than manipulative. An interactive grammar exercise puts communication on a par with correctness, turning the study of grammar into a social activity.

The interactive approach frees the instructor as well as the student. The instructor's role is to act as a coach who organizes, encourages, and guides student interaction. In practical terms, the instructor prepares and hands out group assignments, then circulates from group to group, listening, encouraging, and correcting; when the groups have finished preparing their activities, he or she orchestrates final performances. At times instructors will also participate in a playful give-and-take with students, thus inserting themselves into the interactive process.

Five qualities of interactive oral grammar exercises

Instructors who use interactive exercises in class, and those who intend to make up their own, should keep in mind these five qualities of good interactive oral grammar exercises:

1. They should be *communicative*. Interactive exercises should be integrated into group activities, such as interviews, group games, dialogues, pantomimes, and other forms of role play that encourage communication between students or between the instructor and students.

2. They should be *meaningful*. Interactive exercises should fully engage the students' minds and imaginations. Ideally, students should become so absorbed in the meaningful activity that they learn the grammar point naturally, almost without having to think specifically about it.

3. They should provide a *limited choice*. Interactive grammar exercises should provide students with a limited choice of possible answers in order to allow them to focus their full attention on the meaning of the activity. In most cases this means making a choice between only two forms (e.g., *who* or *whom*, masculine or feminine forms, the simple-past or the past-progressive tense).

4. They should be *expressive*. Students should be encouraged to adopt the accent, intonation, and pronunciation of native speakers as completely as possible. The quality of expression in interactive exercises should be highly inflected, even exaggerated, and should represent the full range of emotions in order to encourage students to forget their inhibitions and truly dramatize the language.

5. They should be *integrated* with other kinds of exercises. Interactive grammar exercises should complement rather than replace traditional exercises. Repetition, substitution, and pattern-practice exercises, for example, are effective tools for language learning at the manipulative level, and they can often be used in conjunction with interactive exercises for the sake of variety. Where class time is unduly limited, a certain amount of manipulative practice that requires thoughtful responses economizes on the time required for students to acquire a foundation for interactive practice. If communicative ability is to be developed, however, there must be practice in using language to communicate meaningful messages, even in limited contexts. (For an interesting discussion of the differences among mechanical, meaningful, and communicative drills, see Paulston 1970 and Rivers 1983a, chaps. 3 and 4.)

Student-to-student interaction

There are two major types of classroom interaction: student-to-student and instructor-to-student. Student-to-student interaction is based on peer relationships, which allow the maximum degree of communication. Any instructor who has witnessed the lively personal interchange between students working together in small groups and experienced the excellent results knows the value of fostering small-group dynamics in the classroom. For the sake of discussion I have divided student-to-student in-

teractive oral grammar activities into three groups: dialogues, poetry
and drama; and information-gathering activities.

Dialogues

Since dialogue represents the most common form of oral communication,
it is not surprising that the dialogue format lends itself so well to interactive grammar activities.

FILL-IN-THE BLANK EXERCISES WITH DIALOGUES

Fill-in-the blank exercises in a dialogue format offers an ingenious
method for transforming a traditional grammar exercise into an interactive one. Students working in pairs are asked to fill in the blanks,
practice the dialogue, and then perform it for the class.

Fill in the blanks with "do," "does," or "did."
A: _____ you want to go shopping this afternoon?
B: I _____ , but I can't because I'm going for a walk with Barbara.
A: But _____n't you take a walk with Barbara yesterday?
B: I _____ .
A: I've never met Barbara. _____ you think she might like to go
   shopping?
B: I _____n't think so. She _____n't do much shopping.
A: That's strange. Why not?
B: Barbara's my dog! Dogs _____n't go shopping very often, _____
   they?

In an interesting variation of a fill-in-the-blank exercise, students are
first given a model dialogue and asked to do a fill-in-the-blank exercise
based on it. This kind of exercise allows students greater flexibility and
freedom than the traditional fill-in-the-blank model.

Ask someone how he or she spends his or her free time. Tell that person
how you spend your free time.
Luigi: How do you spend your free time?
Martine: I read, go to the movies, play a little tennis. And you?
Luigi: I like to meet people like you. Are you busy tonight?

A: How do you spend your free time?
B: _____ . And you?
A: _____ .

TRANSLATION EXERCISES AS DIALOGUES

Translation exercises have generally fallen out of favor in the oral approach to language study. In a class with a homogeneous native-language

background, however, they can provide a lively format for interaction. They are especially useful at the intermediate level and above, when presented as dialogues. The comparison of adjectives is the focal point of the following translation.

Translate the following dialogue into French and then play the dialogue in pairs.

A: What do you think of Gigi and Monique?

B: Gigi is prettier than Monique, that's evident, but Monique is more intelligent than Gigi – much more intelligent.

A: Let's hire Monique, then. Intelligence is more important than appearance.

B: I agree.

As a variation, students may be asked to substitute the names of real or imaginary persons, or they may be encouraged to use the vocabulary of the exercise in original contexts. Caution must be taken, however, with the control of vocabulary in translation exercises, for unfamiliar or overly specialized vocabulary can distract the student's attention from the grammar point in question.

DIALOGUES WITH VISUAL CUES

The use of visual cues in short dialogues represents another useful approach to interaction. Keep in mind that the dialogues should contain natural speech, and the logic of the visual cues should be absolutely clear. Carefully designed visuals can be used to elicit dialogues that stress a number of grammar points; as in the following example.

Look at the model and write three dialogues based on the illustrations below. Practice your dialogues aloud. Work in pairs.

Model
- Tu as **la clé**? Elle n'est pas dans le tiroir.
○ Oh! pardon. Elle est sur la table.
[– *Do you have the key? It isn't in the drawer!*
– *Oh! Excuse me. It's on the table.*]

(Reprinted with permission from C. Benigni and H. B. Hempel, C'est ça, p. 26, Reading, Mass.: Addison-Wesley. © 1983.)

DIRECTED DIALOGUES

In a directed dialogue students are asked to make up their own dialogues based on a defined situation. The flexibility of directed dialogues is somewhat circumscribed, but within those limits they encourage creativity and lead to lively class performances.

Directed dialogue for teaching the verb "to go" and the days of the week
Mike wants to go out with Debbie, but she doesn't want to go out with him. He asks her if she is free today, and she says no. He then asks her about several other days, but she responds by saying that she is busy and is going to various places on those days. Finally, Debbie reluctantly breaks down and says yes. Mike ends the dialogue by exclaiming enthusiastically: "Oh, Debbie, you're fantastic!"

Students may be given the following variation, which allows for a little more creativity.

Raymond F. Comeau

Mike	Debbie
Debbie, are you free today?	

And tomorrow?
How about Monday night?
I suppose you're busy on Thursday night, too.
Oh, Debbie, you're fantastic!

Directed dialogue for teaching the English simple past

A: father/mother   B: son/daughter
Ask what B did last night.

                    Answer A by stating a few
                       things you did.

Ask why B came home at 4:00 a.m.

                    Act surprised: You thought A
                       didn't hear you come home
                       late.
                    Give a good reason or reasons
                       why you came home so late.

Tell B you worried about him/her.

                    Tell A you are sorry you didn't
                       call him/her.

Poetry and drama

Many language instructors who have a fondness for literature enjoy conducting various literary activities associated with poetry, songs, plays, soap operas, or short stories. There can be no doubt that these add variety and richness to the language class, but every effort must be made, in the context of oral grammar practice, to select activities that are simple enough and deal with specific points of grammar.

POETRY READINGS

Poetry is one of the richest vehicles for encouraging students to play with language in a personal way. In elementary classes students can be asked to write original poems after the first week. Below is a suitable model poem that carefully reinforces grammar and vocabulary usually introduced in the first weeks (the prepositions *in, behind,* and *on* and parts of the body).

Dans le parc   (In the park)

Un étudiant dans la classe   (*A male student in the class*
Une étudiante derrière l'étudiant   *A female student behind the male*
                                        student

Un message dans la main	*A message in the hand*
Un sourire sur le visage...	*A smile on the face...*
Une promenade dans le parc	*A walk in the park*
Une main dans la main	*A hand in a hand*
Un baiser sur la joue	*A kiss on the cheek*
Une bouche sur une bouche	*A mouth on a mouth*
Un coeur dans un coeur	*A heart in a heart*
L'amour dans l'air[1]	*Love in the air)*

After studying the poem at home and reading it aloud in class, students are asked to write their own poems using this poem as a model.[2] The poems are then collected and corrected, and some are chosen for a short poetry reading, during which individual students read their poems with the proper solemnity (or lack thereof) to the rest of the class. The originality of the students' poetry and the excitement this activity generates never fail to delight the teacher.

GRAMMAR PLAYS

Plays are not written, fortunately, to reinforce grammar points. Grammar and drama can be brought together, however, for teaching purposes. In grammar plays characters are defined by the grammar they use as well as by their character type. Briefly put, each character is assigned a grammar point and a type by the class. Students are then asked to write an original play using these characters. The following are some examples of grammar types:

Grammar point	*Character type*
comparatives, superlatives	braggart, snob, perfectionist
descriptive adjectives	critic, flatterer
conditionals	character who is constantly regretting past actions
imperatives	commander, boss
past tense	a nostalgic character
future tense	character who lives on good intentions

Each character must use a liberal sprinkling of his or her assigned grammar points without, of course, allowing the grammar to become so obvious that it adversely affects the play. Because of the time required in preparation, this activity can be spread over two or three weeks, with students taking some class time each day to develop their roles.

1 From R. F. Comeau and N. J. Lamoureux, *Echanges* (New York: Holt, Rinehart and Winston, 1982), p. 13.
2 For an approach to beginning English using modeling techniques, see Molinsky and Bliss (1983).

PANTOMIMES

A pantomime is a scene in body language which can be used to elicit spoken or written language. Pantomimes are just as enjoyable for the student mimes as they are for the students trying to guess what the mimes are doing. In practical terms, students in groups of two or three prepare a pantomime and act it out in front of the members of the class, who try to guess, orally or in writing, what the mimes are doing. Pantomimes are very useful for demonstrating verbs and adjectives. Student mimes can even be asked to act out a series of related scenes (e.g., two fishermen go fishing, catch two big fish, bring them home, clean them, and eat them – but they have too many bones!).[3]

Information-gathering activities

Gathering information from people through interviews, talk shows, questionnaires, or guessing games provides a natural context for grammar practice. Since information-gathering activities involve questions, these activities are particularly appropriate for practicing verbs and all the interrogative forms.

INTERVIEWS

Interviewing is a natural interactive activity because it emphasizes group discussion and deliberation. Teams of from two to five students meet to develop a series of questions that can be used to interview a number of candidates for a specific job. The interview is then conducted in front of the class using class volunteers who act as the candidates being interviewed. After the interview has been completed, the interview committee deliberates and selects the person or persons they consider most suitable for the job.

Interviews have the added advantage of being easily associated with a given theme. In a chapter dealing with cuisine, for example, waiters or waitresses may be interviewed for a job in an exclusive restaurant. Other candidates may be doctors (health), athletes (sports), clothing designers or models (clothing), journalists (the media), travel agents (travel), politicians (politics), business people (business), artists (the arts), or language teachers (perhaps a number of language teachers applying to teach your course!).

"RADIO RENDEZVOUS"

"Radio Rendezvous" is a dating game in a radio talk show format. Callers who are looking for persons to date call the talk show host, who

---

3 For a novel approach to teaching French using expressive body movement and verbal expression, see Wylie (1985).

asks them many questions about the kinds of persons they would like to meet (e.g., personality traits, occupation, age, hobbies). The host also asks the callers to describe themselves in much the same way. Members of the class, acting as radio listeners, select the caller or callers they like best.

GUESSING GAMES

Guessing a person's name or occupation, or even what the person is thinking about ("Twenty Questions"), can provide students with a great deal of enjoyment. As part of the normal semester routine students may be asked to choose a rather well-known person and describe his or her physical attributes and accomplishments in front of the class, which then tries to identify the person. This exercise is particularly useful for working with adjectives.

Instructor-to-student interaction

The instructor-to-student relationship, unlike the student-to-student one, is based on superior knowledge and authority. The instructor, as the language expert, knows more than the student and is thus in a superior position. Superiority, however, does not prohibit effective interaction. Instructors who wish to interact naturally with students must demonstrate clearly that despite their position of authority, they are willing to mingle freely, adopt an open and playful attitude toward the students, and accept all kinds of opinions. They must also allow room for students to interact with them. The following are ways in which instructors can interact with their students.

Physical demonstration

Certain exercises lend themselves to physical demonstration. A common way to test students' knowledge of object pronouns, for example, is through transformation or conversion drills using the imperative: *Give the check to Lulu.* becomes *Give it to her.; Don't throw me the ball.* becomes *Don't throw it to me.*

In order to approach this kind of exercise interactively, instructors need only mingle with their class and, pretending to have (or having) a number of objects in their hands, say to individual students, "Here is a/an (object)." The student has the choice of saying, "Give it to me!" or, pointing to a student close by, "Don't give it to me; give to her/ him!" The instructor should choose interesting imaginary objects, such as a diamond, a rat, or a rotten banana to encourage student participation. This technique can also be used with demonstrative pronouns ("Which object would you like – this one or that one?") and descriptive adjectives ("Which lettuce do you want – the wilted one or the fresh one?").

Choral responses

As experienced teachers know, choral responses may be used to introduce or reinforce simple grammar points, such as verb paradigms. Choral responses can be made interactive if there is meaningful and spirited communication between the instructor and the class. In order to introduce the present tense of the verbs *to love* and *to hate*, for example, students may be asked to respond to the instructor's cues by saying emphatically, "We love/hate you!" or "She/he loves/hates you!". Following is a list of some possible cues:

1. You will have three tests tomorrow.
2. Francine will stay in after school.
3. I invite all of you to a gourmet restaurant.
4. But you will pay the bill!
5. George is getting an A in this course.

This kind of playful exercise can be used to introduce or reinforce a myriad of verbs and verb forms. Here is an example of students responding using the expressions "We said hello." and "We didn't say hello.":

Instructor: I saw you in a store yesterday and I was wearing my new purple and orange raincoat.
Students: We didn't say hello!
Instructor: I just won the lottery and I was dying to give some money away!
Students: We said hello!

Creative completions

As stated earlier, language study is a playful activity. Sentence completions can be turned into some of the most playful of grammar exercises. For example, contrary-to-fact sentences of the type "If I were rich, I would buy a new car" should not refer to banal situations that do not capture the full attention of students. Students enjoy imagining unusual and amusing situations that not only fulfill the objective of teaching grammar but also provide entertainment for the class.

Complete the following sentences using the present-conditional tense.

1. If I were a cloud, ...
2. If I were a crazy dentist, ...
3. If I were an airplane ticket, ...
4. If I were an idea, ...
5. If I were a monkey, ...

In reverse, this kind of exercise can be turned into a classroom guessing game. Each student or group of students prepares result clauses in the conditional and the class tries to guess the *if*-clauses.

Here is another example of a creative completion, this time dealing with the negatives *neither ... nor*.

Complete the following sentences using "neither ... nor."
1. An orphan has ...
2. A misanthrope likes ...
3. Eternity has ...
4. An only child has ...
5. Gray is ...
6. A vegetarian likes ...

Contextual cues

A short cue that sets an imaginary context can often be used to elicit a complete response from students. Short cues are particularly helpful for testing verbs and verb tenses.

Cues to elicit the past-progressive tense
Imagine that I saw you yesterday in the following places. What were you probably doing?
1. in a cafe
2. at the ocean
3. in the woods
4. at the mountains

Cues to elicit the future tense
Imagine that you are going to the following places next week. What will you probably do?
1. to the hospital
2. to McDonald's
3. to the country
4. to the White House

Names may also be used as cues, as in this exercise dealing with the present participle.

What did the following people spend a lot of time doing?
Example: Elvis Presley
        He spent a lot of time singing.

1. Shakespeare
2. Benny Goodman
3. Fred Astaire
4. Mozart

The instructor can take advantage of the current interests and natural inventiveness of students by asking them to make up their own contextual cues, preferably in small groups or pairs, and presenting them to the class. In this way an instructor-to-student exercise can be transformed into a student-to-student exercise.

The function of spoken language is to allow individuals to express their feelings, thoughts, and needs to one another. The interactive approach to grammar study attempts to fulfill this function by affirming that grammar work and student interaction should be combined. To every extent possible students should be encouraged to learn the rules of grammar not *before* learning to express themselves, but *while* expressing themselves – in other words, to *perform* rules. Students who have found such practice enjoyable are more likely to try to use what they have learned to express themselves in real-life communication. In short, it is through the interactive approach, with its emphasis on playful group activities, that a simple grammar point or group of related grammar points can be revitalized and, above all, personalized.

Let's act on it

1. Which type of interaction – student-to-student or instructor-to-student – is most consistent with your own teaching style? Would you tend to use both types and, if so, under what circumstances and to what degree? How can one incorporate student-to-instructor interaction?
2. Which grammar exercises in this chapter do you consider most appropriate for the elementary level, and which do you think would work best at more advanced levels? Give a rationale for your choices. Try adapting those you think most appropriate for the elementary level to make them suitable for more advanced classes, and vice versa. Did this work in all cases? If not, why not?
3. In your opinion, what is a creative grammar exercise? Use the definition you develop to index the exercises in this chapter from most creative to least creative. Write an exercise that fits your definition.
4. Indicate which exercises in this chapter you consider most appropriate for the following purposes: testing, in-class activities, homework. Which exercises would also be effective as written exercises, and why?
5. Select five of the exercises you like best in this chapter and plan how and when you will use them or adapt them for a class you now teach.

Annotated reading list

Lee, W. R. 1979. *Language Teaching Games and Contests*. Oxford: Oxford University Press. Describes classroom games for teaching language structure, comprehension, and pronunciation. Chap. 1 presents games based on grammar categories, and chap. 9 deals with miming and role-play activities.

Rivers, Wilga M. 1988. *A Practical Guide to the Teaching of French.* 2nd ed. Lincolnwood, Ill.: National Textbook. Presents numerous practical techniques for language teaching accompanied by concise theoretical explanations. Of special interest are chap. 1, which deals with various forms of dialogue exploitation, and chap. 4, which analyzes traditional and modern oral grammar exercises. Parallel *Guides* (with co-authors) give examples in *German* (1988), *Spanish* (1988), *English as a Second or Foreign Language* (1978), and *Hebrew* (in press).

Rivers, Wilga M. 1983. *Communicating Naturally in a Second Language: Theory and Practice in Language Teaching.* New York: Cambridge University Press. Discusses the most important pertinent theoretical findings of experts in linguistics and psychology on the language-learning process. Of particular interest are chap. 2, which deals with creative grammar use and the two levels of the use of grammar (the level of manipulation and the level of expression of personal meaning); chap. 3, which treats communication drills; and chap. 4, which explores ways of bridging the gap between skill-getting and skill-using.

Stevick, Earl W. 1982. *Teaching and Learning Languages.* New York: Cambridge University Press. A practical and informative presentation of numerous teaching techniques that stress classroom interaction. Chaps. 8–10 suggest useful strategies for enlivening traditional pattern, substitution, and transformation drills.

Wright, Andrew; Betteridge, David; and Buckby, Michael. 1984. *Games for Language Learning.* 2d ed. Cambridge: Cambridge University Press. A number of games in different formats, with an index of the aspects of grammar and types of communication being practiced in each.

6 Interaction of reader and text

Anthony Papalia

From a psycholinguistic viewpoint reading is a problem-solving behavior that actively involves the reader in the process of deriving and assigning meaning. While so doing the reader is drawing on contextual information that contains syntactic, semantic, and discourse constraints that affect interpretation (Cziko 1978: 472–89; F. Smith 1971). Syntactic constraints are provided by preceding words and the syntactic rules of the language. Semantic constraints include the distribution of meaning and relationships of words within a specific language and culture. Finally, discourse constraints are those provided by the topic of the text and its development, each language having its own logical connectives and other elements of cohesion. To predict what they are about to read, readers must be continually involved in integrating the information from these three contexts.

Readers decode print in two ways: semantically (i.e., they identify the lexical meaning of words, but they also create a broader meaning for these words within the contexts of phrase, sentence, and discourse), and syntactically (i.e., they recognize the meaningful structural relationships within the sentence). Fluent readers rely more on semantic than syntactic information except when meaning is not clear. The meanings the reader has derived and created are then recoded in abbreviated form for storage in short- or long-term memory. While reading, the reader is relating what has been stored to incoming information and readjusting interpretations as required. Individual students will employ different strategies while engaged in this activity, some being more efficient than others. Observations and interviews have proved useful in identifying the strategies employed by efficient readers as they extract meaning from texts.

How successful readers interact with the text

To discover which strategies successful foreign-language students use in deriving meaning from a written text, twenty American students who were studying French and Spanish at Clarence High School, Clarence, New York, in 1983–4, were asked to read a passage in the foreign language and to "think aloud" while attempting to grasp its meaning. This technique gave the teacher the opportunity to observe what students actually did when they were reading and to discover the strategies they used in deriving meaning. At the end of the task, students were asked to give their perceptions on how they derived meaning from the written words. The responses reported below indicated that they were employing some useful and efficient meaning-extracting strategies.

David: "First, I pick out the words I know and work around words I don't know. I don't translate every word because some words really are not that important to the understanding of the paragraph. They are just there. For those words I don't know, I leave them out or I put in something that makes sense."

Dan: "First of all, I know this article has to do with baseball so I get myself in the frame of mind of a baseball game or baseball terms that I know would appear in an article like this. I just get myself in the frame of reference for the article. That's the first step. In the first sentence I have to find the subject and the verb. I have to know what those are in order to comprehend the sentence and take it one small bit at a time and just try to piece it together. I read it aloud in my mind. I try to think of what word would sound like it. I pick out cognates and words that maybe sound alike and maybe mean the same thing as they do in English. When I hit a word I do not know, my first reaction is just to go over it and not even look at it and finish the sentence and see if I could figure out the rest of the sentence. If I know what the subject is and know what he is doing, chances are I can fill in the blank. Another way I can figure it out is to say it out loud to myself and see if it sounds like anything I might know in English. If I try these ways and I still don't know what it means, I look the word up in the dictionary in the back of the book."

Bridget: "First, I look for words that I know. Then I look for cognates. So I have all the words I know and all the cognates and then what is left in the sentence I read around and place in the words that would fit there to make sense with the rest of the paragraph or the rest of the sentence."

Myron: "I just try to pick out the words I know and the verbs are the main part, then the prepositions just fit into place and I just have to try to figure out and go around the words I don't know and see if I can make out what it is."

Scott: "I don't have to make constant translations and when I come across a word I don't know, sometimes I can read around it. But if it's a key word (subject), it helps to read past it trying to find out what the rest of the sentence is about and then I can guess. A key word might be further explained or another character might ask a question about it which might bring out a definition or an explanation, sometimes even a description. When I come to a line or even a paragraph that seems out of place, I try to think of what I would say or what the character would say."

For the comprehension of reading passages in a foreign language, these students made the following suggestions to their peers:

– Know the topic of the text.
– Read around words you do not know.
– Make use of all available information in the paragraph to comprehend unfamiliar words.
– Take chances and predict meaning.
– Guess the meaning of unfamiliar words from the context.
– Remember that all words in a reading passage are not of equal importance.
– Skip unfamiliar words that are inconsequential to the meaning of the total phrase or paragraph.
– Try to find that part of the meaning that is determined by the syntax of the sentence.
– Expect the text to make sense and be sequential.
– Do not make constant translations.
– Look for cognates.
– Have confidence in yourself.
– If you are not sure of the meaning of the word, find it in the dictionary.

In addition, these students mentioned that, *when the reading passages concerned topics that interested them, inferencing and prediction of meaning were facilitated*; if too many inferences were required, however, the text seemed difficult and comprehension became an arduous task.

As Dan indicated, inferences often help the process of comprehension. With a text about baseball, he found that by putting himself in the frame of mind of a baseball game, he was able to make inferences and have certain expectations about the content of the text. Many investigators believe that knowledge can be described in terms of schemata, which form an organized framework of knowledge (Carrell 1983; Wessells 1983). As Dan read the passage, he attempted to relate the incoming information to his existing framework of knowledge concerning baseball. Thus, that schema guided the processing of new information and enhanced comprehension: He was using concepts and schemata he already possessed. In comprehending sentences he used semantic, syntactic, and pragmatic knowledge interactively. Comprehension, then, involves the use of *multiple, overlapping strategies*. It requires attention, decision making, and a committal of details to memory, where they interact not only with existing schemata but incoming information. By drawing on his existing knowledge and anticipating related information, Dan was able to draw from the text a coherent sequence through a hypothesis-testing procedure. When the passage was long he tended to forget certain information; he would then go back and reread certain sentences. These reinstatement searches became more frequent when he found the text "hard." He preferred texts that dealt with topics and settings familiar to him. This facilitated inferencing, since he could imagine what the various characters might say or do.

All five student readers utilized cues within and outside of the text to determine its meaning. They sought letter–sound relationships, examined spelling patterns to detect cognates that might give clues to meaning, drew sense from word order, tried to establish meaning from wider contexts, and drew on personal knowledge of the topic and pictures in interpreting the text.

Hosenfeld observed that a skillful reader uses many strategies to attach meaning to the printed text. In her research with Cindy, a fourteen-year-old North American girl, she identified twenty overlapping strategies (Hosenfeld 1979: 59–61). Some of these resemble the ones already presented. Among the successful strategies Cindy employed were the following:

1. examining the illustrations and using information contained in them when decoding;
2. reading the title and drawing inferences;
3. circling back purposefully in the text to check on meaning (cf. Myron's comments earlier);
4. identifying the grammatical function of an unfamiliar word before guessing its meaning.

To discover how students interact with the text, teachers may use a "debugging technique," which consists of asking students in class to say how they solved certain linguistic problems or to "think aloud" while they do certain linguistic tasks. Through this procedure, teachers have some access to their students' thinking processes; this helps them discover where errors are being made so they can provide greater assistance. At the same time, students can learn from each other by incorporating into their repertoire effective strategies that other students have used in solving linguistic problems.

Using the text to facilitate interaction

An analysis of the strategies of the students who participated in the Clarence study supports the view that the teacher must attempt to re-

73

create in the classroom situations in which the students might find themselves and which are meaningful to them. In promoting interaction with the text teachers should:

– provide a meaningful context by discussing in the classroom related topics to aid with inferencing from the text;
– encourage students to learn words for the things they want to know about (Rivers 1981: chap. 14);
– use the message of the text as a point of departure for discussion rather than the syntactic features;
– develop meaning for the text cooperatively by using a problem-solving approach whereby students offer a variety of answers that require a great deal of inferencing;
– create a learning climate where students feel comfortable about making mistakes and are therefore willing to venture interpretations.

Reading comprehension entails more than knowledge of vocabulary and syntax. It also requires ability to perceive the exact nature of the passage being communicated – a deeper form of understanding sometimes called "reading between the lines." Students must learn to detect mood and intentions as well as factual detail. These elements are conveyed by the syntactic and lexical choices of the writer, which devolve from selected register, or level of language and stylistic devices. For these reasons, translating into the native language can create more problems than it solves, unless students have been shown how to interrelate words in context and translate entire meanings, not successive words. If translation is to be used as a technique for elaborating meaning, students must practice using reference tools, like dictionaries, judiciously, so that they are weaned from the tendency to decode items by one-to-one word correspondence – a sure way to muddy comprehension.

For student–text interaction of any depth, students need to acquire the skills of drawing information directly from the foreign-language text without the interposition of their own tongue. This skill is best learned in *progressive* stages, with students practicing regularly with materials that approximate their level of proficiency (Rivers 1981: 368–86). Level of proficiency, however, is not sufficient without the motivational element of material of interest to the students. The problems of fluent reading are numerous enough, without being exacerbated by linguistically difficult texts containing materials to which the students cannot relate.

Too often in the past, reading materials have been selected on the basis of their status as "masterpieces" – an aesthetic judgment that was rarely explained – rather than for their intrinsic interest for a specific group of students of a particular age or background. If students are to acquire fluency in reading, however, they need to be enticed to read materials for the same natural purposes as they read in their native language – for following instructions or recipes; for enjoying letters, jokes, or comic strips; for understanding headlines, news items, and, later, magazine articles; and for savoring short stories, short plays, and so on, before being introduced to what are considered masterworks of the literary heritage. Textbook writers need to concentrate on providing texts that are meaningful for the students, while teachers concentrate on procedures that enhance direct comprehension. What follows is a suggested procedure for an intensive reading lesson that promotes these aims and attempts to develop fluency in reading for meaning and pleasure.

Pre-reading/motivational phase

Pre-reading activities should be selected according to the experience and interest of students and should build on the content of preceding lessons. Expectations in reading are embedded in situations and settings. When a friend receives a birthday card, we infer it is that person's birthday; when a waiter hands a menu to a customer, we expect the customer to order a meal (Phillips 1984). During the pre-reading segment, students should be introduced to situations or a pictorial collage that generates expectations that will be useful in *anticipating and predicting the content* of the passage that will be read. After some discussion students may be asked to develop questions associated with the title of the reading passage or the collage of pictures. In this way, they approach the text with certain schemata in mind and with questions of their own to which they would like to find answers.

Reading of the text in class

The text may be read, in meaningful segments,

– orally by the teacher while the students follow the text silently;
– silently by the students; or
– orally by the students after a silent reading, or after an oral reading by the teacher.

This class or group reading helps develop the habits that characterize fluent reading: *reading in meaningful segments*, not word by word, and *perseverance with a text* in the expectation that later reading will explicate what has not been understood earlier. (When the reading is assigned for home study, the pre-reading/motivational activities should take place in class at the time the assignment is given, to prepare students for the inferencing later reading will require.)

Anthony Papalia

Removal of difficulties

Teachers may aid students in extracting meaning in a number of ways:

- by discussing possible meanings of new vocabulary, giving explanations only when necessary and then, as far as possible, in the target language by using synonyms, antonyms, and cognates;
- by encouraging students to work at meanings through analysis of related stems and examination of prefixes and suffixes;
- by giving or requesting paraphrases of segments in which the problem words occur;
- by encouraging students to draw inferences from the context about structural as well as semantic elements;
- by providing explanations of new structures through paraphrasing or expanding;
- by demonstrating analogies with structures or idioms previously learned; and
- by demonstrating parallelism with native-language structures where applicable.

Activities like these should be followed by a consecutive reading of the complete text to draw together in the whole what has been learned from the parts.

Checking for comprehension

Teachers may involve students in:

- assigning a new title to the reading selection;
- completing true/false or multiple-choice exercises on the content;
- asking fellow students questions that penetrate beneath the surface, beyond the obvious;
- developing a different conclusion;
- developing a dialogue related to the reading selection that brings out the relationships among protagonists.

Advanced students may:

- identify main and subordinate ideas;
- summarize or retell parts of the text;
- discuss the author's intentions expressed in the tone of the passage (examining elements in the text that reveal this facet);
- discuss viewpoints represented by persons in the text and the cultural significance of these viewpoints;
- discuss the temperament and character of persons in the text and devices by which the author reveals these to the reader;

76

- discuss aspects of the content from the viewpoint of different persons in the text;
- conduct group discussion on the participants' awareness of the action and why the author chose to develop the content as he or she did.

Summary

A collective summary may be given by several pupils, cued by the teacher when necessary. At the elementary level, a summary guided by key words written on the board is an effective approach. At more advanced levels, the summary may evolve in a more sophisticated way from reports from student discussion groups.

Assignment

The assignment should come after class consideration of the text and draw together what has been learned from the study of the passage. In this way students learn effective reading skills in a supervised situation that prepares them for individual reading at a more advanced level. Students are given a choice of assignment to increase their sense of involvement. Some pupils may reread the passage and write answers to questions; others may write a summary, use new vocabulary in original sentences, or construct additional questions based on the passage to ask their fellow students; still others may fill in blanks in sentences taken from the text with the correct semantic or syntactic response (a cloze-type procedure that draws together the main idea in a recapitulative fashion). Finally, some may write out their reactions to the passage to be shared with others in a final discussion session, or write their own stories, episodes, or alternative conclusions.

Interactive reading activities

Students should be given the opportunity to relate their own lives, activities, and interests and concerns to the second language and to what is being read in the second language. To provide greater interaction with the text and among students, teachers should stimulate work in groups, where students have the opportunity to work together and learn from each other.

In planning reading activities, teachers will normally consider whether students will profit more from working in large groups or small groups or from working independently at their own pace. Instruction should be tailored to the learning predilections of individual students as much as is feasible. However, in many places, teachers have little choice other than to instruct in large classes or large groups, often for economic reasons. Even within large-group instruction, provision should be made for some small-group interaction or at least interstudent discussion as well as for individual reading.

Small-group work on a reading task stimulates student participation. It provides opportunities to learn how to work harmoniously with others; it encourages open-mindedness about other people's ideas. Students become inquirers – investigators learning from their peers successful strategies for extracting meaning and interpreting content. In small groups, the students have the opportunity to decode and interpret the script, to include personal findings, refine these in association with others, and inject their own reactions. On the cognitive level, those participating in small groups acquire knowledge not only from what they have read, but also through working with other reflective individuals. Through the checks and contributions of others, they learn to relate bodies of knowledge meaningfully, to make cultural observations refined by discussion, and to evolve new and richer interpretations of the material read.

Opportunities for student–teacher interaction, as well as student–student interaction, are greater in a small-group activity than in large groups. Students receive much more attention to their individual problems and feel more personally involved, because they can no longer hide in the crowd. Teachers must, however, plan for small-group work with care. They may begin by promoting activities where students work in pairs on aspects of the text while they circulate among the students to give assistance as needed. Once successful results have been obtained with this approach and students have adapted to more individual responsibility for their work, teachers may develop working groups of three or four students for discussion of more wide-ranging questions and the elaboration of viewpoints to share with the larger group.

To increase student interaction with the text, its author, their fellow students, and the teacher, teachers may select some of the following activities. They are arranged roughly from elementary through intermediate to advanced level.

Interaction between reader and text

1. Students draw a picture to illustrate what was just read or some aspect of it, such as the room where the action took place.
2. Students look for specific information, such as selecting a meal from a menu or identifying times of arrival and departure in airline or railway schedules.

3. Students read a passage and then list three important facts, ideas, or events contained in it.
4. Students read a specially constructed passage and correct sentences that contain wrong information. This is an opportunity to use some humorous sentences that play on similarities in the appearance of words. Students learn to pay careful attention as they read.
5. Students read a story with the ending deleted. They try to make up an ending consistent with the story.
6. Each student is given a comic strip with eight frames. In the first, third, fifth, and seventh frames the dialogue is provided, but in the second, fourth, sixth, and eighth frames it is missing. Students must create meaningful dialogue for these four frames, linking what was said in the preceding frame to the content of the succeeding frame. This activity integrates reading and writing with formulation of oral utterances.

Interaction between reader and reader over text

7. After reading a short descriptive paragraph about something or someone in which the name of the person or object is not revealed, students in small groups try to guess who or what is being talked about or draw a picture of the person or object.
8. A transparency of a reading passage is projected. After a rapid perusal to extract the general tenor, lines are highlighted segmentally and each is discussed for meaning, with the whole group contributing. The lines may be numbered to facilitate quick reference. It is essential to project the complete passage again at the end to draw together what has been extracted from the parts.
9. The first two or three sentences of a passage are shown on the overhead projector. Students then formulate questions to which they expect to find the answers in the completion of the passage. The questions are written on the board. Students finish reading the passage and discuss the answers to the questions.
10. After reading a passage, students supply a suitable title. This can be a large-group activity, allowing students to discuss why they agree or disagree with the titles proposed.
11. Students read a story with the ending deleted. They try orally to make up an ending consistent with the story. Later they may write a summary of the story, adding their own endings. These versions may then be circulated and a vote taken on the most satisfactory ending. Students then compare this ending with that of the original author.
12. Students form their own questions based on a reading selection they

have read and call on other students to answer their questions to check comprehension. This may be a competitive activity among small groups. Students are encouraged to challenge questions they feel distort the meaning. In this way a lively discussion often ensues.

13. Students work together to paraphrase a reading passage without changing the original meaning. This forces students to pay close attention to nuances of meaning and the author's intent.

14. Students in small groups read a series of provocative statements on a major public event, a common experience, or a subject of current interest and controversy. Discussion follows the reading, again integrating reading and oral communication.

15. Students work out as a group a summary of a passage they have read individually. The teacher should cue students where necessary. (Deciding on key words and testing these beforehand is helpful as a preliminary for elementary-level students.) Groups read their summations to each other and discuss the validity of their interpretations.

16. Students in small groups rearrange a series of sentences into a logical paragraph. The sentences should parallel the kind of material read or at least deal with familiar subject matter. They may consist of a rearrangement of sentences from a passage to be read later. This task forces students to discuss concepts and come to certain conclusions by paying attention to elements of contextual cohesion.

17. Sheets are prepared containing questions related to a text being read with a series of multiple-choice responses that require students to make value judgments as they rank the various alternatives. Small-group discussion follows. This activity demands close reading by students as they determine the precise meaning of the alternatives. It also integrates reading with oral communication.

18. Students in small groups are each provided with a card on which an incident is described, but with a different segment of vital information omitted from each card. Students discuss with each other the information they have until they have pieced together the full account of the incident or situation. This is a problem-solving activity that integrates reading and discussion. Students then write out the complete account of the incident as a small-group composition, thus integrating reading, oral discussion, and writing.

Conclusion

In drawing together reader and text, we must continually keep in mind individual interests if we expect the learners to continue reading. Only students who have acquired confidence in reading through materials accessible to them in content and linguistic complexity may be expected to move on with enthusiasm to the great works that are treasured as part of the heritage of another culture. To integrate reading experiences with developing language control, *reading should be continually linked with purposeful communication*, oral and written. To be successful in meeting this challenge, the teacher should (a) provide students with meaningful tasks associated with the reading, (b) develop activities that encourage students to communicate without making graphic or oral demands beyond their competence in the new language, (c) give students, nevertheless, freedom to experiment with the language they possess, and (d) create a classroom environment in which students feel free to express the ideas that have been stimulated by their reading and to work their way toward more and more valid interpretations through the refinement of discussion in a noncorrective atmosphere. In this way, they will come to appreciate reading in another language as a normal element in their new linguistic experience. Experiences with reading, whether in the first or second language, should create autonomous readers who enjoy the stimulation of direct interaction with writers and will continue to read without prodding for their own pleasure and information.

Let's act on it

1. When you were an elementary-level student of a second language, what problems did you have in assigning meaning to a text? How did you overcome these? What advice would you now give your former teachers?
2. List the activities you commonly use in your classroom for developing reading skills. On the basis of what you have read in this chapter, which ones do you now consider useful for promoting reader–text and reader–reader-over-text interaction? How would you adapt the others to increase their interaction potential?
3. What kinds of techniques beyond those discussed would you suggest to discover how your students interact with a text?
4. Gather some data on how your students interact with a text and share these with others in your teacher-training or in-service group. Then formulate some principles to guide you in the selection of reading materials.
5. Given the importance of linguistic and nonlinguistic context in facilitating inferencing, analyze a reading selection from your language textbook and determine what you could do to help your students ascribe meaning to this text.

Anthony Papalia

Annotated reading list

Carrell, Patricia L. 1983. "Some Issues in Studying the Role of Schemata, or Background Knowledge, in Second Language Comprehension." *Reading in a Foreign Language* 1, 2: 81–92. An important piece discussing how research in schema theory has shown that reading comprehension is an interactive process between the reader and the text.

Cziko, Gary A. 1978. "Differences in First- and Second-Language Reading: The Use of Syntactic, Semantic and Discourse Constraints." *CMLR* 34: 472–89. A worthwhile article on the importance of syntactic, semantic, and discourse constraints in deriving meaning from a written text. Discusses their role in the development of the reading skill.

Grellet, Françoise. 1981. *Developing Reading Skills: A Practical Guide to Reading Comprehension Exercises.* Cambridge: Cambridge University Press. Presents a number of useful techniques for teachers and materials developers. It describes and classifies various types of reading comprehension exercises. Reading is considered a constant process of guessing, predicting, checking, and asking oneself questions.

Hosenfeld, Carol. 1979. "Cindy: A Learner in Today's Foreign Language Classroom," in Born, Warren C., ed., *The Foreign Language Learner in Today's Classroom Environment*, pp. 53–75. Middlebury, Vt.: NEC. A useful discussion of the reading strategies a skillful reader used in attaching meaning to a printed text.

Mackey, Ronald; Barkman, Bruce; and Jordan, R. R. eds. 1982. *Reading in a Second Language: Hypotheses, Organization and Practice.* Rowley, Mass.: Newbury House. Discusses theoretical considerations, with a wealth of practical suggestions for ESL or foreign-language teachers interested in the development of advanced reading comprehension.

Phillips, June K. 1984. "Practical Implications of Recent Research in Reading." *FLA* 17: 285–96. An important article that explores how the successful reading of any passage depends upon a combination of linguistic knowledge, cognitive skill, general experience, and knowledge of the world.

Rivers, Wilga M. 1981. *Teaching Foreign-Language Skills.* 2d ed. Chicago: University of Chicago Press. Chap. 9 offers a lucid presentation of the process of reading. Examines the stages that students pass through in developing abilities for fluent direct reading with comprehension of meaning. Very useful as a guide to teachers when choosing reading texts for various levels.

Smith, Frank. 1971. *Understanding Reading: A Psycholinguistic Analysis of Reading and Learning to Read.* New York: Holt, Rinehart and Winston. Discusses a psychological model of reading, maintaining that *prediction* of what appears in a text is an essential part of the reading process.

7 Writing: an interactive experience

Gloria M. Russo

Writing is not necessarily a solitary activity on the part of the author but can be intensely interactive, involving the instructor, other students, and individuals outside of the formal classroom setting. Normally, we write to be read, and our writing improves as we respond to the reactions of others. Our desire to write also increases as others show interest in what we have written. "The desire to write," then, "grows with writing," as Erasmus once observed.[1] Writing skills can be developed through class writing, group writing, individual writing, and community writing – each contributing to the perfecting of the skill. "True ease in writing," we soon find, "comes from art, not chance."[2]

Class writing

Those most intimately involved in the writing process are, of course, the student authors. However, plunging them headlong into the writing process as individual authors is not necessarily the best first step. Class writing, which can be used at any level of language learning, readily sparks enthusiasm among students who are perhaps tired or bored by other language-learning tasks. It consists simply of the students writing on the blackboard a group composition – created by all, corrected by all, savored by all. It is far easier and less intimidating for each student to compose an interesting sentence, logically connected to its predecessors, than to write an entire essay, no matter how brief the latter may be. Since success builds confidence, the budding authors can gradually pass from group work to self-sustained production.

How does one approach class writing? The methods are as varied as the imagination of the instructor. The following suggestions have worked successfully and can serve as springboards for further ideas.

To begin the class composition, the instructor or a student produces an intriguing first sentence, such as "I stared at my friend in disbelief." Note that the sentence does not head in any rigidly specified direction. The students may interpret as they choose the implications of the sen-

1 Erasmus, *Adagia* (1508).
2 Alexander Pope, *Essay on Criticism 11.*

tence and its problem element and embroider on it as the mood of the moment leads them. No two classes will ever produce the same story from an initial sentence, unless the instructor makes the injudicious attempt to dominate its direction. As each student produces a sentence, the thread of the story will twist and bend but never break, demanding more and more imagination and initiative from the class members. Everyone thus learns the power of an opening sentence and, eventually, the impact of a closing one, while passing through the travail of developing a coherent theme.

Class size does not in any way inhibit the production of rewarding class writing. A large class creates a long story, a small class a briefer one. Students who are initially afraid to produce a complete sentence can at least suggest ideas for others to incorporate. Each member of the class can write on the board another student's contribution to the story or help someone else to do so correctly. Students can then take turns reading aloud parts of their group effort, even acting it out if the story lends itself to such an interpretation. Depending on the level and particularly the inclination of the class, mini-dramas and poems can also be written in this fashion (particularly poems that are free in form).

Every effort should be made to keep correction of grammar in class writing in proper perspective and to prevent it from assuming such importance that it inhibits the pleasure of creative writing. For beginning learners the instructor or other students make the corrections orally, without comment, as the student writes at the board. At more advanced levels, the students themselves can comment on each others' work, from both grammatical and stylistic points of view.

Several approaches to student–student correction may be tried. After completion of the creation of the story, for instance, the instructor may underline all errors of morphology and syntax, selecting different students to correct them. Alternatively, a general invitation may be issued for students to go directly to the board to correct the errors of their choice. Or, without having indicated any errors, the instructor may assign one or two students to each sentence to judge whether or not it is grammatically accurate and stylistically appropriate, at which point they will correct any error they may find. Working in pairs is always reassuring and the results are both more rapid and more accurate, especially if the instructor can pair students in such a way as to place, unobtrusively, a student good at grammar with one who is less informed. The instructor can also use the open-invitation technique, allowing all students to correct any, and as many, errors as they can find.

All of these correction techniques, and they certainly represent only a handful, highlight the interactive aspect of class writing. The students, along with the teacher, work together on each segment of the exercise and soon begin to realize that their individual language learning is greatly enhanced by the efforts of the entire group.

Small-group writing

After developing the class writing technique and confirming that the students feel reasonably comfortable with the procedure as well as with their own ability to create in their new language, the instructor will wish to introduce them to individual composition. The transition from one type of writing to the other can be made easier, however, by first passing through the intermediate stage of group writing. The same techniques as in class writing may be used, except that the students work in small groups, producing brief compositions, which they can then write on the board for the appreciation of their classmates. Either at this point or earlier, groups can exchange their compositions for grammar evaluation and adjustments. The compositions can then be read aloud and, if class temperament and cohesion lend themselves to such comparisons, the students can select the story they find the most humorous, the most interesting, the most colorful, the most exciting, or the best written; in this way some accolade can probably be found to compliment each group's effort.

Individual writing

Having moved from class writing to group composition, the students are now ready to fly on their own and undertake sustained individual writing. The initial assignment should be brief – a short paragraph, for example – and fairly well-structured by the teacher in order to avoid panic among the less confident writers. Yet, *the instructor's guidance must remain discreet*; after all, writing is a very personal adventure that becomes stilted and awkward if another intervenes too openly. How, then, does one succeed in guiding fledgling authors without crimping their style or their enthusiasm?

A very simple approach is to offer the students for their early attempts a list of vocabulary words, carefully selected for their relation to a nonstated theme, and invite the students to use half of these in a paragraph. Thus, of ten words loosely linked to one another by some common thread, they may each use any five and create something autonomous and original. The words *suitcase, train, stranger, to stare, to run, to get off, scared, late, laughingly, mysteriously* are obviously linked by the idea of a trip of some kind; students can select individually any five words or more and weave a story around them. Some will produce the standard trip on a train but others, more adventurous, attracted by the words *to stare, mysteriously, scared*, and *stranger*, will create a little intrigue in honored detective tradition. Others, using *late, to run, train, laughingly*, will recount a humorous experience that involved getting on the wrong train because they arrived so late at the station. The possibilities are multiple; the basic structure is there, but the instructor's contribution, although reassuringly apparent, is not oppressive.

As the students' confidence and ability increase, so can the length and complexity of both the composition and the vocabulary list. The instructor may also suggest intriguing titles, with or without vocabulary lists, such as:

"The Cat on the Bookcase"
"Cooking Calamities"
"Thunder in the Cellar"
"Falling Feet First"
"The Unforgettable Lamp"

Note that none of these titles is rigidly subject specific; the students remain quite free to develop the basic idea of *cat, thunder, falling, calamities*, or *lamp* as they choose. Nothing prevents others from concentrating on *bookcase, cellar, feet, cooking*, or *unforgettable*.

In addition, the students can freely develop the topic according to their individual abilities. Hence, for "The Cat on the Bookcase," one student may write a prosaic piece about a figurine of a cat that fell off a bookcase and cost a week's pay or allowance to replace. Someone else may write about a pet that always slept in the bookcase until the day it found its place taken by a kitten. A third author may write about a cat that mysteriously appears on the same shelf of the bookcase whenever the teacher assigns a new composition.

"Cooking Calamities" will inevitably elicit a number of essays on culinary mishaps, but someone with a sense of humor may invent a recipe for *calamities* and explain how to prepare them. Is thunder in "Thunder in the Cellar" a noise in the basement or the name of a pet? Does "Falling Feet First" refer to parachuting or getting out of a bad situation in a lucky way? Why is the *lamp* unforgettable? Is it because of the apparently traditional light bulb that never works because the lamp comes equipped with a genie? Each title is open to as many interpretations as there are students, and the realizations of even the most plodding students will be a far cry from those elicited by the hackneyed "What I Did During the Summer Vacation."

For those teachers or students who may find the transition from group to individual writing too abrupt, a more gradual approach requires individual students to provide at first only the closing sentence, or sentences, for a paragraph already prepared by the teacher or another group. At the other end of the spectrum are those students who will always feel too confined by the structure of a vocabulary list or even a title. For them, the instructor always offers the option of creating a free composition on a self-developed variation of the topic or on a topic entirely of their own choosing. Although teachers may need much patience in trying to comprehend the unexpected, even original vocabulary in such individually devised compositions, these often turn out to be the most rewarding to read.

Evaluating individual student writing can pose some problems. One sticky point is the *question of grammar and style*. Here there are several options. First and foremost, whatever option instructors adopt, they must always recognize and reward the creativity of their student authors. Nothing inhibits developing writing skills more than to see high praise and excellent grades go to the cautious or lazy student whose dull paragraph, written with grammatical precision and little else, repeats the same thing in five different ways. Ready acknowledgment of students' willingness to abandon this unimaginative and prosaic variety of writing is essential to the fostering not only of the ability to write, but also of the desire to do so.

How can instructors make clear that *creativity and imagination count?* If they normally give a letter or number grade for a composition, they can allow a separate grade for content and style that will count for a predetermined percentage of the final evaluation – and a healthy percentage at that. In this way, the final evaluation does not rest only on grammatical accuracy. If instructors give a written evaluation, they can also see that content is recognized with appropriate emphasis. Under no circumstances should grammar be the sole criterion by which a student's writing effort is judged.

A double grammar correction offers the advantages of encouraging meaningful, creative writing and of improving grammar skills. Using this method, instructors underline errors noted during their first reading of the essay. They also label the errors with some kind of shorthand indicating their general category, for example, grammar, vocabulary choice, spelling, or diacritical marks – each category being worth a predetermined number of points. (This method of correction should never be purely subtractive for errors; rather, extra credit should be given for interesting and expressive choices.) The students then reexamine their compositions and correct as many errors as possible on their own. During the second reading, the instructor checks each underlined error. If the student's correction is appropriate, no further work need be done. If, however, an error still remains, the instructor once again deducts the number of points indicated for the appropriate category. All points for both corrections are then totaled and divided by two to arrive at the final grade for the grammar component of the student's writing assignment – divided by two because the student worked twice on the essay. The grammar component is, as stated earlier, one part of the grade. The instructor also takes into consideration the creative and stylistic aspects of the composition in order to arrive at an honest and justifiable grade that reflects the worth of the author's final product (Rivers and Temperley 1978: 324).

Another correction method allows students to exchange compositions and correct each other's errors, or at least indicate them. Alternatively, students can discuss each other's work in order to arrive at the best possible solution to a grammar or vocabulary problem. Such an interchange may well serve as an intermediary step between, or even preceding, the instructor's double correction.

After correction by whatever method, students find it helpful to see a model paragraph on the board incorporating the grammar points with which the group in general has experienced the greatest difficulty: for instance, certain uses of tenses, indefinite pronouns, or appropriate choice of logical connectives and other cohesive elements of discourse. The instructor demonstrates the correct usage in a prose example and asks for student comments. Students can then examine their own compositions in order to see where they had difficulty in expressing themselves correctly and comprehensibly. This part of the exercise terminates with students reading aloud from their own compositions sections that exemplify appropriate use of the features discussed.

Note that throughout the grammar-correcting phase of the writing exercise, the emphasis has been on the *students' active participation*. The goal of written self-expression in the language has never been overshadowed by demands for grammatical perfection.

To encourage students to write more than class exercises, many teachers have experimented with *dialogue journals*, where students write to the teacher when they please on what they please, and the teacher responds (see Rivers, this volume, p. 12). This activity provides the students with the opportunity to write at their own level (and, in writing, levels are very variable). The journal entries should be treated as correspondence and not corrected overtly; rather, the teacher includes in his or her response expansions or restatements of incorrectly or awkwardly expressed ideas. This can be done quite unobtrusively, because of the redundancy of such informal exchanges, the student having, of course, been forewarned to look for help in this way. Even weak students will write more and more if encouraged by the teacher's interest in what they have to say. The material in such journals always remains confidential, however, unless released by the writer.

Poems are particularly useful for individual writing, since they allow for a freedom in word order and choice that, even if unorthodox, may produce very attractive verses. Since the result is intended to be poetic (and poets bend rules even in their own language), unusual expression, far from being censured, may be praised as vivid and imaginative, to the budding poet's delight. (See also Maley, this volume, chap. 8.)

Community writing

Their confidence bolstered by the realization that they can write sustained prose (and even poetry), the students are now ready to combine this skill with their oral ability on a grander scale in community writing. This activity calls upon the students to leave the shelter of the classroom and go into the community to interview, or otherwise contact, native speakers. Their goal is to capture in written form the essence of their interaction with the interviewees.

A community-writing exercise actually involves three written pieces. After the students, either individually or with partners, have decided whom they intend to interview, they submit to the instructor an explanation of their choice of this particular native speaker as worthwhile or interesting to interview. Upon receiving the instructor's approval, they then write a letter in the target language to their subject saying who they are and requesting an interview. Once their request has been accepted, they must prepare their questions and build up their courage to conduct the actual interview, preferably at the subject's home or office.

The written report of their experience may assume one of two forms: question-answer format or straight prose. The former approach is straightforward and reported in the following way:

Student 1:   Mrs. X, where were you born?
Mrs. X: In Quebec City.
Student 2:   Were you an only child?
Mrs. X: No, I have two brothers.

Such a report should always close with a paragraph summing up the personal qualities of the subject to compensate for the terseness of the format. The second format produces a more informative report:

We arrived at Ms. X's home at 2 p.m. She received us in her sunroom where she offered us coffee and homemade cake. In answer to our questions, we learned that she and her two brothers were born in Quebec City....

In this format, students can create atmosphere and flesh out not only their subject but also their own experience.

Instructors may grade these report essays in the same way as individual writing efforts. Once again, the correcting must in no way assume more importance than the writing and the community experience.

For the students, the community experience continues as they share it with their classmates. They distribute a copy of their interview to the other students and discuss with them their reactions to the interviewee. A photograph of the subject, photocopied with the written material, greatly enhances the reality quotient of the report.

The major difficulty in the process of community writing lies in finding suitable interviewees. In a foreign-language situation, instructors can always call upon their colleagues and retired language teachers living in the community. With luck, some willing native speakers, residents in the surrounding area but unassociated with education, can be tapped as subjects. Where there are no such possibilities, the instructors themselves can serve as interviewees.

If enough subjects cannot be found for the number of students involved, a simple and amusing expedient can be called into play. Instructors ask each potential subject to accept several different pairs of students and to assume a new identity for each couple. Thus, Mr. J, a retired language teacher, offers his services for five interviews. For the first he plays the role of a journalist, for the second a pilot, for the third himself, for the fourth a farmer, and for the fifth a mechanic. He could equally well choose to play five well-known contemporary or historical figures from the target culture or the students' own culture. To add a little zest to the classroom part of the community-writing exercise, the student interviewers might relate to their classmates everything about the person interviewed except the name. Once the students have received all the information, they then try to identify the person, asking questions and hunting for clues. The net result is usually a very enjoyable mini-lesson in contemporary events, history, or local affairs.

Interviews may also be conducted by telephone. Persons called upon to give a series of interviews might find this method less taxing. The ultimate interview and writing experience would be one conducted by telephone with a native speaker in the target country. Reduced phone rates at certain hours, coupled with the time differences from one country to another, make this a distinct possibility.

An exchange of letters between students and native speakers is another type of community writing. However, given its personal nature, it is one best left for the students' enjoyment without any intrusion from the instructor for correction. The teacher's role in this instance is merely to locate correspondents and to provide assistance in expression of complicated ideas at the level of expression the student has reached. Even elementary-level students can write down simple facts about their environment and their experiences that will interest correspondents in other countries.

Publication

We write to be read. A term collection (or a monthly class bulletin) of the most successful of the group and individual productions (prose, poetry, and drama), along with interesting interviews, adds to the enthusiasm of the class for writing of various kinds. This collection is distributed to the class and beyond the class – to other classes, the school administration, parents, and friends, even perhaps to the local newspaper for excerpting now and again. In this way, writing is seen as a means of communicating one's thoughts that has no bounds.

As these four types of writing (class, group, individual, and community) indicate, writing in the target language is far from being an inward-looking, restricted activity. Rather, for language students, it can involve lively interaction with one another, with instructors, and with individuals outside of the daily classroom environment. Nor is writing an activity that should be tied to simplistic forms of expression by an overwhelming emphasis on grammatical perfection. Writing is an exciting, challenging experience that permits students to indulge in fantasy, humor, fiction, or fact in the language they have chosen to make their own, while drawing on all their inner resources of imagination and self-expression.

Let's act on it

1. Prepare six composition titles you will use with your class. What were you looking for in working out these titles? For each, show three different ways in which it could be approached.
2. How many distinctly different ways can you identify for attracting interest through the opening sentence of a written composition? What are the components of interesting opening sentences – sentences that invite students to contribute to a class or group composition? Devise five or six such opening sentences that you could use in a composition class.
3. Design an assignment that would lead students to create a group poem. How would you help them find a central theme? How would you stimulate their imagination with regard to the topic? How would you ensure that all the creation was not done by one or two members of the group? What would you do with the completed poem? (See also Maley, this volume, chap. 8.)
4. What are the pedagogical and psychological advantages and disadvantages of group versus individual compositions from the student's standpoint? What pluses and minuses do you see from

the teacher's point of view? Weighing these two, what conclusions can you reach that will affect your future teaching? Remember to take into consideration the objectives of your students and the situation in which you teach. (See also Rivers, this volume, chap. 1.)

5. Design in detail an assignment that will involve students in interviewing native speakers of the target language to find out in which ways they feel their own cultural assumptions and customs differ radically from those of the students' own culture, and the problems they face in adjusting to the contact situation. (See also Robinson, this volume, chap 11.) How might the resulting written report be put to use for a wider audience?

Annotated reading list

Dixon, C. N., and Nessel, D. 1983. *Language Experience Approach to Reading (and Writing): LEA for ESL*. Hayward, Cal.: Alemany Press. Carries the LEA concept (use of the student's own vocabulary, language patterns, and background of experience) over from reading to writing, with special attention to the needs of learners of English as a second language. Considers the four steps of composing: pre-writing, writing, revising, and rewriting for students from Stage 1 to Stage 3.

Gaudiani, C. 1981. *Teaching Writing in the FL Curriculum*. Washington, D.C.: Center for Applied Linguistics. Covers every aspect of teaching composition in a formal classroom setting, with many examples. Examples are mainly in French, but the discussion applies to the teaching of any foreign language.

Raimes, A. 1983. *Techniques in Teaching Writing*. New York: Oxford University Press. Contains a wealth of ideas for activities for class, group, and individual writing at all levels. Discusses use of readings in teaching writing.

Rivers, W. M., and Temperley, M. S. 1978. *A Practical Guide to the Teaching of English as a Second or Foreign Language*. New York: Oxford University Press. Chap. 9: "Writing and Written Exercises II: Flexibility and Expression," gives many ideas, with examples, of how to make writing more participatory. Discusses scoring systems. For examples in French, German, and Spanish, see Rivers (1988); Rivers, Dell'Orto, and Dell'Orto (1988); and Rivers, Azevedo, et al. (1988). For Hebrew, see Rivers and Nahir (in press).

Russo, G. M. 1983. *Expanding Communication: Teaching Modern Languages at the College Level*. New York: Harcourt Brace Jovanovich. Chap. 7, "Communicating Through Writing," gives many suggestions for topic selection and a Composition Point Scale for correction and grading.

8 Poetry and song as effective language-learning activities

Alan Maley

Why poetry and song?

MEMORABILITY

Fragments of poems and songs stick in our minds. The phrases of which they are made up are often particularly poignant or striking, and seem to go on repeating themselves in our inward ear (and even our night-time mind) without our conscious will. Such nuggets, whether in the mother tongue or in English, often remain in the pool of memory long after communicative competence has drained away.

RHYTHMICALITY

One reason for this retention is doubtless that poetry and song are highly rhythmical. Patterns of sound and stress are repeated in regular sequences, and this facilitates their acquisition. Poetry offers a hot-line to the rhythmic heart-beat of a language, so that rhythm 'is not something extra...it is the guide to the structure of information in the spoken message' (Brown 1977).

PERFORMANCE/RECITABILITY

There are very few occasions when the written word can be spoken naturally, especially in choral form. Poetry and song offer a ready-made opportunity for such participation. Unlike drills, which are all too often lacklustre and boring, the learners can read poetry aloud or sing songs as a group without feeling that it is an unnatural process. And the fact that the group performance masks individual error adds to self-confidence.

AMBIGUITY

Almost without exception, any poem means more than one thing. It says something which is plain to all *plus* something which may be privy only to some. It has a 'public' and a 'personal' meaning. In teaching, this is an enormous advantage. It means that, within limits, each learner's

93

personal interpretation has validity. It also means that, because each person's perception is different, an almost infinite fund of interactive discussion is possible.

NON-TRIVIALITY

Because the very function of poetry and song is to enhance our experiencing of existence, in however humble a particular, it follows that they offer significant input for learners. This sets them apart from much other language-learning material: They have a content (affective or cognitive) which really means something and is not simply cooked up for the supposedly fragile digestion of language learners.

UNIVERSALITY

Poetry and song as forms of language use are universal among human beings. No known language is without them. And the themes they deal with are common to all cultures (though the way the themes are dealt with may differ): love, death, nature, children, religious belief – the list is a long one. All language learners are aware of the idea of poetry and of its thematic content. To this extent, poetry is familiar.

PLAYFULNESS

One of the key factors in learning a foreign language is the ability and opportunity to play with it, to test its elasticity. Poetry and song are par excellence the media in which this can be done. Learners can observe and experience what others have dared to do with the language ('he sang his didn't, he danced his did' – ee cummings). Through interactive writing tasks, they can reach out for the limits of the possible themselves. In one sense, the writing of poetry is an ideal task for language learners because of its tolerance of 'error' (Widdowson 1983: 97–106). This is the sand pit where guiltless children can try out their constructions.

REACTIONAL LANGUAGE

In a recent book (Brown and Yule 1983: 11–16) spoken-language uses are divided into 'interactional' and 'transactional'. In 'interactional' language use, people are mainly concerned with social lubrication – making speakers feel comfortable with each other. In 'transactional' language the major concern is with communicating a utilitarian message: giving instructions, stating opinions, describing, and so on.

Poetry and song give access to a *third* type of spoken-language use: 'reactional'. Their main purpose is neither to make people feel comfortable nor to procure a utilitarian result; rather it is to make people *react* personally to another person's verbal sensibility. All literature does this, of course. But poetry and song have the advantage of doing it 'in little space'.

MOTIVATION

There is an obvious motivational element in learning songs in the foreign language. In English, which is *the* language of popular music, this motivational tug is self-evident. Even poetry, however, exerts a motivational force. The realisation that, though relatively inexpert in a language, one can appreciate (to a degree) what is thought to be a 'difficult' use of language, and can even write such language, is a far from negligible morale-booster.

INTERACTION

As we shall see later, the use of poems and songs offers unparalleled opportunities both for teacher–student and student–student interaction. The very fact that no two people will have a totally convergent interpretation sets up the tension necessary for a meaningful exchange of ideas. And this can extend through the phases of preparation, comprehension, planning of follow-up activities, and evaluation of such activities.

Areas of activity

We can group activities connected with poetry and songs into four major stages: preparation, comprehension, expression, and reaction. Generally speaking, all students need to pass through the first two stages to appreciate the poet's intent. They do not need to pass to the second two stages, though it is desirable that they should in order to fully experience the pleasure the poem can provide.

Preparation

Receptivity to a poem is usually improved if students are already 'into' the theme it deals with. In order to get them thinking about the main issues a poem deals with, it is occasionally sufficient simply to say, 'This is a poem about . . . '. But this is rarely the case. The examples that follow show some of the ways of getting ready for the poem itself. They all involve an effort on the individual level before an interactive, sharing phase.

PICTURES

There are many uses for pictures, but the most usual are to illustrate a theme or mood, or to pose a problem for discussion. For example, the photograph in Illustration 1 could be used to lead into poems about loneliness. Individually, students could be asked to note down answers to questions like: Where is this taking place? Who is this person? How would you describe her expression? What do you think she is thinking about? Do you know anyone like this? They would then compare notes in pairs or groups before a feedback session with the whole class.

PERSONAL REACTIONS

These may take the form of memories, opinions, answers to question-naires, or describing personal experiences or characteristics. Here are some examples:

1. *As an introduction to poems on memories*: 'Try to remember some of the earliest things which happened to you as a child. Think of *one* incident which particularly impressed you. Then draw a very simple picture of it. Exchange your picture with a partner. Try to interpret his or her picture. You can ask questions if you like.'
2. *As an introduction to poems on breaking up*: 'Write down three of the most usual reasons people have for falling out of love. Then compare your reasons in groups of four. Do you all agree?'
3. *To introduce poems on loneliness*: 'Different groups should work simultaneously on producing lists to answer each of the following questions. Group 1: What kinds of people feel lonely or cut off? Group 2: What sorts of things do lonely people do or feel? Group 3: What causes people to feel lonely or cut off? Groups report their ideas back to the whole class.'

RECORDINGS

Students can be asked to listen to authentic interviews or 'vox pop' recordings and then complete grids with the key information. Here is an example for introducing poems on waking:

'Listen to these people talking about getting up. Make brief notes on what each one says, using these headings: Waking-Up Time, Getting-Up Time, Dreams, What (S)he Thinks About. Compare your replies with a partner'.

REACTIONS TO TEXTS

1. Often it will suffice to ask students to read a brief extract which bears on the theme of the poem. For example, to introduce poems on waking:

   He came slowly awake with the familiar dry sensation in his mouth. His

Illustration 1. (Reproduced by permission of Blackfriars Photography Project. Photograph by Paul Carter.)

feet were, as usual, swollen, and he had a cramp in his neck. When would they design an aircraft with couchettes? A grey light was filtering through the blind over the window, as they flew into the dawn. And it was cold. He eased the blanket up over his shoulders again and drifted back to sleep. (A. Pal)

2. Students might be asked to compare the poem with another piece on waking, noting down all the similarities and all the differences between the two awakenings.
3. The text may serve as a discussion starter for the theme of the poem. For example, the teacher asks the students to read this passage:

> The smaller birds were at the window now. He recognised the light tap-tapping of their beaks and the soft brush of their wings. The hawks ignored the windows. They concentrated their attack upon the door. Nat listened to the tearing sound of splintering wood, and wondered how many million years of memory were stored in those little brains, behind the stabbing beaks, the piercing eyes, now giving them their instinct to destroy mankind with all the deft precision of machines. (Daphne du Maurier, *The Birds*)

The teacher then asks students to make their own notes in answer to these questions:
a. What is going on? Where is Nat? What is going to happen to him?
b. If mankind were to be destroyed, what species would be most likely to take over the world?
Students compare their answers with a partner.

The preparation stage is not optional. Nor is it a waste of time. On the one hand it allows students time to activate areas of their personal experience the poem is to deal with. They are thus in a state of expectancy. On the other, it provides rich opportunities for interaction, even in advance of the poem itself.

Comprehension

No two people ever understand (that is, interpret) a piece of writing in exactly the same way. Their different personalities, experiences, and memory associations ensure that they will give prominence to different parts of the message, or even ignore some elements as insignificant. If this is true for 'ordinary' reading, it is the more true for poetry, with its richer texture of association and allusion. So we should forget about teaching students *the* meaning of a poem. A reasonable interpretation is a more valuable aim.

Here are some ideas for winnowing out meanings:

1. Read the poem once only. Tell students they should note down any words they recognise, or any words which come to mind in association with the poem. They then work in groups of four to make up composite lists.

   During a second reading they simply check off words on their lists as they hear them and add others which strike them. After this it is worth having a class feedback session, writing up the words which have been noted in the order they were noted. It will often be possible to reconstruct whole phrases of the poem in this way. An alternative procedure at this point is to give a list of all the nouns (or all the verbs) used in the poem, and then to ask students to reconstruct it.

   Finally, give out the text of the poem, and read it aloud again. (The same procedure can be followed for songs.)
2. Students read the poem individually. They are then given two or more paraphrases to read, and are asked to choose the one which best reflects the meaning of the poem. Here is an example:

Scaffolding

Masons, when they start upon a building
Are careful to test out the scaffolding;

Make sure the planks won't slip at busy points,
Secure all ladders, tighten bolted joints.

And yet all this comes down when the job's done,
Showing off walls of sure and solid stone.

So if, my dear, there sometimes seem to be
Old bridges breaking between you and me

Never fear. We may let the scaffolds fall
Confident that we have built our wall.

–Seamus Heaney

Teachers ask which of the following paraphrases of the poem students think is the better. Students discuss their choice with a partner, and then try to improve upon their choice.
- The writer reassures his lover by comparing their relationship with scaffolding and the finished building. Because they have built a solid wall of love, the small disagreements they have (the scaffolding) can be disregarded.
- The writer tells his lover not to worry if the things that first brought them together (the scaffolding) are being lost. They have now built a solid wall of more lasting interests.

The same technique can be used substituting pictures for paraphrases.

3. Students can be given two poems on the same theme. For example:

Fatigue

The man in the corner
all slumped over
looks forlorner
than a tired lover,

forehead dulled
with heavy working,
eyelids lulled
by the train's jerking;

head hangs noddy
limbs go limply
among a number
he dozes simply;

a dumb slumber
a dead ending,
a spent body
homeward wending.
      –Peggy Bacon

Commuters

Tired eyes,
Aching feet,
The commuters scramble
For a seat.

Each night
They go to bed
With heavy heart
And sleepy head,
Knowing tomorrow
They must repeat,
In weary sorrow,
With hurrying feet,
The tedium of today.

Teachers ask students: Are there any words which are used in both poems? Are there any words or phrases which mean more or less the same in both poems? Students then check their notes with a partner.

4. The text of the poem or song is given out as a cloze-exercise, that is, with a number of key words missing. Students have to supply these after listening and discussion in groups.

5. A prose summary of the poem is prepared. Certain key words are removed. The students then complete the summary as a cloze-exercise. This requires continual reference back to the poem.

6. The most common way of getting at an understanding of the poem is through asking questions. But questions of the form 'What is the meaning of . . . in line 3?' are unhelpful. Such questions lack concision, insofar as 'meaning' is left undefined, and even if students were intellectually able to answer they would often lack the linguistic or critical apparatus to do so. Questions which are less obviously about meaning often prove better guides to understanding. Here are a few example-types:

    – Which is the word in the poem which struck you most? Write it down. Compare your words in groups of four.

    – Which do you think is the most important line in the poem? Write it down and compare with your partner.

- There is a 'problem line' in the poem. Can you find it? Compare your answer with a partner. Can you solve the problem together?
- Which do you think are the happy words in the poem? Make a list. Then list the sad words. Compare your lists with a partner. (Alternatively, strong and weak words, warm and cold words, etc.)
- The poem tells a story. Can you make notes on the order in which the events happen? Compare your version with a friend.
- Which of these three titles suits the poem best? Can you justify your choice to your partner?
- Who is speaking in the poem? Who is he or she talking to? What about?
- The poet is making a comparison. What is being compared? Which lines show this most clearly?
- There are a lot of words connected with (for example) the sea in this poem. Can you list them all? Compare your list with a partner.
- Do you think what the poet says in line x is true? Or does the poet mean something else?
- Which parts of the poem move faster and which slower?
- Try to draw a simple picture to represent the poem. How does it compare with the one your partner has drawn?

As a general postcript to this section on comprehension of poems or songs, it is worth stating that the best way of sensing the key areas is to absorb yourself totally in the text. This means reading or listening to it repeatedly until it has given up new layers of meaning. Repeated exposure to a poem or song almost always brings to the surface new ideas for exploitation.

Expression

All songs, and most poems, are meant to be sung, or spoken aloud. It is important, therefore, for students to hear a good model to start with. This may be provided by teachers who feel able to give a sensitive reading of a poem, or play the guitar and sing. Alternatively, there exist excellent speech recordings of poems, as well as a plethora of recorded songs. It is the addition of the vocal element that brings the poem or song to life, so that the importance of providing a first-rate model on first hearing cannot be overemphasised. This is the time when the student can be brought to perceive the song or poem as something pleasurable and even exhilarating.

The extent to which students should themselves participate in singing or reading aloud has been much debated. The following suggestions start with minimal involvement and then progress towards total participation.

1. As the recording is played a second or third time, students are told that they should follow the text and, if they feel like it, sing along (or speak along) with it. Some will; some will not. But generally, with this unpressured approach, most will eventually.
2. If there is a chorus (or a pattern of repeated verses in a poem), students can be asked to sing or speak it chorally. That is after all what choruses are for!
3. Many songs or poems can be accompanied by more, or less, stylised actions or gestures:

This old man, he played one.   I'd rather be a hammer
He played knick-knack on my thumb.   Than a nail.
With a knick-knack, paddy-whack.   Yes I would...
Give the dog a bone,
This old man came rolling home.

This adds an enjoyment factor, especially with younger learners, though adults enjoy it too if you can lure them out of their stuffed shirts.
4. You can have students rehearse singing/reading to produce an aesthetically satisfying version of the song or poem. Two ideas:
   a. Many songs and poems have a chorus or repeated verses, or else are in the form of a dialogue between two or more characters, or else offer the possibility of different lines or verses being spoken or sung by different people. If there is a chorus, the whole group can sing or speak it, leaving the main parts to be sung or read by a single student or a small group. Dialogue poems can be spoken with groups playing the two speakers.

   In poems like this one, groups can be allotted lines to speak as indicated:

   Solomon Grundy   [*whole class*]
   Born on Monday,   [*Group 1*]
   Christened on Tuesday,   [*Group 2*]
   Married on Wednesday,   [*Group 3*]
   Took ill on Thursday,   [*Group 4*]
   Worse on Friday,   [*Group 5*]
   Died on Saturday,   [*Group 6*]
   Buried on Sunday,   [*Group 7*]
   And that was the end   }   [*whole class*]
   of Solomon Grundy.   }

   –Martin Bell

   b. The song or poem can be rehearsed to give maximum expression. For example, in the following jazz chant[1] there would be a grad-

1 *Jazz chants* is a term coined by Carolyn Graham to refer to the choral speaking of highly memorable, impressionistic, freewheeling verse. See her book *Jazz Chants*, New York: Oxford University Press, 1978.

ual crescendo to the word *thunder*, then 'I just wonder at the' would be spoken very softly, and *NOISE* would be shouted.

Mornings

Rustling sheet,
Shuffling feet,
Creaking bones,
Stifled groans,
Chirping, crowing,
Noses blowing,
Toilets flushing,
Bath tubs gushing,
Coffee cups' clatter,
Breakfast chatter,
Neighbours singing,
Telephones ringing,
Radios tuning,
Traffic booming,
Motorbikes thrumming,
Power drills drumming,
Jet planes thunder –
I just wonder
At the NOISE!

Dialogue poems are also good for work on expression, though here it is conveyed more through intonation than volume:

Goodbye

'Don't lie', she said.
'I try', he said.
'My eye!' she said.
'Don't cry', he said.
'I'll die!' she said.
'Oh my!' he said.
'Goodbye!' she said.

With polished performances of poems or songs we are on the borderlands of role-play, which comes into the next section.

Reaction

Songs and poems, as well as being exploited for their own sake, can act as a stimulus for other spin-off activities. Here we shall look at three such activities: role-play, project-work, and writing poems.

Alan Maley

As we have already seen, many songs and poems are dramatic in the sense that there are protagonists who engage in dialogue. The short poem 'Goodbye' (p. 103) is a good example. Students could be asked to work on it in pairs to produce a full version of the dialogue these people were having. This would necessarily involve them in discussing such matters as the relationship of the couple, the event which had brought matters to a head, and the setting in which it was taking place. Each pair could then perform its role-play for another pair. This inevitably leads to discussion and comment. Groups then relay their comments in full-class discussion.

Of course, a poem does not need to include dialogue to offer opportunities for role-play. Sometimes the poem is addressing someone else, as in this fragment:

> What has happened to Lulu, mother?
>   What has happened to Lu?
> There's nothing in her bed but an old rag-doll
>   And by its side a shoe.
> ....
> Why do you wander about as though
>   You don't know what to do?
> What has happened to Lulu, mother?
>   What has happened to Lu?
>
> —Charles Causley

In this case students can work to reconstruct the dialogue which must have taken place.

In other cases they can be asked to project themselves into a situation based on a poem. For example:

Old Age

> There's nobody to help me
> If I want a cup of tea,
> No one to talk to
> Except my old TV.
>
> There's nobody to lift me
> When I can't get out of bed.
> No one to cry on
> Or to stroke my poor old head.
>
> There's nobody to call on
> When I want my shopping done.
> No one to be my friend,
> For all my friends are gone.

Here each pair would be asked to work out a role-play between this person and a young volunteer visitor to old people.

Songs, of course, also open up possibilities for role-play and dramatisation, as does, for instance, the story-line of a ballad, such as 'The Streets of Laredo'. In short, the opportunities for role-play activities based on poems or songs are virtually limitless.

PROJECT-WORK

One of the chief advantages of poems and songs, as we have already noted in the introduction, is that they deal with themes which matter to people. These themes can therefore be readily expanded into more extensive activities. For example, with poems about loneliness or old age the following activities would be appropriate:

— interviews with old people in the local community (hence designing a questionnaire);
— collecting newspaper and magazine articles on the subject;
— interviews with local officials (eg, in hospitals or old-peoples' homes);
— a survey of facilities and special concessions for the aged in the community (eg, hot meals at home);
— proposals for improvements in local care for the old or lonely.

An alternative to exploring the theme is to explore the life or rise to fame of the singer, group, or poet. This might involve the collection of photographs or articles; the collection of other songs or poems by the same group or person; an opinion poll in the local community to establish the current popularity of the subject(s). Again, the result might be in the form of an article, a folder, or a wall-display.

WRITING POEMS

Writing poems is a special way of using language, not necessarily an exercise in perfection. For everyone who tries to write poems it is a case of

Trying to learn to use words, and every attempt
Is a wholly new start, a different kind of failure...

–T. S. Eliot

So there is no reason to feel inadequate if masterpieces are not produced. They rarely are, even by good poets. The important thing is the imaginative and active interaction with the language. It would be unrealistic, however, simply to order students to 'write poetry'. Some guidance and support are necessary. This can come from a number of sources.

— Sharing the writing in groups relieves some of the tension.
— Using a model gives guidance.

105

- Using a fail-safe technique (such as random combinations) leads to worry-proof writing.
- Offering a lead-in – for example, by giving the first and last lines or by setting the structure to be used – limits the number of formal difficulties.
- Using input from the preparation stage provides content – for example, by combining replies to questionnaires to form a poem.

The examples which follow can only serve as an introduction to the very wide range of techniques available.

1. *Group poem.* For example, students work in groups of six. Each member works on one area of sensation: sight, sound, taste, touch, smell, or feeling. He writes a single sentence which recalls an early memory of that area of sensation. All sentences must begin 'I remember...' For example: 'I remember the smell of apples'. 'I remember the feel of a live fish'.

   The group then pools its sentences and arranges them into the most satisfying order to form a poem. They may add a first and a last line.
2. *Working from a model.* For example, using the traditional rhyme 'Solomon Grundy', students work in groups of six. Each pair of students is assigned two days for which they must write the corresponding lines, using the poem as a model but injecting their own ideas and language. For example, the first pair might come up with:

   Solomon Grundy
   Tired on Monday
   Bored on Tuesday...

   The group as a whole has to find the final two lines.
3. *Using a fail-safe technique.* Students work in pairs. They write the theme word (eg, *CONFLICT*) vertically on a sheet of paper. They then work together to write a poem on conflict, each line of which starts with the appropriate letter. For example:

   Constantly quarrelling
   Over small things of
   No importance.
   Fraying the edges of our
   Lives with nagging.
   Impotent rage poisons us,
   Critical and cantankerous,
   Till death takes us away.

   They then compare their poem with that of another pair.
4. *Offering guidance with the structure*: For example, in groups of six, each member is given one verb: *feel, remember, wonder, hope, try, know.* The first line of the poem is given: 'Now that you've left me'.

Each student then uses his or her verb to write a single sentence of the form 'I + verb . . .' (eg, 'I wonder where you are'.) which could follow from the first line. The group then decides which is the best order for their lines, and composes the poem. For example:

> Now that you've left me,
> I wonder where you are.
> I remember the way you smiled.
> [etc.]

At this stage the group can make changes if it improves the poem.

5. *Use of input from the preparation stage.* For example, in a unit of material on memories, students have drawn a picture of a striking incident from their early life. In pairs they exchange pictures. Each person then uses another's picture to write a short poem about the incident. Finally they compare notes.

Conclusion

In recent years there has been much debate about *authenticity of language*. But we have perhaps overlooked one of the most authentic forms of language use, namely, poetry. (Song has had a slightly better deal even if it has been treated mainly as a top-dressing of 'culture' on the cold clay of 'the language'.) Poetry is linguistically authentic. It is also emotionally authentic, and thus provokes an equally authentic and individual response from the reader. Used in the ways suggested here, it can also involve students in authentic discussion and negotiation. When students write their own poetry, an authentic product issues from an authentic process. Perhaps it is worth a try?

Poems in this chapter not otherwise credited were written by Alan Maley.

Let's discuss

1. What criteria would you use for choosing a song or poem to teach a class? What would make a song or poem unacceptable for use?
2. What distinguishes a poem from prose? How do you know the difference? List five distinguishing features, and then compare them with someone else's list.
3. Can you think of teaching situations where you would *not* use poems and songs? Can you justify your view?

4. Is it necessary to tell students *about* a poem (eg, its author, the circumstances in which it was written, its form, rhyme scheme, or metre)?
5. If the answer to (4) is yes, how would you do it in a way that retains the interest of students?

Let's act on it

1. Devise a set of preparation, comprehension, expression, and reaction activities for the poem 'Scaffolding' on page 99. Try these out with a class. How could this set of exercises be improved for another class?
2. Take some newspapers. Cut out enough headlines to provide several groups with about twenty each. Have the groups work on trying to arrange ten of their headlines in the best order to form a poem. What did you learn about selecting headlines for this type of activity?
3. Give a theme word with a generic meaning, such as *love, pain, cruelty, indifference, fun, disappointment*, or let students choose their own. Have the students work in groups of six. Each person should write a sentence starting: 'X is...' (eg, 'Fun is jumping into the fountain with your clothes on'.). Students then try to arrange their six sentences to form a complete poem. What kinds of words were most successful in stimulating the students' imagination and creativity? Was there a difference when they selected their own theme words?
4. Experiment with highly predictable verse forms. Two particularly suitable forms are the *limerick* and the *haiku*.

    The limerick rhymes aa bb a. The first, second, and fifth lines contain three beats; the third and fourth two beats only. The first line always ends with a personal or place name.

    There was a young man from Southend
    Whose troubles seemed never to end.
    And what with the strain
    Of travelling by train,
    He eventually went round the bend.

    Give several groups of students different place names and ask each group to write a limerick.

    The *haiku* consists of three lines, of five, seven, and five syllables respectively. There is no rhyme or metrical scheme. The idea is to produce a compelling image in just a few words:

Among the white hairs
A solitary black one.
Life refuses death.

After explaining the *haiku* form and having students construct one as a class group, let them try in small groups, and then individually. With students there is no need to insist on the number of syllables, provided they can produce a sharp image.

Annotated reading list

Brown, Gillian. 1977. *Listening to Spoken English*. London: Longman. A careful, detailed, and original description of colloquial spoken English as opposed to the 'slow colloquial' form usually met with in language-teaching textbooks.

Brown, Gillian, and Yule, George. 1983. *Teaching the Spoken Language*. Cambridge: Cambridge University Press. Based on the description developed in *Listening to Spoken English* (1977), this book examines the criteria for teaching spoken production and listening comprehension, and for assessing spoken production. Very good examples both of authentic speech and of possible exercise types.

Widdowson, H. G. 1983. "Competence and Capacity in Language Learning," in Clarke, M. A., and Handscombe, J., eds., *On TESOL '82: Pacific Perspectives on Language Learning and Teaching*, pp. 97–106. Washington, D.C.: TESOL. After making an interesting comparison between learner errors and the deviant but accepted production of creative writers, the author goes on to argue for a more tolerant view of the learners' language-learning capacity. The aim is not to conform to a preconceived schema but to work creatively with the language resources at one's disposal.

9 "The magic if" of theater: enhancing language learning through drama

Richard Via

Few would disagree that drama has at last established itself as a means of helping people learn another language. A great deal of our everyday learning is acquired through experience, and in the language classroom drama fulfills this experiential need. When asked what a blind person is, it is very easy to explain in words that a blind person is one who cannot see. How much more effective it is if we blindfold the enquirer, who then tries to perform a simple task, thus experiencing in a personal way the feelings and difficulties of being blind. When we add drama and drama activities to the language classroom, we add a very meaningful dimension to rules and vocabulary.

It is important to give some definitions in order to understand exactly what is meant by the various drama-related terms in present use.

Drama is communication between people. Therefore if our students are doing dialogue work, *and* if they are conveying the intended meaning, as opposed to reciting the lines, they are using drama.

Theater is communication between people for the benefit of other people, which includes play production. It is important to remember that merely reciting memorized lines and speeches is not theater. There must be meaning conveyed – among the performers and between the performers and the audience.

Drama techniques are strategies to achieve either drama or theater, or both. They cover a wide range of activities that are useful in the language classroom. They may be verbal or nonverbal and can be de-signed to accomplish a variety of goals. Most of this chapter will deal with drama, theater, and drama techniques, with a short look at play production at the conclusion.

Setting the scene for language learning: introductory exercises

One of the first things to consider is the classroom atmosphere. There are those who consider this the major force in the success or failure of the language class. Some feel that even the presence of the teacher in the room is such a threat to the whole climate of language learning that

110

students' proficiency would improve if their teachers were removed. Drastic though this suggestion is, it does highlight a problem.

Constantin Stanislavski, the great Russian director, felt that relaxation is important for all actors. "Because of the artificial atmosphere of the stage," he maintained, "in front of a mass of people an actor's senses are often prone to paralysis" (Moore 1960: 27). Language learners often have similar feelings when trying to communicate in a new language. This is especially true when they have learned some structures and have a limited vocabulary. When called upon to speak, all attention is focused on them as if all spotlights were turned in their direction. Tenseness and fear of error can prevent them from functioning at their best. Gallwey (1974: 13) writes of "relaxed concentration," where the focus is on what one must do – in our case communicate in another language rather than be concerned about mistakes or what others may think of our performance.

Actors and language learners alike need an atmosphere that is non-threatening during the learning and rehearsal stages – a place where mistakes are considered normal and where they receive support from all around them. It is the teacher's job to provide the students with this learning environment. The teacher is in the classroom for the security of the students, not the reverse. It is the teacher's responsibility to guide and help the students and to keep them interested and involved.

Proper classroom atmosphere needs to be developed from the first day. I tell my students that the classroom is a language laboratory where they will experiment with the language. As in any laboratory, they must know the ingredients and how they are to be combined in order to succeed. But I also reassure them that in all laboratories there is a great deal of trial and error and guesswork. Mistakes are expected, and help is always available from me and others in the "lab." Next I make sure the students get acquainted, through self-introductions or by introducing each other. I always use the target language – in my case English – but other teachers may prefer to conduct this introductory session in the students' native language.

There are other activities that help break down inhibitions and form a group feeling. Some of these may seem foolish and unsuited to a language class, but the purpose is to create the proper atmosphere. Once students realize that others look "funny" trying an exercise and that they too will look funny, we are on the way to creating a lab where they are not afraid to make mistakes, however ridiculous. I have found the following exercises particularly helpful.

EXERCISE 1: BREATHING

(Students should be in a circle and able to see as many other faces as possible.)

Bend over and exhale as much air as possible. Inhale as you come back up. Hold your breath for a few seconds. With teeth together and lips open and spread, release the air with a hissing sound as slowly as possible. Repeat two or three times.

EXERCISE 2: WALKING

Walk around, using all the available space – but not in a circle like a merry-go-round.

1. Walk as you usually do. Notice as much about the way you walk as possible.
2. How would you walk if you were in water chest high?
3. How would you walk on clouds?
4. How would you walk on hot sand?
5. How would you walk if you were a marionette?
6. Walk naturally and notice how others walk.

EXERCISE 3: MACHINE

In groups of five to fifteen, make an imaginary machine that may or may not have a "real" function. This may be accomplished in two ways:

a. One person begins a movement and a sound; one by one the others join in and fit themselves into the machine.
b. The group is given five minutes to decide on the machine and its possible function.

EXERCISE 4: VOICE

Any voice exercise that does not strain the voice is useful. A stronger voice when speaking another language in the classroom gives confidence to the speaker.

There are no right or wrong ways of doing any of these exercises. Students should not be forced to participate, nor to do them in a certain way. Depending on the language level, instruction and discussion may take place in the target or native language.

Four golden rules for language teaching through drama

Self

Through his work with actors, Constantin Stanislavski has indirectly provided language teachers with a number of useful suggestions. In an elaborate chart he created for a group of directors and actors, he placed *self* in the number one position. He argued that all good acting must express the feelings of the individual. A director should not tell an actor how to say a line or how to perform a particular action. Not only would the actor be unable to achieve the level of the "master," but the imitation would not be believable or "true," since it did not come from within the actor (Hapgood 1963: 42). This concept of self relates directly to language teaching.

Probably all of us who have taught another language have been asked "How do I say this?" My answer was always the same: "I don't know how you say it, I only know how I say it, and that won't help you. You see, I'm an American, a male, and sixty years old. You are Japanese, a female, and twenty. I can't possibly know how you feel in this situation. So you see only you know how you say it."

In oral communication we have moved beyond the idea that vocabulary plus structure equals language. One of the things that needs to be added is Stanislavski's concept of self. It is impossible for someone to be anyone else; therefore language learners need to add their own feelings and desires to any exercise if the language is to express what they wish it to express. This "self" is not to be confused with the strong "individualism" associated with Americans, but refers to the individuality of all individuals. It is excellently expressed in *Improvisation for the Theatre* (Spolin 1963: 391):

Self: Refers to the natural part of ourselves; free of crippling worries, prejudices, rote information, and static forces of reference; that part of us capable of direct contact with the environment; that which is our own nature.

Spolin's definition of self-identity is also useful: "Having one's own place and allowing others theirs; securely placed within an environment; where you are is where *you* are" (1963: 391).

In using drama for language teaching we want to encourage our students to express their own feelings rather than to use the role and new language to hide behind for security. If students are not expressing their own feelings, then their conversation is meaningless. If we train them to pretend to be someone else, a someone who is in turn responsible for any mistakes they make, then we are not only denying them expression of their own feelings, but we are also robbing them of their rights to be responsible for themselves.

Teaching students the importance of self gives them a foundation on which to build their new language. Any other approach requires building a new and artificial foundation, which must be destroyed, as progress is made, before honest communication can take place.

"The magic if" and imagination

Another line in Stanislavski's chart was "the magic if." Since no actor has been everywhere nor done everything, all actors need a technique that will help them arrive at a truthful interpretation. Lewis in *Method or Madness* (1958: 32) presumes that "the magic if" meant that "it is as if." I would prefer to expand it to "If I were in this situation and if I said these lines, how would I say them?"

As language teachers using drama, we can create our own chart, based on that of Stanislavski, but we should include another item besides self and "the magic if," and that is *imagination*. This is somewhat related to "the magic if," but is concerned largely with physical surroundings. When students engage in drama activities, we should allow them time to create in their mind's eye the kinds of clothes they would be wearing, what the furniture might be like, and the total decor of the setting. If, for example, the dialogue takes place in a first-class restaurant, it might be helpful for them to think of a specific restaurant they know. Even if each student imagines a different "elegant restaurant," their manner of speaking will be appropriate. (Of course, often dialogues are of such a general nature that the classroom setting is completely appropriate.)

Thus self, "the magic if," and imagination are the first three golden rules of teaching language through drama. There is one more, which ties them all together.

The final golden rule: the five senses

L. Smith (1983: 77) suggests that language learners should use five "senses" when learning and using a new language. The first is the same as our First Golden Rule, namely, a sense of self; the others are a sense of audience, of relationship between self and audience, of setting, and of goal. In order to relate these senses to a dramatic context of language learning, we need imagination and "the magic if." Smith argues that everyone uses these five senses daily when speaking the native language – in most cases without consciously thinking about them. Sometimes when learning a second or new language, however, we forget that these senses are still with us and that we can use them.

Drama teachers who exhort their students with such phrases as "Put some life into it," "Put feeling and emotion in," or "Make it come alive" are wasting their time unless they give their students more information about the dialogue in order to stimulate them creatively to use these five senses. To give just one example, when students become aware of the five senses and take time to consider them carefully in relationship to the dialogue, a marked vocal improvement occurs in pitch, stress, and intonation. Adding the five senses to "the magic if" and imagination gives our students valuable information to bring their second language to life, a process that should begin on the first day of class.

To take a simple example, let us say the first word to be taught is *hello*, the symbol used as a greeting. Since considerations of structure are irrelevant here, we may be satisfied if students can pronounce it correctly. If, however, we accept the idea that words can and should express the feelings of the speaker, then we need to incorporate the five senses. *Hello* then becomes more than a symbol of greeting and begins to express the inner feelings of the speaker.

We may think of saying hello to a close friend who has been away for a year. The meeting takes place in a restaurant where several other friends have gathered to join the party. Remembering and using the five senses, the students would know how they behave and speak in this situation, how the friend is likely to respond to the greeting, and what kind of relationship they have between them. They would be able to imagine a particular restaurant. The greeting becomes more than a word; it becomes a welcome. The hello resulting from this kind of exercise would be quite different from the recitation of a symbol.

One might ask how this fits in with differences in culture. We always want our students to behave naturally, but that does not mean that they behave everywhere as they would at home. What we are looking for is to discover the emotional feeling of the "hello." Cultural differences would be taken into account with a keen awareness of the person spoken to, their relationship, the setting, and the objective.

"Hellos" can be said in many ways. For the students to discover this, all we need to do is change a few "facts." The students continue to "be themselves," but we change the nature of the character to whom they say "Hello." Perhaps this character becomes an older person: a teacher or a police officer who has had an unpleasant relationship with the student. They pass in a hallway in school and the older person says: "Hello!" The student feels obliged to respond, but the resulting "Hello" is probably not a happy one, nor is its goal to greet or welcome; it is merely an acknowledgment. Students can experiment with different ways to say "Hello" by making slight changes in audience, setting, or goal. Body language will add to the effectiveness of the spoken word to communicate the true feelings of the speaker.

Though body language may vary greatly from one culture to another, changes of expression caused by emotional experiences may be interpreted across cultures and, therefore, these do not have to be taught. Beginners may be allowed to use gestures with the specific meanings of their own culture. At a more advanced level, however, when students know they may be interacting with persons from different cultures, they should learn the appropriate gestures.

Talk and listen

Stanislavski, noting the extreme stress placed upon actors by the "artificial atmosphere" of the stage, said that it is necessary for actors really to talk and listen to each other. In everyday life we often half-listen, but we assume that what we say is fascinating to all and therefore never half-talk, which quite often creates a misunderstanding between speaker and listener. When this occurs in a second language a complete communication breakdown may ensue, with disastrous results.

Listening is the key, yet in many oral classes most attention is given to speaking. A frustrated cartoon character once remarked: "Everyone learned to talk, no one learned to listen!" Many famous people in the theater, when asked their secret of success, state they are good listeners. To be a good actor or a good conversationalist, one must be a good listener. Robert Duvall, the American actor, was once asked if he would give the interviewer an acting lesson. He replied: "Basically, it's 'I talk, you listen. You talk, and I listen.' And four of those things have to be working." This concept of "talk and listen" is integral to teaching language through drama.

Talk and Listen is my adaptation of a technique used by many professional actors to get a full understanding of the play – to reply appropriately to what is said to them, to talk to each other rather than reciting. An additional bonus is that lines are learned through this *Talk and Listen* process, rather than through hours of drilling them into one's head (in other words, memorizing them). West was on the right track with his Read and Look Up approach to language learning. He explained that when one reads a line of dialogue aloud, the words go into one's eye and out of one's mouth with little learning taking place. He believed that if one reads the line without speaking, looks up, and then says the line, the words go from the eye to the brain, where they are processed for a moment before they go out of the mouth. It is in that moment's processing that learning takes place (West 1960: 63–5).

Dialogues should never be learned by an individual alone. A complete dialogue may be read privately by individual students as often as they wish, but only for a clearer understanding of what it is about or to check the vocabulary. At no time should students attempt to memorize the lines. Whenever students are speaking the lines of a dialogue they should be listening to someone and responding appropriately to them. We are all aware that actors who memorize their lines exactly, recite them correctly, and stand in their assigned places are not likely to receive the Critics' Award. It would be good if we could remove the words *memorize* and *recite* from the vocabulary of language classes. We should replace them with *learn* and *communicate*. Rote memorization of dialogues represents poor language learning. When dialogues are learned by heart, a number of things are probably taking place, none of which has anything to do with communication:

1. The student has learned all the lines and says them out loud alternately with a partner; thus there are two monologues.

2. The student speaks when the partner stops speaking, whether the speaker has completed the sentence or not; thus there is no listening except to the sound of a voice.
3. The lines are spoken correctly but without any thought for their content; therefore ideas and feelings are not expressed.

Talk and Listen, at the beginning stages, requires students to make eye contact whenever someone is speaking. For example, A reads his line to himself, then looks at B and *says* the line to B. If he cannot remember the whole line he may look back at the text. Then he looks at B and continues to speak. All this while B is looking at and listening to A, rather than reading what A is saying or preparing how she is going to say her own line. When A has finished his speech, B then looks at her line, reads it to herself, looks at A and says the line, and so on.

It should be pointed out that using the *Talk and Listen* technique will be much slower than reading or memorizing, but the final results will be much better. It is good to know too that each time students go through a dialogue using this technique they are actually going through it twice: once reading and a second time speaking.

Talk and Listen cards are an effective way of introducing this system of dialogue work. Each card contains only one person's lines. This encourages the participants to listen to each other, since they cannot read what is being said to them. In this training period, and especially with beginning students, it is wise to have short sentences and probably not more than four lines for each speaker.

Card one	*Card two*
A: When I woke up this morning...	A: ....
B:	B: Yes, yes, I'm listening.
A: When I woke up this morning...	A: ....
B:	B: You've already said that.
A: I know – I was thinking, so I repeated it.	A: ....
B:	B: Well, when you woke up this morning, what?

Two students may demonstrate to the class how to proceed. The first run-through is to make sure the students are following the instructions for *Talk and Listen*, and to help with any problems of pronunciation. In most cases the beginner is able to use the *Talk and Listen* technique more easily than more advanced students, who have been taught to respond immediately to "keep the flow."

The second time, one student may speak in a high, but unstrained, voice, and the other in a natural, low voice. This often creates laughter among both participants and audience, which is not a bad thing. The purpose of this approach is to demonstrate to the students that a change of tone will give quite a different feeling to the sentence. This can also be demonstrated by having one student talk very rapidly and the other talk very slowly, or by having both talk rapidly; this makes it clear that the speed with which one speaks all or part of a sentence can affect the meaning. In another variation, if culturally appropriate, participants may be asked to touch each other each time they speak.

The students at this point have been unable to give a proper interpretation of the lines because they do not have enough information. In the theater we would want to know the "given circumstances" – in other words, the Wh-questions (the who, what, why, where, and when) – and we might wish to "set the scene" with more details.

Building the scene

For the dialogue on cards in the preceding section, the students may be asked how *they* would say the lines if they were in the following situation:

A has been married to B for five years. They are having breakfast. B is a workaholic who wants to get ahead. A feels that B really should take a vacation and relax. Moreover, A would like to get away from the daily routine. A is in the kitchen when speaking. B overslept a bit and has only ten minutes before leaving the house in order to get to work on time. B is at the table.

A completely different situation may then be created for the same dialogue, in order to point out that language is greatly controlled by the five senses. For example:

A is a young man who has been going with the same young woman for three years, but has not proposed marriage because he wanted to be financially sound first with an apartment or house, a car, and enough money for a good honeymoon. Yesterday he realized everything was in order and that he was ready for marriage. He has brought B to a very nice restaurant. There is crisp linen, fine china, and good crystal on the table as well as flowers and candles. It is a romantic place. For almost three years B has been expecting A to propose, since they seem so ideally suited to each other. B has been to this restaurant on several occasions with A, usually for a birthday celebration.

The interpretations of these two short dialogues will be quite different. Interpretation will vary even more if most of the information given in the second situation is retained but A is given this change:

Last week you met another young woman whom you find more interesting and more attractive. You have brought B to your favorite restaurant to tell her that this is the last time you will be with her.

I should again stress that there is no "correct" interpretation of the dialogue in these situations. The students are asked how *they* would say the lines if *they* were in the situation described, and I am careful to avoid such statements as "I think you should be more concerned, or in a greater hurry"; "I thought you were too gloomy"; or "You were not embarrassed enough." If the interpretation seems completely inappropriate, then the teacher may check to be sure the students understand the situation, or give additional information to guide them. In the first situation, if a student interpreted the workaholic in a rather slow, listless way, it might be that he wanted to indicate the character's need (as the student sees it) for a vacation; there is more to life than work. However, the teacher might remind the student that A is still in the kitchen, and the workaholic, who has not yet had breakfast, has to leave the house in ten minutes. In other words, the student should be given enough information to understand why the character might be interpreted as being in a hurry, rather than being arbitrarily told to be in a hurry.

Though *Talk and Listen* asks the student to make eye contact the first few times when going through the dialogue, this rule changes once the situation has been established. The students should feel free to look at each other or not as they interpret the dialogue, adopting whichever behavior seems appropriate for the roles. Normal body language should be allowed to prevail.

It is not an invariable rule that all *Talk and Listen* dialogue cards be ambiguous in content. However, if you find ambiguity interesting, have two colleagues look at the dialogues you have prepared and suggest where they might take place. Quite often slight changes – for example, in the ages of the characters, the setting, or even the weather – will provide significant differences. The cards may also be used to introduce new structures and vocabulary.

At times, students may be asked to continue the dialogue on their own. If this is too advanced for the class, they work in pairs to write a continuing dialogue. Alternatively, the entire class may be divided into pairs. Each pair may be asked to work as a team – first to use the *Talk and Listen* technique, then to decide in what real-life circumstances such a dialogue might take place. If the class is very large there can be three in each group, with one acting as "director" of the other two.

If you feel that students are not listening to each other, but merely waiting until the speaker has stopped, you can leave some blank spaces on the dialogue cards, for example:

Card one	*Card two*
A: Would you like to go to... tonight?	A: ....
B:	B: To...? I guess so, what time?
A: How about...	A: ....

Richard Via

B: ....

B: At...? That's too..., could we make it at...? I'll meet you at...

A: That's fine, I'll meet you at ...at...

A: ....

When preparing *Talk and Listen* cards for listening comprehension, the teacher should be sure to leave space to ensure that the "blank" word is repeated by the listener.

A: Would you like to go to [the movies]?
B: To [the movies]? I guess so.

For beginning students, you may wish to give multiple-choice suggestions:

A: Would you like to go to [the movies/a disco/a party] tonight?

In this case you may or may not wish to list the alternatives on B's card. Another possibility is to leave it open, but give a clue to what is needed, as in:

A: Would you like to go to (place/event)?

Improvisation

Improvisation is a very useful drama technique, since the focus is on students' ability to use the language they have acquired without the benefit of a script. All improvisations should be goal-oriented or have a problem to solve. This enables students to have something definite to talk about. When students are given general information, such as "two people meet in the street" or "two people meet in a coffee shop," it is difficult to know what to talk about.

I generally start with a group improvisation that gives the students security. A favorite is "The Elevator," a simple improvisation that always generates interest. Four or five students are asked to stand in a small space designated "the elevator." At a clap of the hands the elevator stops between the fourteenth and fifteenth floors of the imaginary building. Students are asked to do what they think they would do in such a situation. One group solved it this way: "What happened?" "It's stopped." "What should we do?" "Let's wait. Someone will notice." I let them wait for a minute or two, then let them "out."

Only two of the five participants had spoken during this improvisation. This is actually a good thing, because only the individuals involved know how they *think* they would behave. The teacher, therefore, must accept every solution given by the participants.

120

Some people worry that, in such a dramatic activity, only those who were in front of the room participating in the activity were involved in any language experience. On the contrary, quite a bit was happening with the audience. Such comments as "Why don't they . . . ?" or "I would do . . . " are being *thought*. A second group, immediately following the first, will probably be much more vocal and active. A third group will more than likely borrow from both groups and add new material. They are able to do this because of involvement with what has been happening, and more time to think before going in front of the others.

The next step in improvisation is to give each involved student a card with specific information, including the goal to be achieved. For example:

A: You work for an advertising firm. You have been very successful and expect a promotion soon. Tonight you and your wife/husband are to have dinner with several important people in your company. Though it is supposed to be a social occasion, you know that it is business. It seems to you that your wife/husband is very slow in getting ready, since you were ready to leave fifteen minutes ago. You must not be late for this appointment.
Goal: To get your wife/husband to hurry and leave.

B: Your husband/wife is a successful young executive and a very hard worker. You realize that he/she is working too hard and takes little time for relaxation. He/she has lost weight recently and tonight seems very nervous. You are going out to dinner with others from his/her office. You would rather stay at home and relax with him/her. You want him/her to slow down.
Goal: To persuade him/her to stay home tonight or to take a vacation.

Another interpretation is possible if husband/wife were changed to friend and/or co-worker.

These improvisations may be performed by several pairs to see if there are different solutions. After students become used to doing improvisations it will be necessary to set a time limit, since usually neither party will give in first. There should always be a discussion about possible solutions and variations. The teacher should be concerned with the interaction (communication, body talk, solution) of the students while it is taking place and take mental notes on language problems, but only on important ones. These should be corrected at the conclusion, without bothering students with every little thing. Students seeing a teacher writing on a notepad deduce that they must be making mistakes, and this can be very inhibiting to spontaneous performance.

Improvisations, as well as *Talk and Listen* cards, may be prepared as written exercises by the students. They make excellent group projects. After performing the improvisation they have created, they discuss the solution and other possible solutions and perform again. When they are satisfied, they write the play script based on the performance.

Richard Via

Play production as language learning

Since my work in language teaching began with productions of full-length plays, I do not want to overlook the value of play production. Dramatic results can be obtained by play production (the pun is intentional), for quite obvious reasons. The production of a play is goal-oriented; language is "real" instead of belonging to a textbook, and language is set in its appropriate cultural setting. Furthermore, all the relevant discussion about direction, character development, movement, and so on, can be in the target language, which provides opportunities for real use of the language in communication. There are also obvious problems in presenting a play, however, including lack of time, not enough space, too few parts for the members of the class, lack of funds, and perhaps the teacher's insecurity as an inexperienced director.

The number one problem is that of time. It is impossible to direct a full-length play, or even a standard one-act play, in the time allowed for most language classes. Normally it is necessary for both students and teacher-director to work on the play as an extracurricular activity. Fortunately, short skits can be successfully performed in the allotted classroom time; and inexperienced teachers may be wise to start with these before attempting a longer play.

As for the other problems, there are many available solutions. Many theater groups, for instance, perform in "available space." This means that the cast adapts itself to whatever space it is given. For teachers, in most cases, the "available space" is the classroom. If there are not enough roles, the play may be double cast; and there is also need for an assistant director, stage manager, prompter, scene shifter, costume assistant, and so on. There are plenty of excellent books available to provide teachers with sufficient knowledge of play presentation (see Annotated Reading List). The play need not involve any expense. Thornton Wilder's great play *Our Town* was written to be performed without scenery or properties and with the simplest of costumes. There are few plays that cannot be performed in this way. This approach is often more effective, because the audience then becomes involved in the creative process of imagining the setting and props.

It is important to remember that all the suggestions made previously in this chapter refer to techniques suitable not only for language acquisition but also for play production. Although in the latter we have to shift our teaching focus from language learning as such (dialogue work) to the goal of a finished production, the techniques remain the same, namely, the creation in the classroom of a nonthreatening atmosphere; the use of the five senses; using *Talk and Listen*; creating "the magic if"; developing imagination.

A short play can be broken down into sections and used as a series of *Talk and Listen* dialogues. As students learn (not memorize) one section, they move on to the next. By combining the sections, they have learned the play or skit. The use of this technique enables different groups of students to work on several short plays at the same time and can lead to the creation of several skits simultaneously.

Let us remember that drama is not a method. It is a technique, or useful tool, that can be a part of any language program. A full semester's work can be built around a drama project, or it can fill five or ten minutes at the beginning or end of a lesson. It encourages the student to view the language as a tool for communication rather than as an academic subject. It can bring life and vitality to the classroom and release the teacher from the trap of routine. With today's focus on communicative competence and interactive language teaching, drama seems to be a viable answer.

Let's act on it

1. What is the difference between using "the magic if" and pretending?
2. According to the author, how is it possible to use one's self when using a prepared (i.e., scripted) text?
3. What are the major differences between learning a dialogue using the *Talk and Listen* technique versus rote memorization?
4. What complications in communication do you foresee arising when the five senses are disregarded?
5. What are the principal factors in a language classroom that might inhibit the use of drama activities as described in this chapter?

Annotated reading list

Maley, A., and Duff, A. 1982. *Drama Techniques in Language Learning*. 2d ed. Cambridge: Cambridge University Press. Provides many examples of activities and improvisations for group work.

Smith, S. M. 1984. *The Theater Arts and the Teaching of Second Languages*. Reading, Mass.: Addison-Wesley. Excellent resource book for play production. All techniques discussed are useful for language learning.

Via, R. A. 1976. *English in Three Acts*. Honolulu: University Press of Hawaii. Activities, short plays, simple production information, and theory of drama for language teaching.

10 Interactive testing: time to be a test pilot

Marlies Mueller

Knowledge must come through action. You can have no test which is not fanciful, save by trial.

Sophocles, *Trachiniae, 592*

Is not all testing, even the most traditional, by its very nature "interactive"? After all, teachers query, students answer. Yet, in its Merriam Webster definition of "mutually or reciprocally active," *interactive* is hardly a term that would occur to the average student in describing the experience of testing. The consumer view of testing is rather that of a one-way street along which one feels prodded, jostled, or dragged by an establishment bent on spoiling what might otherwise be a pleasant student life. Many of our students' definitions of testing would undoubtedly include some colorful adjectives equally applicable to the effects produced by medieval instruments of torture. If, however, we take the audacious step of making testing truly *interactive*, giving both constituent parts of the word their full etymological weight, it can be a lively exchange of stimulating ideas, opinions, impressions, reactions, positions, or attitudes. Students can be actively involved and interested participants when their task is not restricted to providing the one and only correct answer. Why not turn the tables occasionally and focus on the "reciprocal" in the preceding definition by inviting the students to ask the question? A correctly formulated query is as well-suited to demonstrating control of vocabulary and grammar as the traditional, often uninspired and uninspiring response.

To date, it seems fair to say, most testing in the field of foreign-language teaching has not been truly interactive. It suffices to look at the average classroom teacher's bread-and-butter testing, as well as the major standardized achievement tests, to realize that teachers, like generals, typically fight the last war. When audiolingualism was in full swing, testing methods were based on grammar-translation principles: translation exercises artificially constructed around specific grammar rules. Today, when communication-oriented methods and approaches are the vogue, our evaluation practices are, as before, lamentably out of date. Many of us cling almost exclusively to testing stemming from the psychometric-stucturalist era: Discrete-point testing[1] in unconnected sentences, with multiple-choice, true/false, and completion items, is the runaway favorite. Rare indeed is the foreign-language classroom that ever saw a cloze test[2] (so vigorously promoted in the seventies), let alone the "hybrid" or integrative tests that combine natural, communicative language with grammatical and lexical specificity, which have been proposed by Omaggio (1981) for the eighties. Yet it has long been established, as Schulz (1977: 94) points out, that *testing determines the manner in which students learn and teachers teach*. If the communication-oriented methodologies of the current decade are to become airborne, we must all be "test pilots"; we must be adventurous and evaluate our students' progress in ways compatible with our teaching. Thus, many of the testing activities suggested throughout this chapter are first cousins of the day-to-day activities of the interactive classroom. Only when we evaluate both – that is, knowledge of the language *and* communicative performance, or the students' demonstration of that knowledge in concrete situations (Canale and Swain 1980) – will we really test what we teach in a communication-oriented course.

For students to receive the full benefit from interactive teaching, experimenting with interactive tests is essential. Should we, therefore, purge all discrete-point diagnostic testing from our practice? To do so would be as foolish as tossing aside each succeeding teaching methodology in favor of the latest revolutionary approach. Many of our tried and true tests will continue to serve us well. They are convenient, they are easy to score, and they may be assessed more objectively than freer, open-ended global testing. Furthermore, they are remarkably adaptable. All testing techniques offer elements that can be integrated into useful tests for evaluating communicative command of the target language. Canale and Swain (1980: 35) view the "discrete-point versus integrative distinction as a continuum" that ranges from communicative-competence tests to tests of communicative performance. No matter what the format, in testing as in teaching *variety of activity and of pace are crucial* for keeping students alert and interested. Because individual students respond better to some testing techniques than to others, a variety of testing formats will provide all students with broader opportunities for demonstrating both their competence and their ability to perform in the language.

---

1 *Discrete-point* tests focus the attention of the student on specific points, knowledge of which is tested one by one. *Global* (sometimes called *integrative*) tests require exercise of several skills in interaction (see Rivers 1981: 357–8).
2 The *cloze test* is constructed by omitting every *n*th word in a continuous passage of discourse (see Rivers 1981: 377–9). It is considered a convenient measure of overall proficiency.

Marlies Mueller

Individual oral testing

If we are genuinely interested in developing our students' communication skills and in seeing them apply these skills in authentic communicative activities, *oral tests are essential from the beginning* of the language-learning experience. Why then are oral evaluations so gingerly approached? Savignon (1972: 41–9, 82–93) outlines a lengthy process, requiring a native speaker, that might be feasible as part of an overall achievement test administered at the beginning or end of a college career, but that is unsuitable for regular class use. Valdman and Moody (1979) recommend the use of the language laboratory, where conditions for free, open-ended communicative activities are far from ideal.[3] Omaggio (1981) indicates many excellent and useful testing formats for listening comprehension, reading, and writing, but offers only a few suggestions for oral testing, calling instead, in apparent frustration, for workshops and conferences to address this thorny problem. The Interagency Language Roundtable Oral Proficiency Test[4] (developed at the Foreign Service Institute) suffers from difficulties in the transfer of its grading system from government agencies to high schools and universities. Required for entry into the foreign service, the test must be passed at an ever higher level for promotion up the ladder of the government hierarchy. Often a year of intensive study or a tour of duty in a country where the target language is spoken is needed to advance by half a point along the 5-point scale. The American Council on the Teaching of Foreign Languages (ACTFL) recast the scale in a form more suitable for the academic community using the following categories: Novice – low, mid, high; Intermediate – low, mid, high; Advanced; Advanced plus; and Superior.[5] This 9-point scale may obviate this problem of transfer. Nevertheless, if administered as recommended, the test requires two instructors: a native speaker and a linguist. This fact alone makes its frequent and regular use prohibitive for typically large elementary courses.

A perusal of the professional literature points up three major inter-related problems that prevent the frequent, regular use of oral interviews for testing purposes:

1. the large amount of tester's time required per student;
2. difficulty in scheduling the tests;
3. misgivings about rater objectivity in assessing student performance.

---

3 Albert Valdman and Marvin Moody (1979) also describe the Indiana University Foreign Language Communicative Ability Test.
4 Full details of the Interagency Roundtable scale and ratings (originally for the Foreign Service Institute) can be found in Rivers (1981: 368–9, 497–9).
5 For the ACTFL/ETS (Educational Testing Services) rating scale and provisional proficiency guidelines, see Rivers (1983b: 208–21).

Practical problems

The practical considerations of time and scheduling, which have discouraged teachers in the past from persisting with oral testing, can be overcome by planning and organization. The following format has been successfully used at Harvard for the past ten years in the elementary French course.

Once a week half of the students in a relatively large sectioned course (up to 200 students) take a three- to four-minute individual oral test with their section instructors. In a course that is scheduled for one hour on five days per week, the one hour per week dedicated to oral testing has proved to be well worth the loss in class time. Neither students nor instructors are asked to sacrifice "outside" time, and the test administered is standardized course-wide. This format is successful with sections numbering no more than twenty students (only ten students can be tested comfortably in one hour). With a class of twenty students, ten will be tested at scheduled intervals on any given test day. Upon entering the classroom, the student will sit opposite the instructor, who has a copy of the test. As the student responds, the instructor marks the test copy as unobtrusively as possible. To minimize apprehension caused by a wagging pen, students are informed that positive aspects of their performance will be noted as well as negative ones. In general, tests are short enough to allow time for discussing difficulties in the test with the student and pointing out strengths and weaknesses. Grading takes into account appropriateness and comprehensibility of response, grammatical correctness, degree of fluency, promptness of response, and pronunciation when it interferes with comprehension. Although the structure of the test has remained the same throughout the decade, test content has evolved toward ever greater use of interactive elements and communicative activities.

Does this format encourage student cheating? Can students who are tested at 9 a.m. pass on test information to their successors at a later hour? Surely they can, but in this type of test knowledge of the test's content does not particularly determine student performance. Nevertheless, to obviate any advantage of this kind, all students are informed in advance of the general content of the test; consequently, students will have no additional information to pass on after having taken the test. Test items are repeated once upon student request or hesitation. If one student takes longer than expected to complete the pre-timed test, there will be a minimal grade penalty – enough to make normal conversational speed attractive, but not enough to be discouraging. (In practice, 1 point per 100 is deducted for each minute over five minutes on a three-minute test). As each oral test (of a total of five) counts for 5% of the semester grade, a stiffer penalty does not seem warranted.

Should the proceedings of the test be recorded on audiotape? There are certain apparent advantages to this procedure: It permits students, or anyone else, to hear the interview again; it may allow greater objectivity in grading (we will return to this matter later); and it provides a record for subsequent control. We have found, however, that these possible benefits are outweighed by the potential intimidation and discomfort to the students of knowing their first awkward attempts and mistakes in using a foreign language are being recorded, as well as by the considerable additional demands on the time of the instructor, who has to relisten to each oral test.

Fear of *subjectivity in grading* has proved groundless; not once in ten years has a student complained of a lack of objectivity in our oral testing. It seems evident to us that the objectivity of the largely discrete-point format, together with the communicative nature of the content, puts students at their ease.

Content

Specifically what kind of content engages the students' interest and involves them in a meaningful exchange, even at a very elementary level of language control? In testing the forms of the future tense, for example, instead of asking a student to conjugate a verb in the future, we might ask, "Please answer using the future tense":

Will you be going skiing this weekend? With whom?
Will your roommate be working on his/her assignments?
Will we be reading Arsène Lupin on Monday?
Will your parents be going camping this summer?
Where will they go? / What will they do instead?
Do you think I will give you a good grade? Why?

If students have studied verb forms well, this exchange will prove their skill in using them. Many students appear to welcome the opportunity to talk about themselves, their lives and opinions, in the target language, and they often forget that they are being tested and proceed to chat conversationally.

A typical test includes one or two brief open-ended questions, such as "Describe your roommate, using at least five adjectives." *Visual aids* are invaluable in *providing situations, context, and coherence* for oral testing; for example, a student is asked to look at an advertisement and to tell the instructor whether he or she can use the product, explaining why or why not. Later in the year, as they advance in language control, students may be given a subject on which to interview the examiner – for example, eliciting biographical information using the troublesome constructions of *depuis quand* (since when), *depuis combien de temps* (for how long), and *pendant combien de temps* (for how long). Although a three- or four-minute test cannot test everything a student has learned in a two-week period, students tend to study harder than they need so as to have the answers on the tips of their tongues. Consequently, they progress faster in communicative ability than if required to take written tests alone.

Oral testing through a *telephone test* has proved successful and popular. Students are instructed to obtain certain information from an unknown person in the target language via the telephone (an instructor from another class is a useful target). Early in the learning of the language a student may have to find out certain kinds of information during the phone call, such as time and place of events and what happened, a description of the family or of rooms, furniture, or trips to be taken – information that will be recounted in a subsequent oral interview.

If they can be received with sufficient clarity, *short-wave radio broadcasts* from a country where the language is spoken will provide the highly desirable redundancy element of authentic speech and furnish an excellent aural test that can be integrated with the oral interview at a more advanced level. After listening to a broadcast (e.g., for students of English, the BBC World Service Broadcasts or Voice of America programs) or viewing films or videotapes students answer straight content questions or "negative" content questions (in oral or written form) – for example, which adjective or sentence in a series does *not* describe the program or film discussed or the person interviewed. Both kinds of questions can range from the simple ("Who did it?") at beginner's level to the complex ("Which description does not in your opinion characterize the director's intention in making the film?") at the advanced level. Thus, in spite of the formidable objections raised in discussions on individual oral interviews, they can be valuable diagnostic tools and at the same time acceptable integrative, proficiency-oriented evaluations.

Group oral testing

The group oral test offers scheduling as well as pedagogical advantages. From the pedagogical standpoint it is *interactive testing at its best*. Interaction among students increases at an exponential rate through the combination of exchanges offered by the performance of dramatic scenes (either live before the class or in front of a videocamera), debates, discussions, role playing, or other group activities. Where language courses are scheduled to meet three times per week rather than five times, the sacrifice of one-third of that time for individual oral testing during class hours is not practicable. In these situations, oral testing on a one-to-one basis must be relegated to "after hours," where it often presents scheduling problems, or it must be replaced by group oral testing. Two testing

129

sessions per term or semester, which combine group oral testing with other activities, can be scheduled quite easily during class time. A big class can be divided in half for these activities, one group being tested in the instructor's office, while the others write a composition in the classroom or record a prepared skit on videotape at a third location.[6]

For the test, each of several groups of four students prepares an assigned activity – role playing, debating, discussion – that will take a previously allotted part of the class hour to "perform" (e.g., each of three groups of four or five students will receive an ample twenty minutes). Students take on the identity of characters from course materials, or that of an author or a film director, and discuss any one of a number of different subjects from their standpoint. The undertaking challenges not only the students but also the instructor. The latter must try to draw out the shy, tongue-tied, reticent student and cut off, if necessary, the monopolizer, while at the same time noting as much pertinent information as possible on each of the assessment sheets (one per student). From these notes, the instructor completes the evaluation forms after the testing, leaving students the entire time of the test to improve their rating. Where class instructors can work together, two assessors allow for more real communication and less hassle. Debates have yielded excellent results in advanced classes, whereas role playing has proved to be more useful than debates or discussions in elementary- and intermediate-level courses. At the elementary level, students can gradually be eased into performing brief dramatic scenes for each other, starting in the first week. Although these activities may remain ungraded during the first few months, later, when "performers" have acquired enough language knowledge and the necessary confidence, these interactive presentations will be assigned a group grade, shared by each member of the group.

Correction and grading

The scripts for such dramatic performances (a prescribed number of lines per student) may be corrected by the instructor – first in writing and then orally, the pronunciation and intonation being perfected with the help of an audiotape. We have all had the experience of laboring to correct a student's pronunciation, especially at the lower levels, only to hear, with disbelief and disappointment, the student slip back into the old mistake at the crucial moment. This holds true even more when students are under the stress of a graded performance. An all-to-common phenomenon in our classes, it is greatly alleviated during group preparation sessions, when each student's flaws are pinpointed, the entire correction proceed-

6 The writer is grateful to M. Mahler for some ideas for activities included in this section.

ings being recorded on audiotape. Once the students have their own copy of the audiotape, they can practice at their own pace until the correction has "taken." This individualized coaching has proved successful where other methods have failed. Seemingly intractable habits in pronunciation and intonation, even those stemming from first-language interference, have proved to be susceptible to improvement with this approach.

Grades that reflect student progress should be as descriptive as possible (see the Appendix at the end of this chapter). Our evaluations give overall comprehensibility and content a weight of 20% each and preparation of the assignment 10%. The component parts of comprehensibility are separately identified – pronunciation, intonation, grammar, vocabulary and fluency – and weighted at an additional 10%. (In other programs, of course, different ratios will be applied in accordance with the specific objectives of courses.)[7]

The incentives for students to excel are incomparably greater in interactive than in noninteractive testing. Students do not consider it fashionably "cool" to "flunk" these tests, and they work very hard to avoid looking foolish in front of their peers. Initially these tests are not truly global, as an overwhelming emphasis is on the oral component. Later on, as students' linguistic skills progress and correction of scripts becomes minimal, *this type of test is decidedly holistic* in nature by reflecting the students' ability to communicate their ideas effectively both in speech and in writing.

An interactive class activity useful at almost any level is *the test students give each other*. This approximates testing conditions and procedures, but no grades are assigned. Students are asked, as a homework assignment, to pick out difficult vocabulary items and perplexing grammatical forms in order to "test" their classmates in a subsequent class. Thus, during seven or eight minutes, with the teacher as arbiter of disputes, students "test" each other in groups. Because of the irresistible desire to snare their classmates, this "testing" activity encourages students to master the most elusive lexical items and the knottiest points of grammar. The same format can be used for discussing the content of assigned reading. In this form, group oral testing gives students a chance to show how much they have absorbed of the course material and allows them as well to express what they feel and think about issues raised in their reading. As they question others, they reveal how well they have mastered elements of grammar, phonology, and vocabulary.

---

7 Girard, Lussier-Chasles, and Huot (1984) discuss several excellent evaluation tables used in Québec for measuring second-language communicative performance in primary and secondary education as well as on the university level.

Marlies Mueller

Aural testing at the final examination

For today's grade-conscious preprofessional students, the most anxiety-producing part of their education can be the final examinations. After cramming all night, they arrive full of fear that their cherished career plans may be ruined by a dismal performance during the ensuing hours. Test anxiety, which can distort test results so that they are not representative of a student's true knowledge, is particularly damaging to performance in a foreign language. We must do all we can to reduce the level of tension during testing. Interaction, even in the exam situation, is the answer. One way we have found effective has been the acting out by the instructors at the beginning of the examination of a six- or seven-minute humorous skit of their own composition. The laughter and applause as students appreciate the content diffuse the initial stress of the examination atmosphere. For a while the shoe is on the other foot: *We* are performing and they are judging *us*. This is a *triumph of global testing over examination panic*. The content of the skit is based on the reading materials of the course. The students' examination booklets contain multiple-choice questions or statements about the substance of the dramatic performance. Students in elementary classes are allowed several minutes to study these questions and multiple-choice items before the performance to help focus their attention on salient points, but students in more advanced courses are allowed to open their booklets only after the presentation, thus having to demonstrate a higher level of aural comprehension and a longer retention span. A variation of this format that has been used successfully with upper-level students requires students to "interact" with instructors, not merely by marking answers about content and character portrayal in multiple-choice format, but by *reacting* in writing to what they hear and see, responding in full sentences to carefully formulated questions that assess overall language competence. In this way, *testing of listening is combined with testing of writing*.

Some may ask whether all teachers will feel comfortable acting in skits before their students. Possibly not. On the other hand, for many years we have asked our students to act out dialogues and skits in languages unfamiliar to them without considering their personal predilections. The positive results experienced with such activities will surely compensate for the small personal risk to our egos.

Other interactive aural and writing tests that can be given at the final examination, even to several hundred students at the same time, are ones that ask students to *do* something as a result of aural comprehension. This may take the form of asking students to find their way on a map as they follow oral directions; presenting a short crossword puzzle for which the definitions are dictated, with extra clues given at points of difficulty, thus forcing students to listen carefully; giving directions for drawing an object or setting a scene on a stage; asking students to fill out a form for a passport request on the basis of biographical information that is presented with much extraneous material; selecting from photos of three people which one is the villain from aural information supplied; and, in courses that combine the study of literature with language instruction, identifying in written form literary quotations given orally, ascribing author; title of book, play, or poem; and name of character. The instructor may play an audiotape of brief opinion-poll interviews and ask students to isolate the information pertinent to the announced objective of the poll by filling out a grid classifying the opinions as favorable, not favorable, no opinion, undecided. Students may write down the essential parts of a taped telephone message that they are presumably taking down for their roommate. Commercials from radio or television may be read or played and students required to write a paragraph assessing the offer in terms of their own taste or situation. Students may be asked to locate on a train schedule a particular connection indicated orally by the examiner, or to identify rooms on floor plans of houses or apartments and then draw in furniture according to the examiner's directions. Personal messages in the classified section of the newspaper may be read and students asked to write down whether they can meet the desires of the writer and the reasons why they would or would not feel like responding. The reader will be able to think up many more active tasks of this type that *involve students in reacting and interacting in the examination situation.*

Tests of writing

The present emphasis on both grammatical accuracy and ability to use all four language skills in actual communication means that writing has regained some importance in language learning. Much as we might grimace at the prospect of stacks of papers to correct and evaluate, instead of merely to mark and grade as with discrete-point tests, our students need practice in expressing and defending their opinions, thoughts, and desires in writing in ways that reflect their understanding of the foreign language and their ability to use it – from the application of simple grammar rules to recognition of subtle sociolinguistic norms. Our aim in drafting writing tests should be to provide a meaningful context whether for discrete-point or global testing.

A written examination for an elementary language course that incorporates all the foregoing features and obtains consistently positive feedback from students may be described as follows.[8] North American (or British) students studying French as a foreign language are asked to imagine that they are French students traveling in North America (or Britain). They are to reply to a letter from their instructor in Paris who has never been abroad. In the letter, the instructor asks many questions about North America (or Britain) – touristic, social, and political; questions about the student's educational experience, classmates, student life, and so on. (Alternatively, learners of English as a foreign or second language from country X imagine they are British or North American students traveling in X. They reply to a letter from their instructor at their home institution, in Britain, Canada, or the United States, who has never visited X.) This type of testing reflects a real-life situation for language use and gives students a chance to play the guide to a foreigner, to discuss their own country and university with pride, as well as to voice frustruations with their way of life and criticize negative aspects of their own culture if they feel so inclined. Answers are not a string of disconnected sentences but form part of a meaningful context, as students express what they feel and write about matters they know intimately.

Personalized tasks relevant to the students' lives can constitute contextualized writing tests that, nevertheless, are *good diagnostic tools*. For instance, in order to test the students' command of the modals, they may be asked to imagine themselves applying for a summer job and list what they are able to do and what they would like to do within the constraints of the position. If carefully constructed, this type of test can guide students to use specific grammatical and lexical items in an interesting and thought-provoking context. Asking students to react to statements and opinions has similar positive qualities. Students may be asked, for instance, to react to a paragraph that recounts the hypothetical misfortunes of another student/teacher/roommate/celebrity. In order to test the command of the subjunctive in French, for instance, the beginnings of reactive sentences are provided (*I am happy that . . . , I am sorry that . . . , I am surprised that . . . , I was afraid that . . . , The teacher should forbid them to . . . , We all wish that . . .*). Visual aids, such as advertisements, cartoons (humorous ones are particularly appreciated), notices for concerts, museum openings, or films, are simple and effective means of eliciting written (or oral) information from the student in an interactive format, at the same time that they allow the evaluation of reading comprehension, vocabulary acquisition and retention, as well as general writing skills.

The advent of *computer-assisted testing* will surely have a revolutionary impact on our testing practices. We are told that it will soon be

8 The writer is grateful to Margaret Beissinger for suggesting this format.

possible for testing to be at once individualized and interactive: individualized, because the level of difficulty can be continually adjusted as the students proceed, so that they will encounter the fresh wind of challenge at every turn but not be discouraged by question after question beyond their reach; and interactive because it presupposes a tester wholly responsive to the candidate's ability, such as can normally be provided only by oral testing on a one-to-one basis. Once voice recognition has been perfected, the approximation will be even closer to this situation. Such individualized testing poses evaluation problems. These can be met by setting achievement levels for different groups of items and establishing the level at which the student ceases to cope with the material (see also Dow and Ryan, this volume, chap. 15).

For most of us, the synthesis of interactive, personalized testing via computer with, in all probability, video technology is still some way down the road. However, we can recruit among our colleagues some enterprising souls willing to enlist as test pilots for the many forms of interactive testing at present available to all. Communicative testing through weekly individual oral tests with authentic, meaningful context; group oral tests based on scene dramatization, debates, and discussions; lively person-to-person aural testing; and meaningful, personalized writing – all can be inserted into the most traditional formats. They may take us a long way toward modifying students' potentially negative attitudes toward testing and make it an interesting and enjoyable experience.

Let's act on it

1. What difficulties would you have in implementing weekly oral tests for your course? What would you propose as the best compromise in your situation?
2. What would be your criteria of evaluation for group oral activities? What problems, other than those discussed, should be considered? Design some activities of your own and suggest ways of evaluating them.
3. Take a discrete-point test and transform it into an interactive test. Try it out on your students. What was their reaction? What were the advantages and disadvantages?
4. What interactive techniques for testing grammar or vocabulary, orally or in writing, are you currently using? How successful have they proved to be? What improvements to this testing would you now suggest?
5. At which level of language learning do you feel it is most desirable to offer interactive testing: elementary, intermediate, or advanced?

Why? In what ways would such testing differ at the different levels?
6. Propose some scenarios for testing in one activity:
   a. listening and speaking;
   b. speaking and writing;
   c. listening, speaking, reading, and writing.

Annotated reading list

Canale, Michael, and Swain, Merrill. 1980. "Theoretical Bases of Communicative Approaches to Second Language Teaching and Testing." *AL* 1, 1: 1–48. In order to determine the feasibility and practicability of testing communicative competence of students enrolled in French as a second language programs in elementary and secondary schools in Ontario, Canale and Swain establish a set of principles for a communicative approach and then briefly suggest some implications of their theoretical framework for second-language teaching and testing.

Clark, John L. 1983. "Language Testing: Past and Current Status – Directions for the Future." *MLJ* 67: 431–43. A concise historical overview of foreign-language testing, with suggestions for future development of tests for performance-based language instruction.

Girard, Claude; Huot, Diane; and Lussier-Chasles, Denise. 1984. "L'Evaluation de la compétence de communication en classe de langue seconde." *ELA* 56: 77–87. The authors describe innovative testing instruments and evaluation tables measuring communicative performance. These proposals are suitable for primary and secondary schools as well as for the university level.

Omaggio, Alice C. 1983. "Methodology in Transition: The New Focus on Proficiency." *MLJ* 67: 330–41. Definition of the proficiency-oriented method or approach proposed by ACTFL and ETS.

Omaggio, Alice C. 1986. *Teaching Language in Context: Proficiency-Oriented Instruction.* Boston, Mass.: Heinle and Heinle. Chap. 8, "Classroom Testing," offers many excellent suggestions with examples of communicative testing, particularly for reading comprehension and writing.

Rivers, Wilga M. 1981. *Teaching Foreign-Language Skills.* 2d ed. Chicago: University of Chicago Press. Chap. 12, "Testing: Principles and Techniques," discusses the principles of construction for aptitude, proficiency, achievement, and diagnostic tests and describes traditional as well as modern techniques (from discrete-point to integrative testing) as they relate to various course objectives. Rivers (1988), chap. 10, describes proficiency-oriented tests.

Rivers, Wilga M. 1983. *Speaking in Many Tongues: Essays in Foreign-Language Teaching.* 3d ed. New York: Cambridge University Press. Chap. 10, "Testing and Student Learning," advocates student-centered testing: establishing testing criteria consistent with the students' aims and purposes in learning a foreign language.

Russo, Gloria M. 1983. *Expanding Communication: Teaching Modern Lan-*

guages at the College Level. New York: Harcourt Brace Jovanovich. Offers techniques and suggestions for involving students in communication activities that exercise all four language skills while stimulating student creativity.

Appendix: Oral Evaluation Form*

Student's name:

Harvard University
Department of Romance Languages
Evaluation Scale: Oral Examination

I. OVERALL COMPREHENSIBILITY
   1. Barely comprehensible
   2. Comprehensible but requires concentrated effort
   3. Comprehensible with moderate effort
   4. Easily comprehensible
   5. Approximates target-language norm

   A. Pronunciation
      1. Pronunciation patterns almost exclusively from native language
      2. Mixed target-language and native-language pronunciation patterns; native-language patterns predominate
      3. Native-language pronunciation patterns occasionally apparent
      4. Native-language pronunciation patterns rare
      5. Approximates target-language norm

   B. Intonation
      1. Intonation patterns almost exclusively from native language
      2. Mixed target-language and native intonation patterns; native-language patterns predominate
      3. Native-language intonation patterns occasionally apparent
      4. Native-langue intonation patterns rare
      5. Approximates target-language norm

   C. Grammar
      1. No control of grammatical elements
      2. Minimal control; obvious interference from native-language usage
      3. Moderate control; some interference from native-language usage
      4. Good control; interference from native-language usage rare
      5. Approximates target-language norm

   D. Vocabulary
      1. No vocabulary control
      2. Minimal control; obvious interference from native-language usage

---

*Some sections of this form adapted from Table 10–1: Evaluation Scale: Conversation, in Russo (1983), p. 92. For a discussion of percentages that may be allotted in various combinations, see p. 131, this chapter.

3. Moderate control; some interference from native-language usage
4. Good control; wide range of vocabulary
5. Approximates target-language norm

E. Fluency
1. Halting speech pattern
2. Moderately halting speech requiring concentrated effort on the part of the listener
3. Adequate fluency
4. Good fluency
5. Approximates target-language norm

II. CONTENT
1. Shows minimal understanding of texts, questions, etc.
2. Moderate understanding
3. Good understanding
4. Very good understanding
5. Excellent grasp of concepts involved

A. Preparation
1. Questions or activities have not been prepared
2. Moderately good preparation
3. Good preparation
4. Very good preparation
5. Excellent preparation

B. Mistakes

_____

_____

_____

Section III   The wider world

11 Culturally diverse speech styles

Gail L. N. Robinson

Through television, international travel, and telecommunications in to-day's world, we frequently find ourselves in front of, face to face with, or voice-to-voice with people from different language backgrounds, people with different values, and people with different speech styles.

The psychology of person perception teaches us that the success of encounters largely depends on how all parties in the interaction behave and how the behavior is perceived by the viewer, listener, or speech partner. To the degree that we perceive the speech style of another people as similar to our own, we tend to evaluate those people positively and behave toward them favorably. In turn, such positive attitudes and behaviors trigger positive reactions and behaviors on the part of our speech partners. In interactions between people of different cultures, speech-style differences may be more readily perceived than similarities, with negative reactions as a result (Robinson 1985: 49–72). Effective communication between people of different cultures requires more than an "awareness" of how or why people from different cultural backgrounds interact in particular ways. Successful and positive interactions, person to person, take place when participants in the interaction have developed not only respect for diverse interaction styles but, perhaps more importantly, when they have developed multiple interaction skills, including multiple speech styles, themselves; that is, when people can be good talkers *and* good listeners, when people can speak directly *and* indirectly, and when speakers can happily engage in equal, or reciprocal, conversations and unequal, or nonreciprocal, conversations. To the degree that each person has a larger repertoire of interaction skills, speech partners will perceive each other more similarly, evaluate each other more positively, and behave more favorably. After developing diverse speech styles, a direct speaker will no longer judge an indirect speaker as "beating around the bush," nor an indirect speaker judge the one who comes immediately to the point as being "blunt and overbearing."

Diversity in interaction not only involves communication through verbal speech factors, but also through such paralinguistic elements of speech as pitch, stress, intonation, speed of speech, and frequency with which certain meanings are conveyed. For example, the frequency of status markers within a conversation (be it through level of speech, lexicon, or tense markers) conveys the importance of status within particular cultural settings (cf. Robinson 1981: 39). Equally important is body language, such as posture, facial expressions, and gestures, which may accompany speech or convey messages directly without speech at all (Hall 1959; Laver and Hutcheson 1972; Morris et al. 1979). Additionally, different cultural assumptions about the purposes of particular interactions and expected outcomes of encounters affect interaction.

Multicultural understanding takes place as individuals *become* multicultural to some degree – that is, when individuals have multiple ways of interpreting things and possess multiple interaction styles that correspond to different cultural styles. (See Robinson 1985 for a theoretical discussion of how culture is acquired and the processes involved in multiculturalism.) This chapter identifies some factors to consider in developing diverse speech styles and provides examples of strategies that are useful in teaching and learning different interaction skills; it leaves aside for the present the important areas of paralinguistic elements of speech, body language, and cultural assumptions.

Factors to consider in developing diverse speech styles

In cross-cultural interactions, the way people structure conversations, forms of agreement and disagreement, the degree of speech reciprocity, and turn-taking conventions are particularly important (see also Kramsch, this volume, chap. 2).

Speech reciprocity

Speech reciprocity refers to a variety of speech dimensions that cause a conversation to be symmetrical or asymmetrical. For example: To what extent do different speech partners initiate the conversation? Who initiates subsequent questions or topic changes? Does each of the speakers talk or pause the same amount of time? What is the pattern of interaction? For instance, does speech interaction form a back-and-forth pattern of short chunks or does it appear more "linear," with each speaker continuing for longer chunks? Is the pattern a combination of both, because of speaker differences? Does the speaker respond to what a former speaker has said, or does the speaker switch topics? Do the speakers talk about the same kinds of things, that is, are they equally public or private in what they disclose or choose to talk about? Although the degree of reciprocity between speech partners of the same culture may vary among individuals, differences in reciprocity tend to be much more pronounced between people of different cultures.

American students in a course on cross-cultural communication, at the University of California, Berkeley (1983), as well as American, Asian, and European professional participants in a workshop on developing diverse speech styles organized in 1984 by the Society of Intercultural Training and Research at George Mason University, were asked to observe various conversations. Observers were asked to identify similarities and differences in reciprocity and to consider what might account for the differences. Some participants attributed differences in speech style to personality – for example, introverts versus extroverts, listeners versus talkers, considerate people versus selfish people. Others attributed such behaviors to philosophy. They felt that "reciprocal" speech was associated with a philosophy of equality and democracy, and nonreciprocal speech indicated "hierarchy." Many felt that the differences in such speech behaviors originated in the socialization practices of particular cultures.

It was interesting that some American and European participants were offended by the terms *reciprocal* and *nonreciprocal* speech. They argued that since *reciprocal* was positive and *nonreciprocal* was negative, the terms themselves were value-laden and unfair. However, some Asian participants did not perceive nonreciprocal speech in negative terms at all. Rather, they felt that nonreciprocal behaviors reflected polite speech habits that were appropriate to different situations, such as conversations among business associates as opposed to friends, conversations among people of different status, and conversations between people of different gender. These comments themselves indicate how "cultural" these kinds of speech behaviors may be.

Such focused observations and discussions are important steps in developing diverse interaction skills. They provide awareness exercises that may productively be followed by skill practice.

Conversation structure

Another factor to consider in developing diverse interaction skills refers to the way people structure their arguments. For example, do people present their main point first, followed by elaboration and supporting information, or do they present a general picture first, saving the main point until sufficient background information has been given? We often refer to this aspect of conversation structure as *directness* and *indirectness*, and this tends to be associated with particular cultural values. For example, have you ever become impatient with someone you thought too wordy, who gave unnecessary background details instead of getting right to the point? Have you ever been offended by someone who was too direct and blunt? Developing skills of directness and indirectness, as appropriate to different cultural situations, decreases negative judgments about interactions with others.

143

A related aspect of conversation structure is the way in which people express agreement and disagreement. Speakers of some languages are hesitant to say no. For them, cultural etiquette favors avoidance of direct negation. For example, a Japanese speaker may accept an invitation rather than offend the host. According to certain cultural conventions, verbal agreement, even if it is not meant, is preferable to directly offending the speaker with a refusal. From a North American perspective, such behavior constitutes breaking a commitment and may be negatively evaluated. In contrast, the directness of North American questions and refusals may be evaluated as a slap in the face by Asians.

In a similar vein, Asian speakers often agree or disagree with speakers' assumptions rather than with the direct information in a statement or question. North Americans might facetiously refer to this as the "Yes, we-have-no-bananas" syndrome. For example, suppose an ESL teacher asked a Japanese or Korean student about his or her family, using a negative question in English, as in the following example.

Commonly misunderstood Asian responses to negative tag questions
Question: You don't have any sisters, do you?
Asian response: No.
Implied meaning: "Yes, I agree with your assumption. I don't have any sisters."

Question: You don't have any sisters, do you?
Asian response: Yes.
Implied meaning: "No, I disagree with your assumption. I have (two) sisters."

In these languages, the listener is agreeing or disagreeing with the speaker's assumption. By contrast, a speaker of English in Japan or Korea frequently conveys equally unintended messages. English speakers agree or disagree with the information in the statement, regardless of how it is stated or what is assumed by the speaker. Using the same example:

Question: You don't have any sisters, do you?
North American reply: Yes.
Implied meaning: [regarding the information about my sister] "Yes, I have (two) sisters."

Question: You don't have any sisters, do you?
North American reply: No.
Implied meaning: [regarding the information about my sister] "No, I don't have any sisters."

It is easily understood how such differences in conversation structure may cause miscommunication. One solution is to avoid short, one-word yes or no answers to tag questions and to use complete-sentence replies instead. Clearly, developing diverse ways of structuring conversations, appropriate to different cultural settings, will also improve interaction.

Making input "comprehensible"

Miscommunication may also occur because the listener simply has not heard the speaker correctly. What the speaker intends to communicate is not always what is understood by the listener. What listeners "hear" in turn affects how they feel and behave toward the speaker, including how they expect him or her to respond verbally, paralinguistically, and through body language. Although misunderstood messages may occur in any interaction, they are particularly likely to occur between people from different language and cultural backgrounds who have different speech conventions. The important question is, How may such misunderstood messages be avoided?

Krashen (1981) suggests that making input comprehensible is the solution to the problem of acquiring a new language. Although no one would deny that sending and receiving comprehensible messages is essential to "communicating" and "acquiring language," the critical question for our purposes is, What makes input comprehensible from the perspectives of the speaker *and* the listener?

SPEAKER PERSPECTIVE

Speakers may make their own speech more comprehensible in a variety of ways. For example, speakers may

1. simplify speech by avoiding complex sentences, using instead short sentences, simple syntax, and frequently used vocabulary;
2. make the message redundant, that is, convey the same message more than once through paraphrasing;
3. speak slowly to allow the listener (who may be mentally translating) to process what he or she has heard;
4. pause often to allow the listener time to ask for clarification or respond to the information;
5. use gestures to reinforce messages.

LISTENER PERSPECTIVE

Listeners may also elicit more comprehensible input through a variety of means. For example, listeners may

1. give the speaker signals, through gesture or speech, that they understand or are having difficulty;
2. interrupt the speaker and ask for clarification;
3. ask the speaker to slow down and pause more frequently;
4. check their own comprehension through paraphrasing what they think they heard.

145

Gail L. N. Robinson

Although the foregoing ways of making input comprehensible are in-tuitive or automatic to some, different cultural conventions in speech may inhibit their automatic use by others. Differences in turn-taking conventions may be particularly inhibiting. These include such factors as the length of pause needed to indicate completion of a thought or turn, and permissibility of conversation overlapping and interrupting (e.g., speaking before the former speaker has completely finished or sufficiently paused). A Japanese listener in an English-speaking situation, for instance, may be more hesitant to interrupt the speaker or ask for clarification than a North American in a Japanese-speaking situation. Moreover, a North American speaker may be less likely to pause between sentences or questions when speaking to a foreign speaker than a Jap-anese speaker in a similar situation, because of their respective familiar speech styles.

To overcome cultural constraints that inhibit comprehensible input, listeners and speakers of all languages and cultural backgrounds may benefit by using certain strategies. Equally beneficial is familiarity with diverse ways of structuring conversations and comfortably engaging in interactions that are at times reciprocal and at times nonreciprocal, as appropriate within particular cultural settings and situations.

Useful strategies

The activities that follow are examples of useful strategies for developing diverse interaction skills. They are in no way exhaustive. Many of the strategies were developed by students in cross-cultural communication classes at the University of California. They are intended for use within culturally homogeneous groups (such as foreign-language classes) or within culturally pluralistic groups (as in English classes in English-speaking countries or intercultural training sessions). Optimally, all par-ticipants play each role (A, B, or C) at some time to practice a variety of speech styles. The somewhat facetious titles or comments that follow are reminders of the culture-bound values that are often attached to these styles; they are, in themselves, mnemonic strategies.

The first strategy, *Monitor* (1), is aimed at identifying general differ-ences in speech styles. *The interrupting game* (2), *Did I hear you cor-rectly?* (3), and *Give me a chance* (4) are aimed at making input comprehensible for both speakers and listeners. *Kill the conversation* (5), *Keep the conversation going* (6), *Equal participation* (7), and *The good listener* (8) provide practice in reciprocal and nonreciprocal speech styles. Finally, *Don't beat around the bush* (9), *Don't be so blunt* (10), and *"Yes, we have no bananas"* (11) develop skills in diverse conversation structures.

Identifying general differences in speech styles

(1) MONITOR

Robert Burns once wrote, "O wad some Pow'r the giftie gie us / To see oursels as others see us!" *This activity is aimed at developing an awareness of different factors in speech styles* and how we judge the speech acts of others. It is a good activity for introducing students to diversity in speech styles.

Directions
1. Divide the class into thirds and label them A, B, and C.
2. Instruct the A's and B's to pair off and begin a conversation. (They may introduce themselves or speak on a designated topic.)
3. Privately instruct the C group to observe the conversation between the A's and B's. One observer joins each pair and observes factors in each partner's speech style. (These observations may be "open" to see what participants notice on their own, or they may be "cued" by providing an observation sheet, based on factors such as those described at the beginning of this chapter.)
4. After five minutes, the entire group comes together. Each partner A introduces partner B to the class and paraphrases everything he or she has heard. Then partner B does the same with regard to A. (Through this experience, partners A and B begin to realize some dimensions of their own speech, especially with respect to reciprocal/nonreciprocal factors.) Then the C's make observations about the conversations.
5. Discussion follows in which the factors in speech styles that have emerged are summarized and extended.

Activities for making speech comprehensible

(2) THE INTERRUPTING GAME

Silence is not always golden! *This activity accustoms listeners to ask for clarification.* Through lively team competition, participants practice interrupting the speaker in a purposeful way. At the same time, participants may practice listening-comprehension skills focusing on particular linguistic goals.

Directions
1. Divide the class into two teams.

147

2. Read to the class a passage containing a certain number of nonsense words. Each time a nonsense word is heard, someone must interrupt you and ask the appropriate Wh-question: Who? Where? What? Why? When?
3. Rules: Anyone can interrupt at any time. The first person to interrupt with the correct question scores a point for his or her team. The team with the most points at the end of the passage wins.

Example of a passage with nonsense words:
Jack and *bilper* [Who?] went up the *burle* [What?] to fetch a pail of *plepods* [What?].
Jack fell *derge* [Where?] and broke his *hern* [What?], and Jill came tumbling *bimper* [When? Where?].

Note: The linguistic goal of the exercise may vary. For example, the goal could be auditory discrimination of the minimal pair "l/r." A passage with several words containing l's and r's would be chosen. Participants would be instructed to shout "Excuse me!" each time they heard an "l." A correct interruption would increase their team's score. However, an incorrect interruption (when no "l" was present in the word) would decrease their team's score. The game could be replayed, this time with interruptions based on "r."

(3) DID I HEAR YOU CORRECTLY?

We have all heard the cliché "None so blind as those that will not see." We may extrapolate to "None so deaf as those that will not hear!" This is a simple exercise in *paraphrasing* to check one's own comprehension.

Directions
1. Participants write down a paragraph extending an invitation related to a specific situation. For example, they invite someone to visit them to work on a particular project in their country.
2. Partner A invites partner B.
3. Partner B checks his or her own comprehension by rephrasing what partner A has said (e.g., "You mean you would like me to ... ?").
4. Partner A confirms the invitation or restates it if it has been misunderstood.

(4) GIVE ME A CHANCE

Time out for listening! This is an exercise in *pausing* and *responsiveness to what others have said.*

Directions
1. Pose a question regarding an appropriate topic. (With limited English

speakers, a two-page reading related to a controversial issue may be provided. In this way, students will have a common background for discussion. Questions such as "What is culture?" provide a starting point for discussion at the beginning of a course.

2. Divide the class into groups of three or four.
3. Rules: No one may speak a second time until everyone in the group has spoken once. There must be a pause of seven seconds between speakers. All speakers must refer in some way to what a previous speaker has said.
4. Assign the role of facilitator to one student in each group. The facilitator ensures that the rules are not broken. (Rotate the facilitator every five minutes.)
5. After fifteen minutes, the class comes together. Someone from each group summarizes the group's opinions.

Activities for developing reciprocal and nonreciprocal styles

(5) KILL THE CONVERSATION

Some have called this activity "the killing conversation." In this game, participants deliberately kill the conversation by asking closed questions (e.g., "Do you have any animals") or by responding with short answers (e.g., yes/no) and long silences. When the roles of partners A and B are switched, those accustomed to killing a conversation with silence see their own behavior in an exaggerated form. Conversely, those accustomed to initiating (or hogging) the conversation practice an exaggerated form of keeping quiet. In a more serious vein, all participants practice *nonreciprocal speech*.

Directions

1. Instruct students to write down five short, unrelated questions to ask different people in the room. "Closed" questions that request responses to yes/no or Wh-questions are particularly appropriate. Written questions increase the activity's success for nonnative speakers by ensuring they have something to say. However, written questions are not necessary for native speakers of the language.
2. Divide the class into two groups, A and B.
3. Instruct the A's and B's to form pairs.
4. Partner A asks each of the unrelated questions of partner B.
5. Partner B responds with as short an answer as possible. (Partner B may not give any additional information or ask a question in return.)
6. The group discusses how they felt while acting as partner A and partner B.

149

(6) KEEP THE CONVERSATION GOING

This is typically called "conversation American style." Some students often refer to it as "the three A's of conversation: answer, add, and ask." The aim of this activity is to practice *reciprocal speech*.

Directions
1. Instruct students to write down one question to ask someone in the room. Alternatively, the group or instructor may nominate a topic or topics for discussion. Open-ended questions and controversial issues facilitate this activity: for example, "What is your opinion about people living together before marriage?"
2. Divide the class into groups A and B.
3. Instruct the A's and B's to form pairs.
4. Partner A addresses a question to partner B.
5. Partner B must answer the question, add some more information, and ask a related question of partner A.
6. Partner A then answers, adds, and asks, and so on.
7. The group discusses what they learned about each other and contrasts the way they felt in this activity to how they felt in the previous activity.

(7) EQUAL PARTICIPATION

This activity also develops skills in reciprocal speech styles. It inhibits "conversation hogs" as well as "conversation underdogs." The competition between different teams discourages silence in order to win points for one's team. However, the rule of equal participation among members of one's own team discourages conversation dominance. As such, it is a particularly useful exercise for a culturally pluralistic group.

Directions
1. Assign a reading or provide a short handout on a current controversial topic, for example, "Do you think abortion should be legal? Why?"
2. Divide the class into two teams. The instructor/student facilitator begins by asking one team the initial question only. Anyone from the team may answer, and then pose a related question to the opposing team. From then on, the teams respond alternately unless they lose their turn through silence.
3. Rules: A team member who successfully answers a question and then asks a new question scores a point for the team. However, any silence of five seconds or more results in a point for the opposing team. No member of a given team may speak a second time until each person

on that team has spoken once. The first team to reach x points wins. (X is the number of students on a given team + 5.)

(8) THE GOOD LISTENER

This activity could also be called "therapist" or "ethnographer," because the skills developed are similar to those needed in these occupations. These skills require the listener to focus attention on the speaker's input rather than on the listener's input; to ask a few, open-ended questions; to continually probe the speaker's responses for elaboration; and to seek to identify the speaker's feelings as well as thoughts. What results is an interview rather than conversation. The interviewer generally initiates most of the questions, although they always derive from what the speaker has just said. The activity illustrates the *positive uses of nonreciprocal speech*. (The usefulness of this technique in obtaining cultural information and as a process for developing cross-cultural understanding is elaborated in Robinson 1985: chap. 6.)

Directions
1. Partner A, the interviewer, begins with an open-ended general question: "How does it feel to ... ?"
2. Partner B responds.
3. Partner A asks for further elaboration: for example, "What do you mean by ... ?"
4. The interview continues for fifteen minutes or more, depending on the level of the class.
5. The interviewers write down a summary, including what they learned about the speaker's culture; what they learned about the speaker personally; what they had in common with the speaker; what they learned about themselves and about their own communication style.
6. If the persons interviewed are in the class, they too may write a summary of how they felt during the interview.

Activities for diversifying conversation structures

(9) DON'T BEAT AROUND THE BUSH

This activity is aimed at structuring information directly, or *getting right to the point*. Some students have called it "What's your bottom line?".

Directions
1. The class is divided into A's and B's.
2. The instructor/facilitator distributes a short paragraph to the A's, which contains a request in the fourth sentence: for example, "I've

151

been working a lot lately. There's too much homework and not enough time to relax. What do you like to do in your free time? Perhaps you'd like to go to the movies sometime – maybe this Saturday night?"
3. Partner A reads the paragraph aloud, making the request of partner B.
4. Partner B rephrases it directly, structuring the paragraph so that the main point comes first. For example, "Do you mean: Would I like to go to the movies Saturday?"

(10) DON'T BE SO BLUNT

This activity is simply the reverse of the preceding one. Participants practice indirect ways of structuring conversation. In particular, students practice polite indirect refusals by avoiding yes/no responses.

Directions
1. Students write down a direct request, beginning with "Will you ... ?" followed by one sentence of explanation. For example: "Will you lend me your car? I have an important errand to run today."
2. The class is divided into partners A and B.
3. Partner A makes a direct request, such as the one in step (1). Partner B responds indirectly, explaining the circumstances and replying in the third sentence without using the words *yes* or *no*. For example: "I have been very busy lately too. Sometimes I don't use my car in the afternoon. However, I will be using it today."

(11) "YES, WE HAVE NO BANANAS"

This exercise provides practice for those who have difficulty with *tag questions and negative questions* in English. (As teachers, we don't have difficulty teaching this, do we? Yes, of course we don't!)

Directions
1. The class stands up and forms a circle.
2. Throw a ball to a student and ask, "You don't have a ball, do you?" The student with the ball must respond, "Yes, I do."
3. The student with the ball throws it to another classmate across the circle, asking the same question, until all have practiced at least once.
4. The instructor then asks a question about something a student has. For example, "José, you don't have a watch, do you?" The student (who has a watch) answers, "Yes, I do." That classmate then asks another classmate a question based on the truth, following the same structure, until all students have practiced once.
5. The classmates now try to fool each other. They can ask questions that are true or that they know to be false. Students must give an

honest reply. For example, "You don't have two heads, do you?"
"No, I don't!" or "You don't have ten fingers, do you?" "Yes, I do."
6. The game may be continued with "be" verbs. For example: "You aren't shy, are you?"

Conclusion

Although we have claimed that the study of other languages and cultures broadens the learner's understanding of the foreign people involved, this aim has fallen far short of fulfillment (Robinson 1978). Perhaps we have thought that our perspective and the perspectives of the learners could be broadened without personal change. Some may fear that learning diverse speech styles will undermine their own personality and identity. The latter is not necessarily so. Change of this nature may be viewed as an additive rather than a subtractive process.

The foregoing activities will certainly not change anyone's speech style overnight, but they do provide examples of strategies that are useful in teaching and learning diverse styles. In this way, individuals increase their own repertoire of behaviors, so that teachers and students alike can communicate more effectively in the wider world of different languages and cultures.

Let's act on it

1. Introduce yourself to three people and speak for five minutes. After the meeting, briefly write down your first impressions about these people. What things were your impressions based upon? Notice if your comments are shaped by differences or similarities with yourself or things you aspire to. Notice also how quickly first impressions are formed.
2. Observe interactions between people of different cultural backgrounds. Write down and explain one example of how different ways of structuring conversations led to miscommunication.
3. Observe the degree of speech reciprocity among three sets of speakers. Is one speaker dominant in initiating questions or directing the conversation? Do the speakers speak the same amount of time? Is the form of interaction in short chunks or lengthier paragraphs? Do the speakers respond to each other's comments or do they switch topics? What other indicators of reciprocity can you identify? What were your reactions to each of the conversations and the speakers involved?
4. In the three conversations observed in (3), what factors do you

think contributed to the degree of speech reciprocity in each situation? Consider the topic and setting of the conversation, the social roles, age, gender, and cultural background of the speakers. What other contributing factors did you observe?
5. Monitor your own speech – for one day or up to one week. Engage in at least two conversations with speakers of different languages. Notice, write down, and discuss what strategies you automatically use to make your speech more comprehensible to others, and to check your comprehension of others. Describe your feelings and opinions about the speech partners involved when the speech was comprehensible and incomprehensible, respectively.

Annotated reading list

Goffman, E. 1967. *Interaction Ritual: Essays on Face-To-Face Behavior*. Garden City, N.Y.: Doubleday. Focuses on patterns of behavior, social roles, and rituals involved in interactions.

Morris, D.; Collett, P.; Marsh, P.; O'Shaughnessy, M. 1979. *Gestures*. New York: Stein and Day. Provides a practical survey of European-based gestures and their meanings.

Pifer, G., and Mutoh, N. W. 1977. *Points of View*. Rowley, Mass.: Newbury House. Provides motivating readings on thought-provoking topics with discussion questions and exercises for English as a second language and foreign-language programs. It is suitable for university and adult learners.

Robinson, G. L. N. 1985. *Crosscultural Understanding: Processes and Approaches for FL, ESL, and Bilingual Educators*. Oxford: Pergamon Press. Provides an in-depth theoretical discussion for educators and university students on cross-cultural understanding from the perspectives of anthropology and psychology, applied to FL, ESL, and bilingual programs. The discussion includes how culture is acquired; how we perceive and interact with people of different cultures; how positive attitudes and behaviors may be encouraged and negative behaviors decreased.

12 The use of technology: varying the medium in language teaching

Karen Price

A variety of technologies assume a natural place in language teaching, since language use is itself a multisensory experience. Some technologies permit us to see and hear language in a cultural context as well as observe the impact on language meaning of things like real time, word stress, and gestures.

The greeting "How are you today?" can be presented in a variety of mediums:

Print: "How are you today?"

Audio: We hear the phonic chain, with stress and intonation for the particular meaning intended.

Video: We observe one individual greeting another and saying, "How are you today?" with gestures appropriate to the culture.

Methodological considerations

Many developments in language teaching have evolved from a growing awareness of the different mediums with which we can work. Individual teaching styles as well as methodological approaches distinguish themselves in part by the mediums used for presentation of language, production of language, and monitoring of student output. In the Silent Way, for example, the stimulus for language is visual when the teacher points to a color on a chart, and the instructor's feedback to the student is in a paralinguistic medium, by means of hand signals and gestures (Gattegno 1972).

Available technology – tape recorders, slide projectors, overhead projectors, videotape recorders (VTRs), as well as drawings, pictures, and the ever-trustworthy chalkboard – makes it possible for the language teacher to present language in more forms than just speech and print. We can substitute one medium for another, as when we give feedback in the form of hand signals rather than through verbal correction, or we can alter or eliminate a medium (when we turn the sound down on a videotape to draw students' attention to visual aspects, such as the body language of the participants), or we can use three mediums instead of just one (as in the case of captioned television, which uses audio, print, and nonprint visuals).

Language takes many forms: spoken, written, kinesic (body language). We need the many technologies at our disposal to present language effectively in the context in which it occurs. We can present language and monitor our language learning in more than one medium. Changing the usual medium of presentation and feedback is an important key to interesting and creative teaching.

Different approaches tend to urge the use of one medium over another or to the exclusion of others. The dilemma facing language teachers is the fear that perhaps there is one "best way" that is presently unknown to them. Particular methods emphasize specific techniques that draw on a given sensory mode – for example, aural in Suggestopaedia (Lozanov 1978) or visual in the Silent Way – and then report an overwhelming success with students that staggers our imagination as we think of our own, more modest achievements.

Choice of medium

The choice of a particular medium depends on several things, including:

availability of materials: Audiotapes and radio broadcasts; television programs; commercially produced video; or newspapers and magazines, cartoon books, and the like.

availability of necessary equipment: Tape recorders, projectors, videotape recorders, videodisc machines, radios, or satellite dishes.

type of language lesson planned: Does the instructor intend to focus on spoken language or written language? Can use of particular mediums assist the students in transferring their knowledge from, for example, aural to visual recognition of language forms or vice versa? Through which medium will materials best enhance the student's understanding of cultural referents, or of the features of formal and informal language?

The effective use of any medium in language teaching depends on the role the message in that medium plays in the language-learning situation (e.g., as model or stimulus), the content of the materials, and the ways these two interact within each student's language-learning experience. Teachers can use technologies and materials effectively in innumerable ways, depending on the aims of the program and the learning preferences of the students.

Materials in the classroom: as model and stimulus

The point of departure in a language class, from the point of view of materials and the medium(s) in which they occur, is the words and bits of language played on a tape, written on a chalkboard, or printed in newspapers and on product packages, labels, coupons, flyers, price tags, or hiding in fortune cookies. These act as models. Pictures, tapes, articles in newspapers and magazines, and video (including television broadcasts) all give the language learner a feeling for the diversity of use of another language (variety of accents or differences between formal and informal language) and provide information on the life and habits of the people (the cultural setting and referents). All of this provides a context within which to situate language.

Models alone cannot meet the learner's needs, however. Listening to Japanese radio every day for many years will not produce a speaker of Japanese. Only during interaction with the model – reflecting, verifying, clarifying, asking questions, consulting classmates about it – does the language begin to make sense.

Language can be presented as a stimulus – a springboard for interaction. Language can provoke. A classroom structured so that learners interact with each other as well as with the model will be even more effective if language interactions are structured in different mediums.

How can the teacher structure interactions between students and language in different mediums?

NEWSPAPERS

Language puzzles and word games arouse student interest. The newspaper's anagrams, even the acronyms, dare us to unscramble them; crossword puzzles challenge us; stories cut into strips beg to be reordered. Newspaper photographs separated from their respective captions tease students into matching photos and captions from the shuffled array. A newspaper can also be a resource for planning an evening out on the town, with students scanning movie listings, restaurant advertisements, and the calendar of events. They can also compare the content and viewpoint of foreign-language newspapers with those of native-language newspapers – a natural starting point for lively discussion.

Supplemental materials in a medium different from that in which the language was first presented can be useful. We can read the news, listen to the news before reading it, or listen to news we have read. We can listen to the news while working with a transcript or partial transcript. An excerpt may be taken from a television news program and students set to work as a group, drawing out the general idea of the news story and the viewpoints of the people they are watching. The groups will then discuss their conclusions.

COMBINING MEDIUMS

Context may be presented in one medium and the task structured in another. For example, an audiotape of various city sounds may be played while students identify the situation and time of day; later they can role-play a possible situation to the accompaniment of the tape. Similarly, a sequence of odd sounds may act as a stimulus for students to tell or write down an accompanying story.

INFORMATION GAPS

An interview or story may be selected from a TV broadcast, radio program, or even from a magazine or newspaper. After the class has been divided into groups, each group is supplied with certain portions of the text only (on tape or in print). As a group the students then piece together the sequence, soliciting information from each other before going over the entire material.

If you are videotaping a class activity, you can create an information gap in the following manner: Several rowdy students enter the room dressed bizarrely and solicit money, favors, or advice from several students before leaving. Then the surprised students discuss what they saw, hotly debating who said what to whom, how the intruders were dressed, and what they themselves were doing when the interruption began. Students arriving late who missed the staged episode are an asset. They can play the role of arbiter and ask questions. After discussion, the videotape on which the whole incident is recorded can be replayed, giving students an experience of the unreliability of eyewitness accounts. The unexpected and the controversial never fail to provoke absorbing interaction.

ELICITING STUDENT–STUDENT INTERACTION IN A VARIETY OF MEDIUMS

Working in pairs or small groups, students (1) examine and classify photographs from home or arrange a collage for a guessing competition; (2) listen to tape-recorded interviews with community leaders, or native speakers of different occupations, and prepare discussion notes for other students or oral presentations on the content, or they write essays for a class newspaper; (3) plan as a group the videotaping of some activity for which only a limited amount of videotape, audiotape, or film may be used. The negotiations involve language practice.

ANALYZING GROUP DYNAMICS ON VIDEO

A class discussion is videotaped. Students discuss who participated the most, or the least, or who would not yield the floor. In terms of discourse analysis, students examine the nature of the interactions among their classmates, asking such questions as: Did students corroborate, ignore, contest, or agree with the remarks of their classmates? Were they able to fill pauses and use fill-in expressions as native speakers do? What gestures did they use and were these appropriate for the language used? What was their interaction style? Was it culturally appropriate? (See Kramsch, chap. 2, and Robinson, chap. 11, this volume).

INTERACTING WITH THE COMMUNITY

Students in a second-language environment may be sent out with a cassette player to record such daily events as announcements over loudspeakers in supermarkets, department stores, train stations, bus stations, and airports. These provide interesting material for students to decipher at home or in class.

In situations where students can meet native speakers of the target language, excursions into the field with a videotape recorder or cassette recorder in hand prove stimulating and amusing. Authentic language is brought back to the classroom for clarification and sharing with peers. Students may be sent out to accomplish specific tasks, such as short interviews with speakers of the target language. They prepare questions and their own self-introductions in advance, working in pairs or small groups, before setting out in company. Members of the group can help the main interviews by assisting in positioning the microphone or camera, asking additional questions, taking notes, and later transcribing the tape. Even for elementary and low-intermediate students, this activity is motivating and satisfying. At this level, they prepare interview questions from material they have studied.

The foreign-language teacher helps by suggesting ways of finding native speakers through embassies, consulates, airline offices, church organizations, ethnic restaurants or bookshops, *au pair* agencies, or bilingual schools. Brainstorming by teacher and students may produce a surprising number of locations and events likely to attract native speakers of the foreign language, such as the local screening of a foreign film; students can conduct an opinion poll as people leave the theater. (See Strevens, this volume, chap. 13, for further suggestions.)

MULTIMEDIA TASKS

Students enjoy working on multimedia activities. A group creation of a mock television or print commercial leads students to consult advertisements on the radio, on TV, in newspapers, or on billboards. Much discussion takes place in the planning stages, and students practice the language of negotiation when it comes to the design of the situation, the writing of jingles and dialogues, the reading of first drafts, and finally the use of camera, microphones, or pen and paper when creating the commercial. This activity, as well as the creation of soap operas, newscasts, class newspapers, skits, plays, musicals, and so on, forces the learner to work in more than one medium and practice a variety of language skills: listening, speaking, reading, writing, scanning, browsing, negotiating. The emphasis should be on the process rather than the product.

MUSIC AND SONG

Music and song lead naturally to language-learning activities involving different mediums. Pronunciation and intonation are easily assimilated through songs in the target language. Working with popular music may involve reading about the singer, listening to interviews with the singer on radio or TV, watching rock videos, or singing with a record. Motivated to learn the words, the learner may struggle with the record alone, replaying phrases and writing down the text as accurately as possible, comparing what has been taken down with other students' texts. The teacher may make this process less arduous by supplying a cloze-type version with blanks for the students to fill in as they listen. (See also Maley, this volume, chap. 8.)

LISTENING, VIEWING, AND READING WITH A PURPOSE

The instructor's role in facilitating comprehension and language learning is to help the students start with a "shared script" – an understanding of the assumptions, crucial lexical items, and cultural referents in the material – and then to suggest that students look, listen, or read with a purpose. In simple terms, this may mean asking the students to listen for the next day's temperature in the weather report or to ascertain the total cost of a vacation described in a travel magazine. Before viewing an entire tape of an episode in a soap opera, students may be encouraged to identify characters, context, and situation in the early frames or to seek out the key elements in a crucial scene. Viewing the picture without the sound helps focus students' attention on information they can infer from the visuals alone and the contributions these make to the general atmosphere and tone. Listening to the audio track of a videotape with the picture blacked out focuses students' attention on the audio, without the complications of processing the visual. Video material or films should never be played straight through in the hope that students will get some value from them. Teacher and students should play around with various parts and various elements, so that the student is prepared gradually for the quite difficult experience of comprehending consecutive authentic material of some length.

STUDENT-CREATED PRODUCTS

Student-made audio or video recordings of role plays, negotiations, business case studies, debates, speeches, and interviews with visiting native speakers can provide a record of language-learning progress. These student-created products can become the basis for further learning when studied attentively with a critical, analytic intent. The viewers must learn to interact with the tape. Playing back an entire class session, no matter how entertaining the content, is tedious and often boring. For this reason, it is advisable for the instructor to take note, in the playback session, of linguistic moments worthy of attention and jot down the corresponding counter numbers. With these points of reference, the instructor can efficiently locate and play selected segments. Some instructors prefer to forego the playback in class, scheduling individual or small-group playback sessions with students to review particular segments of the tape. Other instructors leave playback sessions to the student, requiring a subsequent written report on particular aspects of the session. In this case, instructors may wish to specify particular grammatical issues or lexical or phonological problems the students should study in the tape, identifying these by counter number. (This procedure is also useful with audiotapes.)

VIDEO FEEDBACK

A natural extension of the widespread use of tape recording to let students hear their own performance, videotaping of interactions in the classroom is an effective way for students to obtain immediate feedback on their nonverbal as well as verbal behavior. Unlike film, videotape requires no developing, so classroom interactions can be played back immediately.

Since part of the value of video feedback lies in its immediacy, many instructors and students like to place the monitor facing the participants so that all may see exactly what is being recorded on the tape as it is being recorded. This immediate feedback is surprisingly effective in motivating students to monitor their speech and gestures in ways they cannot in a traditional classroom setting. Students should also view their tapes as soon as possible after recording so that they can learn immediately from their performance. As with a book, they can skim or ponder, rerunning their performance at will.

Technologies

Available technologies make it possible to present verbal and nonverbal material via auditory and visual mediums in varying combinations. Videotape is not only the most flexible of available technologies, but it also incorporates all the benefits of audio.

Karen Price

Videotape

Videotape has numerous advantages over film. Videotape can be stopped at any point for asking and answering questions. Many models of videotape recorders have a "freeze-frame" or "pause" capacity, which allows the picture to be stopped so that students can refer in detail to sections of the tape. Segments can be replayed whenever participants wish. Short scenes are easily located on videotapes either by using counter numbers or by fast forwarding or rewinding while watching the picture.

The increasing availability and simplicity of video equipment designed for the home market has eliminated the need for specially trained personnel and the consequent financial and scheduling considerations. Instructors and students can easily set up and operate the equipment themselves, which allows both for more spontaneous and timely use and for appropriate focus during the taping. The question of focus is important, because the atmosphere and even the content of the tape are enormously influenced by the positioning of the camera in relation to the focal points of the taping session, for example, opposite, behind, or to the side of the students or teacher.

Students overcome initial self-consciousness quickly as they get into the session and as taping sessions become more frequent. Having students or instructors operate the camera also helps reduce the participants' inhibitions concerning the equipment.

Practical information on video equipment

The video equipment necessary for adequate taping and playback is becoming more and more affordable with the increase in production of video systems for the home market. The teacher will need:

- *An inexpensive camera* (preferably color). Automatic features, like light-level adjustment, encourage instructors to experiment with this medium. A camcorder combining a VTR and camera is useful.
- *A videotape recorder*: The slower the tape speed one uses, the more economical the system will be, since less tape stock is required.
- *A color television or color monitor*. Television sets are quite adequate for playing back videotapes; monitors (which cannot tune in TV channels) provide better pictures.
- *A microphone and floor stand*. An omnidirectional microphone, plugged directly into the videotape recorder and placed on a floor stand, will usually yield higher audio quality.
- *A tripod*. A light, inexpensive tripod may be adequate for the camera but is recommended only for less rambunctious classrooms or for situations that do not require rapid setup and transporting of video equipment. In the latter case, a cart on wheels is advantageous.

– *Videotapes.* When no longer needed, tapes may be reused by recording over old material.

FORMAT

Videotape recorders (VTRs), also called videocassette recorders (VCRs), exist for a variety of different cassette formats. The four international standard tape formats are U Matic (3/4″), Beta (1/2″), VHS (1/2″), and 8 mm. A cassette of one format will not play in a machine of another format; that is, a Beta cassette will not play in a VHS (an acronym for Video Home Systems) machine.

Moreover, different broadcast standards exist in different countries. This means that a tape produced in one country cannot always be played back on the machine of another country. Incompatibly formatted color tape can, however, sometimes be played back in black and white. The three major categories of national standards are NTSC, PAL, and SE-CAM. Within these categories, there exist further subgroups that may also be mutually incompatible. Special playback equipment, or tape conversion at special production centers, can overcome this problem.

INDUSTRIAL VERSUS CONSUMER MODELS

The cheaper consumer VTRs are quite sufficient for schools and have proved to be durable. In some cases, the consumer item is identical to the industrial model but costs less. Moreover, features that are standard on consumer VTRs, such as fast search with picture, remote control, still framing, and tuner/timers for off-air recording, are generally available only on the best industrial models, which cost up to six or seven times as much.

TAPE SPEEDS

Both VHS and Beta videotapes can be recorded at different speeds, which thereby determine the number of hours of video on the tape. Slower recording speeds are advantageous, in that they permit two or three times as much material to be stored on the same amount of tape. More-over, visual search in fast forward and rewind is usually possible only with the slower-speed recordings. Material originally recorded live or off-air at normal speed may be dubbed at slower speed for more efficient and economical storage or simply to permit fast-speed scanning. As in audio, quality is somewhat less for video at slower recording speeds, but the difference is visually imperceptible unless the copy is several generations removed from the original. Finally, tape speed must always be checked against the speeds the machine can play back, even in the case of expensive industrial machines, which cannot always play back commercially available tapes.

The longest tape is not necessarily a bargain if the tape is going to be viewed in a manner placing wear and tear on the tape (i.e., stop-fast forward-stop-play-rewind-play, and so on). The longer tapes are not as durable as the shorter ones.

OPTIMAL TAPE STORAGE

Tapes will last up to twenty years if carefully handled and stored at relatively constant, cool temperatures. Tapes can have new material rerecorded over old material a great many times, although repeated rerecording along with demanding playback styles will eventually lead to perceptible deterioration of the image.

PURCHASING TAPES

Ordering video- and audiocassettes in bulk (even in quantities of as few as ten) from a large wholesaler or order house will reduce the total tape cost. Both kinds of 1/2″ tapes (Beta and VHS) are less expensive than 3/4″ tapes and take up far less shelf space. The quality of videotapes varies from brand to brand along with cost. Low-quality tapes are a poor investment.

FREE SOURCES OF VIDEO MATERIALS

Free sources of materials for language teachers include a vast array of sources of commercially produced videotapes from government agencies (aerospace, promotional, and military), tapes produced by large corporations promoting their products, the Red Cross, universities, consulates, and libraries. Videotapes can be obtained for rental or purchase through a wide variety of distributors, clearinghouses, and agencies. Video exchange programs, set up by educators throughout the world, are another way to obtain foreign-language broadcasts.

Some spin-offs of video technology

SATELLITE RECEPTION

Satellite and local off-air taping yield a great variety of language materials. Consumer VTRs have built-in tuner-timers that may be set in advance to record from a particular TV channel at a specified time. Satellite dishes do not require a massive expenditure. Many foreign-language classrooms in the United States enjoy daily broadcasts from all over the world – from Eastern and Western Europe, Africa, Central America, Japan – and English classes abroad frequently use British, Canadian, or Australian Broadcasting Corporation and Voice of America programs.

Obtaining a particular program may be easy, but instructors should be aware of legal constraints involved with off-air recording, not only in the United States but also via satellite. A 1984 U.S. Supreme Court ruling does not protect instructors in the United States who wish to use the same off-air recording in their classroom semester after semester.[1] The U.S. Congressional Guidelines of October 1981, which stipulate the erasing of videocassettes after a certain period, still apply.[2] As for broadcasts recorded via satellite, some countries have "open skies" policies, others do not. Instructors should exercise caution in this area and keep themselves informed of developments and regulations in their own country and elsewhere.

CAPTIONED TV

Captioned TV makes it possible to work with three mediums simultaneously: video, audio, and print. Many kinds of programs, originating in the United States as well as abroad, are captioned in the same language as the audio. To see the regular broadcasts with captions, all one needs is a special decoder connected to a TV set.

In 1981, Price and Dow conducted a study at Harvard University to determine whether nonnative English speakers could benefit from captioned materials originally targeted for the hearing impaired. Would it be possible for foreign speakers to process both aural and visual cues and attend to captions without getting bogged down, and if so, would this be equally true for all of the ESL population? Results showed that viewers, regardless of educational level or language background, benefited significantly from captioning, even with one viewing.

An excellent source of material is off-air recording of general TV

1 The January 17, 1984, U.S. Supreme Court Ruling, *Sony* v. *Universal City*, No. 81–1687, provides no clear guidance to educators for the use of videotaped, copyrighted material. The decision was limited to the in-home, noncommercial use of video recordings.
2 The fair-use guidelines, published in the October 14, 1981, *United States Congressional Record*, were developed by a Congressional committee chaired by Robert Kastenmeier. These guidelines, applying only to off-air recording by nonprofit educational institutions, permit schools to record programs for subsequent instructional use, but the recording may be kept for ten days only; recordings for faculty preview may be held for up to forty-five days. All off-air recordings must be erased or destroyed immediately at the conclusion of the designated time limit, or else licensed from the appropriate owners.

programming that is captioned.[3] It provides the authenticity of situations badly needed for language learning and enables the viewer to acquire more of the cultural script while relating aural material to the written form. It also exceeds in technical and artistic quality most budget-conscious educational productions.

Two new mediums – teletext and videotex – permit TV viewers to interact with information (graphics and print, but no audio) on the television screen. Both use a small keypad that hooks up to the TV set and telephone line, opening up a world of information indexed by broad topics, such as news, sports, money, education, games, shopping. The user selects one topic and then gains access to more specific information.

Teletext permits the viewer to select materials of interest and read them on the screen, pausing, browsing, and rereading at will. Videotex goes further, enabling the user to "talk" to the system through the keypad – for example, to order items and services from the electronic shopping catalogue or to create graphics and printed messages on the screen and electronically send them to another videotex subscriber.

In addition to immediate communication with the real world, videotex provides subscribers with more traditional educational programs, some in foreign languages, which record student responses to items on the screen and provide feedback. "Flashcard" programs permit students to create their own lessons, typing in questions and answers for themselves or electronically swapping questions and answers with a classmate. The questions are displayed in random order on the screen until all questions have been correctly answered. The possibilities for teaching language through this new medium are too vast to enumerate, but current applications include word puzzles, cloze tests, adventure games, and even opportunities for students at different locations to work together to create a newspaper.

Random-access mediums: video and audio

Although the addition of computer control enhances the use of videotape recorders and cassette recorders by adding the option of random access, perhaps the most promising medium is the videodisc. Up to 54,000 images can be stored on the disc and then accessed as either still frames or moving pictures. The existence of two audio tracks makes it possible to have alternate or bilingual audio materials.

3 Captioned TV shows are always identified in some way. *Closed*-captioned TV shows, which require a decoder to enable one to see the captions, are marked CC or ⌷ in United States TV program guides. Other captioned materials that do not require a decoder are listed as *open*-captioned or OC.

Unfortunately, lack of vision and experience have prevented videodisc, invented in the 1890s, from realizing its potential. Questions of production and design aside, the major problem in launching this medium is that it offers more possibilities than can be taken advantage of without significant experience in complex programming and production. The realization of these possibilities requires expertise in a design format with which relatively few educators have had experience. Even the few existing basic techniques for script design[4] are subject to debate, depending on one's assumptions about language learning and teaching.

The random-access feature of the videodisc is made possible by a microprocessor. The same access to nonlinear points in the audio medium is also possible using audiodiscs. This medium, too, remains as yet unmined by the foreign-language profession, because of the failure of many teachers to appreciate the potential of random-access mediums and to take the time to master their design complexity. The advantage of the audiodisc is that it provides the same service as existing audiotape, which is easy to record but has search times slower than those of the audiodisc. Until there are affordable machines that permit audiodiscs or videodiscs to record, their use for language teaching is limited to the playback of prerecorded materials. Eventually, however, these random-access mediums offer the exciting potential of putting students in control of their learning experience through interactive programming. (See Ariew and Frommer, this volume, chap. 14.)

Conclusion

Language teachers have had the good sense to use available technologies for centuries. Comenius created his picture and word lessons in the seventeenth century for the teaching of Latin. We know that the forerunner of the slide projector was used as early as the eighteenth century, and even a bonafide language course using phonograph records, text, and pictures was in use in Paris in the early 1900s. Language teachers have long understood the power of presenting language in various mediums to elucidate meaning, facilitate memory, alleviate boredom, and impress their visiting supervisors.

So what constitutes the "effective" use of technology? Surely the image of a lone student late at night at the language laboratory – hunched over the console and drooling repetitions into the microphone – is enough to make us realize that we should be evaluating the nature of

---

4 A script design is an outline of all audio and visual content and its location on the disk. It may also include a description of potential access patterns via the computer program (if the disk is to be computer-controlled).

specific situations and not the effectiveness of "technology" in language learning. Effective use of technology in language teaching has to do with the role and content of audio and visual materials and how these interact with each student's language-learning experience.

Let's act on it

1. Consider the following lesson plan and determine the number of mediums used and in what applications (i.e., as model, stimulus, or feedback): Students watch a captioned TV program about the techniques of wine tasting and then conduct their own wine tasting, writing up their conclusions in the form of a newspaper article.
2. How can audio or video recordings be used in the correction of student errors? What problems do you see? How may these be resolved?
3. What factors must be taken into account in planning which mediums to use in a given teaching situation?
4. Consider the mediums currently used in your language-teaching program. What does this suggest to you about the assumptions you are making concerning the teaching of the language?

Annotated reading list

AECT (Association for Educational Communications & Technology), 1126 16th Street, NW, Washington, DC 20036. For up-to-date sources of directories, handbooks, conference proceedings, and periodicals related to the use of technology in education, this is an excellent place to start.

Fanselow, John F. 1977. "Beyond RASHOMON – Conceptualizing and Describing the Teaching Act." *TQ* 11: 17–39. A thought-provoking article that should motivate language teachers to be more conscious of the mediums, agents, and "moves" involved in the teaching act.

Future Systems, Inc. *The Videodisc Monitor.* Falls Church, Va. Although expensive at $197 per year for twelve issues in 1986, this is the most comprehensive periodical to date publishing articles on video, video conferences, new product releases, and ongoing projects.

Lonergan, Jack. 1984. *Video in Language Teaching: A Practical Handbook for Teachers.* Cambridge: Cambridge University Press. Deals with numerous language activities and techniques that rely on the use of video in the language classroom.

Richards, Jack C. 1983. "Listening Comprehension: Approach, Design, Procedure." *TQ* 17:219–40. A very readable article that prompts the reader to reexamine listening comprehension before applying mediums to the teaching of it.

Utz, Peter. 1982. *The Video User's Handbook*. 2d ed. Englewood Cliffs, N.J.: Prentice-Hall. An excellent guide to the technical aspects of video equipment for the rank beginner or more experienced user.

13 Interaction outside the classroom: using the community

Peter Strevens

In the elegant city of Bath, a dozen young students, of a dozen nationalities, are pushing one of their group through the streets in a wheelchair. They visit restaurants, shops, public lavoratories, discos, markets, schools. At each place they look at the facilities, or lack of them, available to handicapped students. They talk to local inhabitants, shopkeepers, and city officials about the problems. Eventually they collaborate, under the guidance of their English teacher, in producing a 'Wheelchair Guide to the City of Bath'. For those students, one major segment of a ten-week course in English as a foreign language has taken them out of the classroom and into the surrounding community, immeasurably widening their experience of the foreign language by giving them well-motivated, socially-conscious reasons for talking and interacting with a broad range of people in addition to their teachers. And they have found the task absorbing, educational, worthwhile.[1]

In the city of Norwich – not so architecturally elegant, perhaps, as Bath, but a splendid and lively place – a group of a dozen young German teachers of English is compiling a dossier of materials describing life in Norwich over a period of a month. They select from the local newspapers items for future classroom use, back home in Germany, that will show their secondary school pupils some interesting, authentic, topical aspects of life in Britain today. They talk to shopkeepers, city councillors, local celebrities, local noncelebrities but interesting people; they make tape recordings of others. They watch TV, especially for items of local significance. They select particular news items – a proposal to close a post office or build a new road; a crime; the signing of a star player by the local football team – and follow day by day the way these items are treated by the local press, radio, and television. They visit local pubs – a great deal! – and notice what is being talked about.

By the end of the month these young teachers have had an unparalleled quantity and breadth of experience of English, the whole of it gained through interaction with members of the local community. They have also prepared quite staggering quantities of classroom materials for fu-

---

1 I owe much of my thinking on this topic to colleagues in the Bell Educational Trust, notably Diana Fried-Booth, Keith Morrow, Dave Allan; also to Christoph Edelhoff of Giessen, West Germany.

ture use. I envy their students, and wish I could have been taught with a similar dedication and authenticity.

In Toronto, a particular class of immigrant children gets regularly bussed to and from school. The bus driver is a Polish immigrant whose own English is strictly limited. But it is closer to the beginning level of the students than is the English of most people they meet, so he does not threaten them by having a native-speaker command. And anyway, he is their friendly daily driver. The children themselves do not realize it, but the teachers have cottoned on: The children learn a very great deal of their English from the bus driver's relaxed and caring talk, as well as from the dinner ladies and the unpaid helpers who aid with arrangements. In this instance, the responsible teachers understand the valuable additional help the children are getting through their inescapable contact with the community.[2]

In Yorkshire, a teacher of French has noticed that quite a few native speakers of French, from Belgium and Switzerland as well as from France, live and work nearby. So the teacher starts a club, a Cercle Français. Two or three times a month there are visits from French-speakers to talk about themselves, their work, their life back home. As a result of these simple contacts the French embassy becomes interested and informs the teacher of cultural activities that might become accessible: French films on loan; a French rugby team due to play a match nearby; how to link up with a school in the South which because of its location is able to receive directly French television broadcasts; and so on.

The underlying and unifying points from these case histories are simple. (1) There are nearly always valuable resources to be found in the community outside the classroom, resources which can greatly increase the enjoyment of the pupils and can provide opportunities for real interaction – interaction with a real-life point to it, unlike most conventional classroom interactions, valuable though they are. (2) Because the opportunities are outside the normal, everyday format of the class, the learners can often find a role or an involvement which makes them, the students, the interactors with a source of language, bypassing the teacher, who otherwise is almost always not only the mediator but the intermediary, the inescapable other participant. (3) Because the teacher has been seen to take initiatives to provide something interesting, something extra, his or her stock with the students goes up, and that in turn seems invariably to produce an improvement in the students' willingness and intention to learn.

Once the teacher starts to think about the resources available from

2 My source of information and inspiration in this aspect of using the community is Jean Handscombe, of North York School Board, Toronto.

the community, the list of possibilities becomes a long one, though its exact composition depends on the educational level, the type of community (eg, rural, metropolitan, industrial, a port, or a tourist centre), and the status of the target language in the community: Is it principally a foreign language or a second language?

Among resources and activities that might be considered are the following.

PEN-PALS

Many schools encourage pupils to correspond with a native speaker of similar interests. Some investigation might turn up pen-pals who actually live in the local community, as opposed to 500 or 5000 miles away.

TELEPHONE FRIENDSHIPS

When there are speakers of the desired foreign language living nearby, it can be helpful to arrange phone friends. A foreign national is asked to strike up an acquaintance with one or two or three individual learners and to make regular phone calls – however brief they may have to be at first – once a week, twice a month, or at whatever interval is most convenient.

NATIONAL CULTURAL AGENCIES

These include, for English, the British Council, US Information Service, or the Canadian Cultural Services; for French, the Alliance Française; for German, the Goethe Institute. Most languages being learned will have some back-up available through the embassies concerned. Sometimes they need to have suggestions put to them (such as some of the ideas mentioned later in this chapter), but embassy cultural staff are normally very willing to help.

THE LOCAL BUSINESS COMMUNITY

For the principally-learned languages, at least, there are generally native speakers among the business community who are happy to discuss with teachers what help they can give. There are almost always foreign-trade connections, too. There may be an olive oil importer from Spain or France, an onion trader from Britanny, a terrazzo businessman from Italy. Is there a general import business in the town? Do they receive regular visits from German salespeople of cars, of pharmaceuticals, of heavy engineering; from Italian suppliers of food, or wine, or cars once again; from Latin American or Spanish business representatives. If so, will they make an arrangement to be available for students to talk to them, to see what they are dealing in, perhaps to pay a visit to the warehouses or the docks to show the students some aspects of business or commerce in a foreign language?

SPORT

Are there any visits from foreign teams or individuals? Students who play tennis or watch football can find it exciting to meet players from both countries. More difficult to organise, but not impossible, is the obtaining of recordings of sporting events in the target language. TV commentary on the Tour de France cycling championship, for instance, or Cuban baseball, or German football matches can be a fruitful source of interest. (Again, the embassies may help.) Best of all, going to watch a visiting team, and getting one of its members to come to school next day, can arouse a great deal of interest.

COMMUNITY RADIO, TV, PRESS

In many places there is a community speaking the target language which is sufficiently large in number to have its own newspapers, radio programmes, even TV programmes. Such media activities are a marvelous resource, and media people are generally more than willing to make contact with language-learning programmes.

TWIN TOWNS

Particularly in Europe and North America, many towns and cities have 'twinning', or 'sister city', arrangements with one or more towns in another country. These can nearly always lead to involvement, to the teachers' and students' advantage, since that is their basic function: to interpret the life and times of each town to the other.

FREQUENT TRAVELLERS

Certain occupations carry the probability of extensive travel and therefore of foreign contacts. Are there any airline pilots or cabin crew nearby? Are any of them foreign nationals, or do they at any rate know of contacts? The list can be endless – sailors, diplomats, some university staff – and is limited only by the ingenuity of the teacher. The local community should always be regarded as a foreign-language resource. The problem, then, is to identify the most effective ways of tapping this resource.

One necessary dimension of involvement with the community should be *the students' interests*. It would be fatal for teachers to organise elaborate events with the foreign community which the students find totally boring. But if the students' own interests form the starting point for investigations into what the community can provide, the outcome is likely to be more useful. And students *are* interested in many issues that have a foreign dimension. They are learning French? – They will certainly be interested in discussing hunting and sealing in French-speaking Quebec. Can the teacher get magazines and newspapers from Quebec dealing with the subject? Students of Italian have views on divorce and abortion in a Catholic society, on the preservation of Venice, on the paparazzi. Other languages will have their own issues. If there are native speakers in the local community, the implications are simple. If not, an effort may have to be made to bring in appropriate information, texts, recordings, people, from the wider community.

Once the teacher starts to investigate the possible resources in the community, it quickly becomes clear that the students' contact can and should be *participatory*. There is not much benefit in finding, let us say, a Spaniard with a cork import business who lives locally, if he is invited only to come and give a talk in English about his work. The value of the community as a resource rests on fresh opportunities for interaction, for communication, for participation, by the students themselves.

Project work can fit in very well with such principles. Not only is project work usually popular with students, but the very act of collaborating with other students, in the language they are learning, increases the quantity of interaction. Some teachers are loth to admit that students can get help from each other: Teachers have an uncomfortable feeling that they can remain in control of the teaching (and learning) only as long as they dominate the talking. My experience points strongly in the opposite direction. As long as the teacher is available to help when difficulties of expression or comprehension arise – for example, on a project involving contact with the local community – students can and do build up their language very noticeably through collaborative work.

Fifteen years ago teachers were fighting a battle to have classroom furniture unbolted from the floor, so that the grouping of students could be flexible and permit a range of new classroom activities. Today we can see that informed teaching encourages us to regard the community *outside* the classroom as an equally liberating potential.

This liberating potential has two sides. One side is its value in creating interest, impact, and variety, and therefore in encouraging the students' desire and intention to learn; the other side is the learning value of interaction. If one maintains that comprehension contributes largely to *receptive* learning but the leap to *productive* learning requires an additional practical effort on the learner's part, then the use of the community as a resource provides extra opportunities of involvement that require and encourage interaction by the student.

Let's act on it

1. Make a list of users of the foreign language in your locality, under headings such as (a) embassy or consulate; (b) academics and teachers; (c) commercial or professions; (d) others. Make a programme for contacting as many of these as possible, and expand the list into a directory, giving names, addresses, phone numbers, and so on, and noting what each might contribute to long-term programmes.

2. Some of the major "transnational" industrial and commercial firms make publicity and training films and videos in the language of the principal countries where they operate. The local head-quarters of oil companies, international communications firms, manufacturers of automobiles and heavy vehicles, airlines, shipping firms, or banks may be contacted. Ask for showings of their promotional or training films or videos and for copies of their publicity literature or instructional manuals in the appropriate foreign-language edition. Share what you have been able to find with fellow-students and colleagues and discuss how they may best be used.

3. Approach the Cultural Attaché of appropriate foreign embassies in your country. Ask about possible visits from touring artists, theatre groups, speakers, exhibitions. Also inquire whether they have helpful contacts to suggest from the commercial and business interests of their country in your locality. What other sources of this type can you think of in your locality?

4. Contact the relevant foreign national tourist authority, national airline, national railway organisation, national shipping lines, broadcasting and television organisations. Ask them for free publicity information, posters, photographs, programmes, and other material, especially printed in the foreign language concerned. Discuss how these might best be used in some project. See also Melvin and Stout, chap. 4 in this volume.

5. Write to the Cultural Attaché of your own country's embassy in the foreign capital city. Ask for suitable contacts in the foreign country in order to establish exchange visits, pen-friends, reciprocal holidays, or exchange of realia (newspapers, magazines, books, postcards, tapes, and disks). If you are able to make your own cassette or tape recordings, films, or videos, offer to exchange them with an equivalent institution or individual in the foreign country.

6. Some countries maintain an overseas cultural service which would be glad to help you: the United States Information Service; Canadian Cultural Services; the British Council; the Alliance Française;

the Goethe Institute; the Dante Institute. Make sure you are known to any such body in your country as a person eager to receive help of every relevant kind. Ask a representative to come to your training class to discuss what can be made available to you and under what conditions.

7. Find out from the group of students with whom you are presently working which aspects of life in the surrounding community they would be most interested in investigating. Help each of them to develop a project, interesting to them personally, which would give them access to people in this sector in an unobtrusive and culturally acceptable way. See also Russo, chap. 7 in this volume.

14 Interaction in the computer age

Robert Ariew and Judith G. Frommer

Interactive computer-assisted language learning

Anyone who has used a computer, for whatever purposes, realizes that the computer is essentially an interactive device. It is, therefore, a most appropriate aid for language learning that has interaction as its goal. Although not yet capable of carrying on a natural conversation with a user, the computer does have a responsive capacity that endows **computer-assisted language learning** (**CALL**) with certain advantages.[1]

The advantages of CALL

Different types of CALL **programs** have evolved over the last few decades as **computer-assisted learning** (**CAL**), or **computer-assisted instruction** (**CAI**), has become more prevalent, but all of them possess common characteristics related to interaction. This can be demonstrated by comparing a simple drill program to a similar written exercise. Taking as an example a CALL English drill in which "They are arguing" must be transformed from the affirmative to the negative, a student keying in "They no are arguing" would know immediately not only that a mistake had been made, but also why the answer was wrong. Depending on the program, the student might have more than one try to get the answer right, with each incorrect answer triggering an appropriate explanation. After a predetermined number of tries, the right answer would appear on the screen. Table 1 illustrates such an exercise.

Although more interesting CALL materials exist, as will be explained, the simple example in Table 1 makes it easier to point out the advantages of CALL, which can be summarized as follows:

Interaction. The student transmits a message and receives one in return.
Immediate feedback. There is immediate notification that a mistake has been made.
Error analysis. Specific errors are identified and explained.
Self-correction. Clear error messages help most students to achieve the satisfaction of reaching the correct answer in the end.

1 Words printed in boldface are defined in the glossary at the end of this chapter.

Reinforcement. Students are encouraged by congratulatory messages for correct answers.

A similar written exercise would not have these features. Although written exercises can be creative and original, they are not instantaneously interactive, and immediate feedback is rarely provided. Even when answer keys are given in the back of the book, students often do not check their answers or do not notice that they are incorrect. When answers corrected by the teacher are returned, many students look only at the score and usually have already forgotten the exercises.

Although the computerized transformation drill in Table 1 does not involve an oral exchange of language and represents limited use of the computer's capabilities, it demonstrates that CALL can be more positively interactive than exercises done in the classroom or language laboratory. This is because *the computer responds to or interacts directly and continuously with the user of a CALL exercise.* Since students using CALL work at their own pace, which is not possible in oral exercises in class or with a fixed-speed tape in the language laboratory, CALL activities approach individualized instruction – personalized learning that maximizes the opportunities for individual input and response and, therefore, interaction. Students can make an infinite number of mistakes without trying the computer's patience and, while using the CALL program, spend time only on their own mistakes without having to listen to the teacher explaining something they already know. Finally, the computer *guarantees privacy*: If scores are not recorded and saved for the teacher, only the student knows what mistakes have been made; the rest of the class and the teacher are not aware of an individual's performance and a student is not embarrassed by public errors.

Sophisticated CALL lessons, consisting of activities at several levels of difficulty on related grammar points, provide even more individualization of learning. More flexible than textbooks, workbooks, or tape recorders, these programs do not follow a predetermined sequence, but allow students to control their own progress, selecting options from a **menu** as to what they will practice according to their interests or perceived level of proficiency. A program may also offer suggestions for review or advanced exercises based on the student's previous performance. With this CALL feature, known as **branching**, the computer becomes even more responsive to the student, enhancing the interaction between them.

The computer's **graphics** capability distinguishes it further from other pedagogical tools. With graphics, an activity can be cued through color drawings or animations. Referring to the transformation of "They are arguing" to "They are not arguing," the screen could present two animated characters arguing and two who are not. The presentation would

TABLE I. SAMPLE CALL ENGLISH DRILL

Try Answer		Message
1	They no are arguing.	"No" is not the right word and is not in the right place. Try again!
2	They are arguing not.	"Not" is in the wrong place. Try again!
3	They are not arguing.	Excellent!
	Not they are arguing.	"Not" should be placed between "are" and "arguing." The correct answer is: They are not arguing.

be forceful because the images associate the target language with the event depicted, rather than with the native language. In addition, the animated graphics hold the students' interest and act as a motivating force (Gareth 1984:147–56).

Types of CALL programs

Writers about CALL usually group CALL programs into four categories: the drill and practice type of program already mentioned, tutorials, simulations, and games. Although these classifications may have sufficed when computers were first used in language learning, they no longer cover the wider range of formats made possible by improved technology and increased experience. To the original four types of CALL programs, we will add two others: contextualized activities and tool programs.

DRILL AND PRACTICE PROGRAMS

Drill and practice programs consist of mechanical manipulations of words or sentences, using the same types of exercises as one uses in class, such as transformation and substitution drills; or in textbooks, such as multiple-choice and fill-in-the-blank questions. These exercises, in which items are usually limited to single sentences eliciting one-word answers or substitutions, can be based on verb conjugation, as in the example in Table 1, on a grammar point, or on vocabulary. The value of drill and practice programs depends on the accuracy and relevance with which vocabulary and structures are used and on the quality of the error analysis in the program.

CONTEXTUALIZED ACTIVITIES

Contextualized activities require greater involvement by students than occurs in drill and practice exercises. Consisting of units of text longer than word or sentence items, these programs stress understanding and creative use of the language rather than merely eliciting correct and automatic responses. Activities of this type are cloze passages, in which every *n*th word is missing and must be replaced; paragraphs in which sentences must be reordered (thus requiring understanding of the complete text); or stories containing erroneous or misplaced words that must be identified and changed. Students must not only understand the material but often, by completing it, actually contribute to its meaning. Contextualized activities are especially important in foreign-language learning, because they emphasize the language content along with structure. For example, in the area of reading comprehension, students may be presented with a passage and then asked to participate in activities that demonstrate their understanding. They may reorder randomly presented sentences according to the sense of the passage, choose the best rejoinder to complete a thought expressed in the passage, or fill in words to complete a passage similar to the original. Through these activities meaningful and thoughtful interaction between computer and student is achieved.

TUTORIALS

A tutorial presents new material to students and then questions them about the information. A computer tutorial can present explanations of concepts or rules, supplemented by charts, illustrations, or examples, just as textbooks do. Then, as a follow-up activity, the computer can check on the student's comprehension by proposing exercises or questions. Unlike text-based tutorials (i.e., explanations in a textbook), the computer can present dynamic illustrations, such as animations, graphics in color, or words that change visually on the screen to demonstrate the effects of a grammar rule. The follow-up questions take advantage of the immediate feedback that the computer can provide. In tutorials that branch, the order of presentation can be determined by the students' conscious choice or by their performance on follow-up activities.

SIMULATIONS

Simulations present a situation with which the student must interact, playing a role in what is happening on the screen. A scene or action is portrayed by graphics or by a computer-controlled videotape or **videodisc** player, and at certain points the student is called upon to make key decisions. The student's decisions or answers determine the content and sequence of the student–computer interaction. Although until now this type of program has been most successfully and extensively used in job training and science courses, it has potential for foreign languages.

GAMES

Games involving vocabulary or culture may be played in the target language. Some are like the video and computer games that children and students already play in their native language. Adventure games, for example, in which the user interacts with a program to solve a mystery or to survive in an imaginary environment provide an excellent CALL experience for students. Requiring decision making on the part of the players and including a great deal of text display, these games promote comprehension skills and thoughtful response. At the same time, they stimulate interest in the new language by associating it with an enjoyable, leisure-time activity. Even simple word games, such as "Hangman," provide good CALL materials.[2] Many of the contextualized activities already mentioned can be transformed into games by the addition of a scoring option. Teachers should be aware, however, that some games are really drill and practice programs to which a scoring option has been added. They should look for games that require comprehension and creative contributions from students.

CALL activities presenting larger units of content (i.e., paragraphs rather than words or short sentences) and demanding problem-solving skills involve students to a greater degree and are, therefore, more interactive. Unfortunately, the state-of-the-art CALL **software** is such that student input to date consists for the most part of selecting from multiple-choice responses or typing a few words, since assessing sentence-length answers requires sophisticated programming and microcomputers with extremely large **memories**, which are not yet readily available. This does not necessarily limit the potential for interaction, since, as indicated previously with regard to contextualized activities, this depends as much on the context of the question as on the form of the answer. As CALL develops, with advances in **artificial intelligence** and answer-judging, the potential for more natural interaction will be greater.

In fact, the more elaborate CALL packages usually involve elements of more than one type of CALL activity. For example, there are software packages that begin with a *tutorial*, a short grammatical presentation interspersing questions to ensure comprehension. The presentation can include *simulation* if it shows graphically how the language works. A *drill and practice* exercise then allows the student to practice the gram-

2 In "Hangman" the computer challenges the user to identify a predetermined word. A number of blanks, equivalent to the number of letters in the word, appear on the screen and the user begins by typing a letter, continuing in like manner to guess all the letters in the word. If the typed letter matches a letter in the word, it will replace the corresponding blank on the screen; if the guess is incorrect, one line of a stick figure of a hanged man is drawn on the screen. The user has as many tries to spell the word as it takes to make such a drawing, winning if he or she guesses the word before the drawing is finished. The computer is the winner if the picture is completed.

181

matical concept with many examples. Finally, the last part of the package is a *contextualized activity* or a *game* that rewards quick recall.

Tool programs, such as word-processing and **database** management programs, are another type of program which, though not created for CALL, can be used in language learning. Word-processing programs perform editing functions, helping students with their writing in the foreign language in the same way as they help them in their native language. They can check words used against a dictionary stored in memory, advising students of incorrect vocabulary or gender. They can also check for capitalization and punctuation, reminding students of French that months and days of the week start with small letters, students of Spanish that questions must be preceded by a punctuation mark, and students of English that adjectives of nationality must be capitalized. With these programs, composition writing becomes a dynamic experience in which the student learns to modify a text continually in order to improve it. Thus far, these programs exist mainly in English for use with the predominant **micro-computers**, but they are sure to become available for other languages in the near future.

Data bases can be used to provide a *grammar reference source* for students. Complete verb conjugations or verb-tense usage may be stored on a **disk** that students can access when writing compositions. Database information can also be used for cultural studies of target-language countries. If instructions for the use of the data base are in the target language, the students will be learning functional language while increasing their cultural knowledge. Few such programs are currently in use, in part because of memory limitations.

Computers and oral interaction

The CALL programs discussed thus far can improve grammar, vocabulary knowledge, reading comprehension, and even, to some extent, writing skills, but all are silent, except for computer-produced nonverbal signals or music. Although microcomputers can produce synthesized speech, the quality is not yet sufficient for learning new languages. Storing high-quality digitized speech takes up too much computer memory to be feasible on a microcomputer, the predominant CALL hardware. In addition, artificial intelligence is not sufficiently developed to allow computers to engage in natural conversation with users. It is unlikely, therefore, that students will be "talking" to a computer in the near future. In spite of this, computers are still capable of helping students to improve oral interaction skills, both listening and speaking. With currently available hardware, CALL software can include audio and visual components, thereby bringing CALL activities closer to real-life interaction.

Interfacing a tape recorder with a microcomputer can provide stimulating, interactive *aural comprehension exercises* for students (Wyatt 1983). An audio interface permits immediate verification of comprehension while students are listening to tapes, rather than delaying such verification to a later class period. The taped material can be divided into segments interspersed with comprehension activities, such as multiple-choice questions, so that students know immediately whether or not they have understood the tape. The tape recorder can be controlled automatically by the program or by the student's depressing a key on the keyboard. A listening exercise of this type can be programmed so that the student cannot go on to a subsequent section unless the questions in the preceding section have been answered correctly or unless the student has achieved a high enough total score. With more sophisticated audio-interface devices, the program allows students to repeat segments of the audiotape at will.

Videodisc players can also be interfaced with microcomputers to provide CALL with interactive *audiovisual materials*. The videodisc has an advantage over audio and videotape because it is composed of frames, or disc locations, that can be identified by a frame number. This allows the computer to give instructions to the videodisc player to select and display a specific frame in any area of the videodisc almost instantaneously. Film slides, audio information, text, graphics, or computer instructions can all be recorded on a single videodisc.

Interfaced tape recorders and videodisc players provide *speech production* for the computer, but they do not solve the problem of speech recognition. There are, however, *voice recognition interfaces* that match short segments of speech heard to similar segments stored in the computer's memory, making it possible to use the computer to improve pronunciation and intonation. In a typical exercise, the student first repeats a word or sentence after a native speaker, and then sees a schematic drawing of both utterances displayed on the computer **monitor**. This allows the student to compare his or her speech with that of a native speaker. The student may try a number of times to approximate the intonation and sound quality of the native speaker, using the computer display to keep track of progress.

CALL and the syllabus

In order for CALL's capacity for promoting interactive language learning to be effective, CALL materials must be integrated into specific curricula. This can be done in a number of ways.

First, *an entire course* may be presented via the computer. Although this is what many teachers are afraid of, fearing they will be replaced by machines, such courses are rare and have proved to be less successful than those with greater student–teacher contact (Chambers and Sprecher 1983: 22). Since free exchanges, either written or oral, are not yet possible on the computer, it would be difficult to maintain that an effective foreign-language course could be created with CALL as the only means of interaction. However, there are cases where complete CALL **courseware** is an appropriate solution: in distance learning, for instance, where the student is isolated from the educational institution, and with less commonly studied languages for which no language instructor may be available.

Well-designed CALL courseware, consisting of individualized, self-paced drill and practice with branching and adequate error analysis, may be used as required material and *coordinated with a textbook*, as is the case with workbooks or lab manuals. This type of approach can eliminate in-class grammar drills and writing practice, freeing class time for more meaningful, communicative activities. Thus, the computer not only replaces passive homework with interactive exercises, but increases the amount of interaction that takes place during class time.

CALL programs of all types may be used in many ways to supplement or enrich the learning situation. Initially, it may be necessary to introduce CALL as nonrequired individual work, so as not to force it on either students or teachers. Continuing this type of approach, however, may perpetuate the idea that CALL is a frill (Holmes 1984: 103). It is preferable to include stand-alone CALL modules in a syllabus as *an integral component of course materials*. They should be introduced by the teacher and followed by appropriate classroom activities, as are other adjunct materials, such as texts, films, or cultural supplements. According to a number of CALL users, assigning a compulsory, though limited, place in the curriculum to CALL may be the best method of implementation: compulsory to give it credence; limited because, as we have seen, it cannot replace the essential human interaction that confident language use requires (Hartley 1984; Holmes 1984: 104).

Regardless of the role CALL software plays in a course, it may be used *individually on a student's personal computer or in a computer laboratory*. A computer in the classroom can be *a work station* at which teams of students work together. If the video display can be shown on a larger screen, a whole class can cooperate in finding the answer to a question or playing a game. Although CALL does not respond individually to each student in these group situations, it nonetheless promotes interaction by stimulating communication among the students who are using it (Higgins and Johns 1984: 35).

The bug in CALL

CALL's great potential to foster interactive language learning has not yet been fully realized because of a variety of problems in the areas of software, hardware, instruction, and administration. First, there is a *lack of high-quality software*; this can to some degree be attributed to the newness of the medium: Standards of acceptability and criteria for effectiveness have not yet been established. At present, drills are the primary type of computer software used in language teaching, and many of these are routine programs that are nothing more than electronic workbooks (Higgins and Johns 1984: 43; Holmes 1984; 98). Drill programs can be useful when they are flexible and provide feedback, adding to the student's learning experience; unfortunately, most commercial software for microcomputers consists of short, mechanical exercises having little educational value. To a great degree, the computer has been used most often to do what is already done, instead of for activities that have not yet been done because they *require* a computer.

It is only recently, however, that significant numbers of machines of one kind have been purchased by school districts, colleges, and universities, thus providing a sufficiently large market to interest publishers in developing educational software. Recognizing the growth of the "**hardware** base," more and more publishing concerns are now offering good-quality CALL courseware for a variety of microcomputers.

Since publishers have been slow to provide adequate software, many institutions interested in CALL have been striking out on their own, using their favorite computer – **mainframe, minicomputer** or microcomputer – so that the software and **courseware** they produce can be used only by those having access to exactly the same system. This multiplicity of systems and their **incompatibility** is another reason why CALL has not yet achieved its potential.

The instructional and administrative problems, really the same problem from two different points of view, can be summed up as *resistance to change*. The use of the computer as a learning aid necessitates a change in attitude on the part of the teacher and a change in organization on the part of the institution. Many language teachers, formed in humanistic disciplines, do not understand computers and find them frustrating and threatening. Many are accustomed to directing and managing learning. Language teachers need to realize that the computer can aid them in their task rather than supplant them, freeing them from much repetitious explanation and direction of practice. To profit from CALL they may have to change their approach and devote classroom time to interactive activities that stimulate real communication.

Many institutions have not yet recognized CAL as a serious and integral part of the curriculum. On the organizational level, this means that they do not provide computer laboratories so that students can conveniently use CAL if it is available. In addition, by not recognizing the creation of high-quality courseware as worthy of promotion and tenure, they discourage faculty from contributing to advancement in this field: Teachers cannot be enthusiastic about a time-consuming endeavor for which there are few professional rewards and for which released time is rarely available. Finally, institutions cannot expect teachers to excel in an area for which most of them have not been trained. It will be evident that institutions place a high value on CAL(L) when they provide training courses for their current staff and require **computer literacy** from incoming teachers.

CALL program development

Most current CALL activity can be divided into two main categories. Some institutions are developing software for the newer and more powerful microcomputers and interfacing the microcomputer with various devices, such as videodiscs, videotape, and audiotape. Others are concentrating on creating high-quality software using the hardware they already possess.

In the first category are the software packages applying *videodisc* technology to the teaching of foreign languages, such as those that have been developed at Brigham Young University in Utah. One consists of a film recorded on a videodisc, which is used with a computer program. The film is interrupted at certain intervals, and questions are asked that require comprehension and a sensitivity to the cultural content of the audio and visual segments presented. If the student cannot answer the questions, the video segment is shown again. If the students' answers are still wrong after two tries, a transcript of the scene is shown (Meléndez 1980: 11–12).

The second Brigham Young videodisc project, *Montevidisco*, is a simulation-type program that attempts to approximate a realistic linguistic situation in a target-language environment. Montevidisco provides for a conversational exchange between the student and characters in filmed scenes that are recorded on the videodisc and controlled by a branching program. After watching a segment on the video screen, the student chooses from a series of responses. This choice determines what the characters will do next (Schneider and Bennion 1983: 44–6). With this material, students interact with and control the computer to a greater extent than with other materials, because they enter into and become part of the story, determining to some degree its outcome. Consequently, it is possible for students to use and reuse this material, creating different stories with each passage.

Another videodisc project is the University of Utah's Video-computer Courseware Implementation System, which allows educators to create and modify interactive CAL materials for a mainframe computer without doing any actual programming (Brandt and Knapp 1982). In addition, the Massachusetts Institute of Technology's (MIT) Project Athena is preparing multifaceted materials for use with videodiscs and the more powerful microcomputers that should be available in the 1990s. The MIT stand-alone modules concentrate on reinforcing skills necessary for conversational interaction, although they do not attain the level of natural discourse.[3]

Other institutions are writing more modest courseware that takes advantage of the computer's special capabilities without using the most advanced, and hence the most expensive, hardware. The many articles appearing in journals, such as *System* or the *Calico Journal*, attest to the increasing involvement of schools and universities in CALL software.[4] A specific example is the Pennsylvania State University French department, which has prepared *modules*, based on French folktales, that combine animated color graphics and simple audio interfacing (Ariew 1984: 43–7). Higgins and Johns discuss numerous word games in which the video screen presentation shows movement, rather than duplicating static text. They also explain computer-generated games in which the text produced by the computer depends on student answers, as opposed to the usual drill and practice materials with a fixed sequence of questions (Higgins and Johns 1984: 46–50, 53–62).

CALL: What's ahead?

Advances in computer-assisted language learning are clearly tied to advances in computer hardware and software. To answer the question

3 Based on a presentation given by Claire Kramsch and Douglas Morgenstern of MIT at the 1985 CALICO Conference in Baltimore, Maryland.
4 The *CALICO Journal* is the periodical of CALICO, the Computer-Assisted Language Learning and Instruction Consortium. For information, write to CALICO, 3078 JKHB, Brigham Young University, Provo, Utah 84602 USA. For information on *System*, described on its title page as "An International Journal of Educational Technology and Applied Linguistics," write to Pergamon Press Inc., Maxwell House, Fairview Park, Elmsford, NY 10523 USA (for North Americans) or to Pergamon Press Ltd., Headington Hill Hall, Oxford OX3 OBW, United Kingdom. *System* published a special CALL issue in 1983 (vol. 11, no. 1) and another in 1986 (vol. 14, no. 2).

"What's ahead?" we must first establish trends in hardware development. Computers are becoming both smaller and more powerful. In the last few years there have been significant increases in storage capacity, both in memory and in disk storage. (For example, the Apple II, which started as a 16K memory machine, evolved into the Apple IIe with 128K.) The processors are becoming *faster and more powerful*. As we have escalated from the 8-**bit** to the 16-bit and 32-bit microprocessors, speed has increased significantly. These trends will certainly continue in the years ahead.

Because of the primary trends of more power, more storage, and smaller machines, there will be secondary effects that will have a strong impact on CALL. Larger memory spaces will mean room for more and *more complex programs*, and *better graphics and animation*. One can predict "conversational" programs where the student and the machine will interact on a particular topic in a foreign language. The machine will have the basic facts of the topic and the appropriate pragmatics and basic rules of communication (including rules of discourse and linguistic rules), thus allowing the machine and the student to conduct a written conversation. The exchanges will *simulate actual interaction* that might take place with native speakers, including linguistic ambiguities and cultural and political orientations. These activities will make it possible to provide "laboratory" experiences on specific topics.

The increased dynamic memory and disk storage will also make possible *high quality audio storage and retrieval*. Interactions that include an audio component for cuing will become commonplace. The intelligibility of the voice will increase as the available storage space increases. Students will be able to hear high-quality conversations in foreign languages. They will be able to have words, phrases, or sentences repeated instantly. Using the keyboard, they will be able to ask questions about computer-generated oral messages or written text freely, and receive information in return. Eventually, they will be able to take part in a conversation as audio recognition technology advances. One prediction is that voice recognition will advance to such a degree that by the year 2000 natural language in spoken form will be the normal mode of communication with the computer (Chambers and Sprecher 1983: 186).

Another hardware innovation will be the linking of microcomputers into **networks** in order to share common resources. Networking will also offer new opportunities for interaction by allowing students to communicate with each other and leave messages for the teacher.

Sophisticated **authoring systems** or **template programs**, by allowing teachers having no programming knowledge to write programs tailored to their students' needs and interests, will increase the availability of higher-quality software. Students may even be able to participate in the creation of the materials, thereby becoming involved in the teaching–learning process and in greater interaction with the language.

One can also predict programs with very *sophisticated answer judging*. Students will be able to obtain detailed explanations (linguistic, cultural, or pragmatic) of errors and suggestions to remedy their problems. Specially designed activities may be dynamically presented to the student, based on performance. Levels of difficulty of activities will vary constantly to address an optimum level of comprehension and learning. Making many errors will reduce the level of difficulty, while interacting successfully will increase the sophistication of the interaction to challenge the students and to help them reach higher and higher levels of competence in communication.

Finally, increased storage capacities will mean more sophisticated graphics. *Images of near-photographic quality* will be stored, retrieved, and manipulated quickly. One can imagine programs that use realistic graphics to place the student in a realistic situation. The program would alter the image by adding or removing elements according to an interaction. For example, if the situation called for buying a piece of clothing, the student would select its color and size, pay for it, and all the while would be able to see the item, the color chosen, the money used, the cashier, and other details on a color monitor. Such graphics will enhance student–computer interactions by making them realistic and plausible.

What's ahead, then, is new technology that will allow language learning to involve active communication. The fulfillment of this exciting prospect will depend on the ability of educators to create, or have created for them, suitable CALL courseware. Progress in CALL will also be a function of teachers' readiness to adopt new attitudes and approaches toward language teaching that will allow students to learn at their own pace in their own way.

Let's act on it

1. What features would you look for in selecting a microcomputer for use by your department and students? What preparatory activities would you need to initiate to precede its actual introduction?
2. Read one issue of some computer journals (e.g., *CALICO Journal, Educational Computing, Electronic Learning, Journal of Computer-based Instruction, MacWorld, PC World, Personal Computing, System*) available from your library or newsstand and write a report justifying a subscription for two of these journals for your department.
3. If CALL is already in use in your department, evaluate some of the

courseware being used, paying special attention to error analysis, individualization of learning, and variety of activity. Is the software of the "electronic workbook" type or does it use the computer's capabilities well?

4. Imagine that you have the services of an experienced programmer. Design a CALL program (simulation, tutorial, or game) that would help students learn how to make polite requests.

5. What aspects of language learning do you think are least provided for in the classroom? In what ways could CALL help with these? (Be specific in your discussion.)

6. Suggest ways in which microcomputers could be used to help students improve their writing skills.

Annotated reading list

Chambers, Jack A., and Sprecher, Jerry W. 1983. *Computer-Assisted Instruction*. Englewood Cliffs, N.J.: Prentice-Hall. Provides background information and explanation of CAI, as well as advice on choosing hardware and on writing and evaluating software.

Davies, Norman F. 1985. "Getting Started with Microcomputers – A Practical Beginner's Guide." *System* 13, 2: 119–32. Useful information and suggestions about obtaining hardware and software, and finding out more about CALL.

Harper, Dennis O., and Stewart, James H., eds. 1983. *RUN: Computer Education*. California: Brooks/Cole. Numerous readings on all aspects of CAL, with selections by Papert, Bork, Chambers, and others.

Higgins, John, and Johns, Tim. 1984. *Computers in Language Learning*. Reading, Mass.: Addison-Wesley. Designed for language teachers who want to know how computers can be used in their profession. Emphasizes creative ways of using the computer and provides programs that may be copied.

Holmes, Glyn. 1984. "Of Computers and Other Technologies," in Jarvis, G. A., ed., *The Challenge for Excellence in Foreign-Language Education*, pp. 93–106. Middlebury, Vt.: NEC. Brief overview of current state of CALL.

Olsen, Solveig, ed. 1985. *CAI and the Humanities*. New York: Modern Language Association. Useful overview of various aspects of computer-assisted instruction.

Glossary of computer and CALL terms[5]

artificial intelligence: Branch of computer science concerned with developing systems that can perform intelligent tasks, such as interacting in natural language, playing games, and answering questions.

5 Definitions are based on information from Spencer (1979) and the glossary in Chambers and Sprecher (1983).

authoring language: Special-purpose programming language that facilitates development of **CAL** programs. Examples are **PILOT** and **TUTOR**.

authoring system: **Template program** that provides the structure of a **CAL** exercise, activity, or lesson, which instructors can use with no programming knowledge since only content and pedagogical specifications must be entered.

BASIC (Beginners All-purpose Symbolic Instruction Code): Easy-to-learn programming language available on most microcomputers.

bit (binary digit): Smallest component of computer-stored information, indicating a two-choice situation.

branching: A feature of CAL programs that enables the students to move from the linear program to review previous work or to skip to more advanced exercises. This may be an automatic procedure based on the student's previous performance.

bug: Program error that causes the program to "crash," that is, to malfunction.

byte: One character – letter or digit – of information stored in the computer, usually 8 **bits** long.

CAI or CAL (Computer-assisted instruction or learning): Use of computer-controlled programmed sequences to provide instruction.

CALL (computer-assisted language learning): **CAL** restricted to the teaching and learning of a language other than one's native language.

central processing unit (CPU): Computer circuitry to control interpretation and execution of instructions; "brain" of the computer.

chip: Small integrated-circuit package containing many logic elements. The invention of the chip made the **microcomputer** possible.

computer language: Set of rules, characters, and structures used to prepare computer **programs**; programming language.

computer literacy: Capacity to understand how computers function and to use them for one's own purposes.

courseware: CAL **software** intended for a specific course.

cursor: Moving, sliding, or blinking symbol on the screen of a microcomputer or computer terminal indicating where the next character will appear.

data bank, data base: Collection of data used and produced by a computer **program**. Large amounts of information that can be accessed via computer.

debug(ging): Process of eliminating errors from a **program**.

disk drive: **Peripheral** device that receives a **floppy disk** so information on it can be accessed by the **central processing unit** according to **program** instructions.

disk(ette): See **floppy disk**.

file: Collection of related sets of data treated as a unit by the computer.

191

floppy disk: Small flexible disk, usually about five inches in diameter, and used for storage of data and programs with a **microcomputer**. (See also **disk drive**.)

graphics: Displays, drawings, or pictures on the video screen of a computer.

hardware: A generic term used to describe the electronic and mechanical components of a computer system.

incompatibility: Computers are incompatible when **software** produced by one cannot be used with another. Incompatibility is a characteristic of most **microcomputers**.

(to) input: To introduce data from the keyboard or an external storage medium (floppy disk, tape) into the computer **memory**. Data entered into the computer are called **input**.

interface: Device for, or the action of, linking two pieces of hardware.

K: The symbol for the quantity 1024. It is used to indicate the number of **bits** that can be stored in memory. Microcomputers are usually described in terms of their memory size, e.g., a 512K Mac.

mainframe: Large, powerful, nonportable computer usually requiring sophisticated support equipment.

memory: Internal storage unit that stores information the **central processing unit** uses when actually running a program.

menu: List of choices appearing on a computer's video display **terminal**. The user depresses a key, touches the screen, or clicks the **mouse** (on some computers) to determine the program sequence that will be executed.

microcomputer (micro): Desktop computer; also known as a "personal" or "home" computer.

minicomputer: Medium-size computer, between **mainframe** and **micro**.

modem (modulator-demodulator): Device permitting computer to communicate by telephone with another computer.

monitor: Display screen of computer terminal or **microcomputer**.

mouse: Small handheld device that allows user to interact with a microcomputer without using the keyboard. The Apple Macintosh was the first mouse-controlled computer.

network: Two or more interconnected computers that can communicate with each other electronically.

operating system: **Software** controlling the general operation of the computer, as opposed to **programs** performing specific functions.

output: Data transferred from a computer's memory to some storage or output device, such as the computer screen or a floppy disk. Also, data produced by the computer as the result of a program, as opposed to initial data, or **input**.

peripheral: Computer components external to the **central processing unit**: **disk drives**, printers, and auxiliary storage units.

personal computer: See **microcomputer**.

PILOT: A popular authoring language.

PLATO: CAI project started at the University of Illinois at Urbana-Champaign in the mid-1960s with support from the National Science Foundation and Control Data Corporation(CDC). Used the **TUTOR** authoring language on CDC mainframe computers. System commercially marketed by CDC.

program: Set of sequenced instructions that cause a computer to perform specific operations.

random-access memory (RAM): Main computer **memory**. Information can be written into and read out of RAM and can be changed at any time by a new write operation, but the contents are lost each time the power is shut off.

read-only memory (ROM): Computer **memory** consisting of data permanently encoded during the manufacturing process. Data can be read from this area, but none can be written into or added to it.

software: Generic term to describe the computer instructions, **programs**, and codes that enable the computer to function, as opposed to **hardware**.

storage: Synonym of **memory**.

template program: A CALL program that instructors can adapt for use with specific material. The structure of the program is predetermined but the content can be changed.

terminal: Input/output **peripheral** device connected to the computer, but which may be in a remote location: another room, city, or even country.

time-sharing: Sharing of a computer facility by several users for different purposes. Although each user is actually serviced in sequence, the high speed of the computer makes it appear that the users are all handled simultaneously.

TUTOR: See **PLATO**.

transportability: Capacity of **software** to be used on computers of different types and makes; also referred to as *portability*.

user-friendly: Computers, **peripherals**, and **programs** that permit the user to interact with them without special training.

videodisc: Disk that looks like a 33 rpm record. A single-sided videodisc, consisting of 54,000 frames, is capable of storing video images as well as computer instructions and text.

15 Preparing the language student for professional interaction

Anne R. Dow and Joseph T. Ryan, Jr.

For centuries the wisdom and the technique of law and medicine have been acquired through the study of past legal cases and clinical work, respectively. Since the early 1920s, case study has been the preferred method of managerial training at the Harvard Business School, and it has spread to the fields of government and education as well. In the past ten years, English as a second language (ESL) teachers at Harvard, having used the case method in the context of designing English for special purposes (ESP) courses at the professional schools, have found it to be an excellent way to teach foreign languages as well.[1]

The case method provides the ultimate in an interactive technique, involving as it does interaction between the student's experience and the case content, the student and other students, the student and videotape, the student and members of the business community, and the student and the teacher. It is task-oriented and purposeful, the goal being to find the best solution and support it in order to persuade others of its merit. It is highly motivating because of its relationship to real-world problem solving and interpersonal strategies. It is not insulting to mature professionals and challenges highly motivated younger students. It emphasizes cooperation in both study groups and the classroom, in which students build on each other's ideas, but it may also be constructively competitive. Since there is no one "correct" answer, it is the antithesis of traditional passive memorization. The emphasis is on process rather than product.

What is the case study method?

Instead of presenting theories, the case study method gives students materials to make them think purposefully. A case is a set of data concerning a real-life decision-making situation. Students are expected to analyze the facts presented and, based on their own experience, come up with a recommended course of action. Exposure to many such particular situations builds a body of experience in a field for "observing

1 The authors wish to acknowledge the following past instructors in the ESL programs at Harvard for their contributions to the evolution of the business case study elective described herein: Lucy Caldwell-Stair, Maryann Piotrowski, Gloria Mason, Ashley Goldhor-Wilcock, and Mary Wright-Singer.

coherent patterns and drawing out general principles" (Gragg 1951: 1). It is, therefore, inductive rather than deductive, and decisional as opposed to expository.

An example of the case method used in a language program

The business case study course offered as an elective in the Harvard Summer School intensive program of ESL is a multiskill professional course designed to simulate a business-school environment. Cases are read in English. Students then think about the cases they have read and prepare a written analysis to be used in class. They are encouraged to meet in small study groups to discuss cases: not in order to reach a consensus, but to refine, adjust, and amplify their own thinking. In addition, they may plan bargaining strategies for mock sessions in class. Students then meet as a larger group in class, not only to present their analyses, but to discuss and defend their recommendations. This involves careful listening to the ideas of others as well as expressing one's own ideas clearly and effectively in English.

Who should take a business case study course?

The "right" students for a case study course are those who want to be there. Self-determination is an important factor in the success of education, as in any other human endeavor, and the fact that teachers are free to design such courses and students to request them as electives produces a great deal of ego investment with high dividends in energy. Since the case study method taps student experience, the classroom interaction benefits from the presence of individuals with business experience and expertise. It is then possible to include others without experience as long as they demonstrate a high degree of motivation. Those already accepted for professional schools should be given priority for places in an ESP course, since this preselection implies not only appropriate experience but a high degree of motivation. In general, students with relatively outgoing and aggressive personalities fare better in this type of course, although it may serve to train more reticent individuals in the kinds of skills needed for professional interaction.

Description of the business case study course

The business case study course at Harvard meets two hours each day, five days a week, for approximately seven weeks. The first hour daily is either a discussion of an assigned case or an interactive role-play activity – a simulated bargaining session, presentation, or sales meeting – related to the previous day's case. In one seven-week course in 1984, twenty-one cases and four supplemental articles were used. Eleven of the cases were followed by bargaining sessions. Five of these sessions and the discussions of another five cases were videotaped to provide feedback for students.

A *teacher–student contract* should be established at the beginning of the course. Stress is laid on the high level of preparation required of both teacher and student. In the program described, students are informed on the first day that the final grade for the course will represent a breakdown typical of most business-school case courses.

Fifty percent of the final grade is based on *class participation*. A daily diary summarizing students' in-class comments on the case will help the instructor pinpoint skills needing improvement, gauge student progress, and calculate the grade. Grading class participation rigorously prompts the student to speak in class and also realistically replicates the pressure to produce under which students will be expected to operate in the business world. It is wise to stress the importance of quality rather than quantity of contributions in order to reduce the "empty barrel" and "echo" effects, which may slow things down. The weighted emphasis upon speaking in class promotes improvement in reading and writing as well, since effective participation requires that students read the case thoughtfully and prepare an analysis. Not to have done so is usually embarrassing.

Twenty percent of the course grade is based upon written assignments, which serve as tests. Following the same routine as at a business school, the student has a limited amount of time to read a case and write up *an analysis, including an action plan*. These assignments provide feedback about reading speed, ability to manage time, and mastery of the elements of an analysis. For the student who expects to study at a North American business school, these tests provide an opportunity to assess one's ability to cope with this type of pressure.

The final 30% of the course grade is based on written out-of-class assignments. One is *an action memo* (10%), the other *a sales territory redistribution report* (20%). Both are due on the day for which the students prepare the case. Since these cases have to be prepared anyway, students do not regard the writing assignments as extraneous. Class discussion is of a higher quality when there has been written preparation of a more real-world nature than the usual short analyses; students, feeling satisfied with the depth and control of material, are encouraged to maintain that degree of quality in other cases. The written analyses prepared for class discussion of all other cases are rated by the instructor on a scale from 1 to 10, but these ratings affect the final course grade only if they are better than the performance in class and on other written assignments.

Components of a case analysis

The following outline is typical of the approach that most students use to do a case. It has three advantages. First, it organizes an unwieldy mass of complicated material into an orderly pattern from which a student can develop a solution. Second, the student can use it to present the case in class. Third, if challenged, the student can use it as a reference to locate substantiation for points with which others disagree. Just as there is no one correct answer for a case, so there is no one correct analysis or analytical format. This type of outline is in general use, however, and lends itself conveniently to tackling the typical components of a case.

Business case analysis: standard outline
   I. Summary
      A brief description of what is going on: Who is acting? Why? What has the result been?
  II. Problem
      A succinct, one-sentence statement.
 III. Cast of characters
      A. People
         1. Name
         2. Job title
            a. experience, if relevant
            b. influence or attitude, if relevant
         3. Relationship with the problem
      B. Institutions or events
         1. Name
         2. Influence on events
  IV. Chronology
      What happened in sequential order (as it relates to the problem). Facts only. No evaluations here.
   V. Issues
      What important aspects of the situation are in conflict or are relevant to the problem at hand? This is the component where evaluation is done. For example, a case might include such issues as:
      A. Company culture
         1. Independent decision making
         2. Centralized decision making
      B. Organizational change
         1. introducing a new person
         2. introducing a new procedure
  VI. Options
      List possible courses of action. Evaluate each one.

    A. Course of action
      1. advantages (or pros)
      2. disadvantages (or cons)
VII. Recommendations
    A. A statement of the action you support.
    B. Enumeration and explanation of the reasons for your recommendation.
    C. An outline, in as much detail as possible, of an action plan to solve the problem in the case.

In general, students will find that the best way of dealing with a case is to read it three times. The first reading should be quick – perhaps only the first paragraph in its entirety and then the first sentences of the rest, primarily to identify the problem. The second reading should be careful; students underline information related to the problem. After thinking about what they have read and how it relates to the problem, the students then begin their analyses, extracting information they need from the case to fill it out. After completing the analysis, the student should read the case a third time to check that nothing significant has been omitted, and to verify the facts, listing the source for each by page, paragraph, and line number. These notations serve as a handy reference when citing information if challenged.

Having students turn in a case analysis for each case is an efficient means not only of checking but of challenging them to improve their reading and writing skills. Preparing a summary, identifying the problem accurately, and listing pertinent facts concerning the people and institutions involved with the problem test reading comprehension as well as logical analysis. Writing about this material in an organized, effective, and grammatical manner is a test of written skills. Careful execution of these two tasks elevates the quality of class participation, since it forms the basis for anticipating the ideas expressed by others as well as for expressing one's own ideas clearly, persuasively, and succinctly.

SAMPLE CASE

The sample that follows, although compact, displays the narrative qualities typical of many cases used in North American business schools. It may be used on the first day of class to teach students how to write out a case analysis.

Bob Smith
The first National Bank of Littleton, Massachusetts, has received a loan application from Bob Smith. He wants to borrow $20,000 to start a shoe store

in his hometown. From the application itself and from conversations with people in Bob's hometown, the loan officer has the following information to consider.

1. Born on a farm in western Massachusetts.
2. Mother died when he was 6 years old.
3. Delivered newspapers after school as a boy.
4. Worked while in high school as a grocery clerk every Saturday.
5. Bought his first car for $300 at 18.
6. Used his car to deliver groceries for the local store.
7. Served in the army as a private for two years; no promotions.
8. Fined once (at 19) for speeding; no other criminal record.
9. Applied at 22 to a bank for loan of $10,000 to start a shoe store in his hometown; bank refused him the loan.
10. Worked as clerk in shoe store for six years; promoted to assistant manager after three years.
11. Has just applied at 28 to bank for loan of $20,000 to start a shoe store in his hometown.

Before looking at a completed analysis of this case, some comments about student reactions to it will show advantages and disadvantages of using the case method for an ESP class. For the inexperienced student, this overwhelming array of disparate material may appear confusing. For the experienced student this case may appear to be too easy or to lack sufficient information for making a decision. Both groups need reassurance that the purpose of the case method is to develop the analytical skills required to assess options and make a reasonable decision. Cases will always contain either too much information or not enough. Concern with that aspect is a diversion from the essential purpose of the method: to develop the analytical skills needed to make a case recommendation. For example, item nine of Smith's résumé tests a student's reading comprehension of ambiguities stemming from use of the indefinite article with the word *bank*. Will the student focus on the important point that Smith's application was turned down, or get lost in a tantalizing digression about *which* bank Smith applied to and was eventually refused by? Such provocative vagueness may actually prove an advantage to the case teacher, however. It promotes discussion and provides an opportunity for the inexperienced student to offer opinions that a more explicit, technical exposition might discourage.

This case also involves *cultural ramifications*. Since these cases have been written for American students at American business schools, various cultural assumptions are inherent. Although this may present a challenge for the nonnative teacher, it is valuable from the student's standpoint to learn about cultural assumptions and appropriate behavior along with vocabulary and syntax. In the Bob Smith case, his part-time work as a teenager would be viewed by a North American as an admirable example of the work ethic. To many of the foreign students studying at a North American university, the idea of a teenager working in a grocery store is incomprehensible. Being outside their experience, it may be disregarded, or even looked upon as evidence of lack of interest in his studies or extreme poverty. To some students, Smith's traffic violation at the age of 19 would indicate a dangerously irresponsible personality, whereas to others it might seem an irrelevant youthful escapade.

Finally, this case has great potential for some realistic *role playing* – one of the hallmarks of a good case for the foreign-language teacher. After the case has been presented and discussed, some students will recommend turning down Smith's application. The teacher will then ask one student to take the role of the loan officer and announce the bank's decision to another student playing Bob Smith. Not only is this an effective opportunity to develop speaking skills, but it is also one of the common classroom devices used in actual case-method classes to which students must become accustomed.

Now that you have read this case, look again at the standard analysis outline (p. 197), and write your own analysis in this form. When you have done this, compare it with the sample below.

SAMPLE CASE DONE IN ANALYSIS FORM

Case analysis: Bob Smith
  I. Summary
     Bob Smith has applied for a bank loan of $20,000. He wishes to open a shoe store in his hometown. He is an experienced salesperson in the shoe business.
 II. Problem
     The bank loan officer must decide whether or not to approve the loan based on personal data and the professional history of Bob Smith.
III. Cast of characters
     A. Bob Smith, assistant manager in a shoe store; six years' experience in shoe sales. Age 28. Denied loan of $10,000 for the same purpose at 22. Has worked consistently since childhood.
     B. Loan officer. Works at First National Bank of Littleton, Mass. Has to make decision about Smith's loan application.
     C. First National Bank of Littleton. Denied Smith's request of $10,000 for a shoe store six years ago.
 IV. Chronology
     A. Smith applied at 22 for loan of $10,000 to start shoe store in hometown. Bank refused him loan.
     B. Smith worked as shoe clerk for six years; promoted to assistant manager after three years.
     C. Smith has applied at 28 for loan of $20,000 to start shoe store in hometown.
     D. Bank loan officer must make decision about loan application.

V. Issues
   A. Salesperson/assistant manager versus owner of business
      1. How do their responsibilities differ?
      2. Does being a good salesperson mean having the experience to be an owner?
   B. Business experience versus business education
      1. Which provides better preparation for being a store owner: practical experience, book knowledge, or a combination?
   C. Smith's potential for success as an owner
      1. Experience
      2. Drive and ambition
      3. Ability to handle $20,000
      4. Promotion to assistant manager

      (Note: the goal here is not exhaustive coverage, but selectivity. Notice the absence of any reference to Smith's arrest, where he was born, etc.)

VI. Options
   A. Refuse the loan
      + Avoid risk of possible loan default if Smith's store fails
      − Lose interest income and possible future business
      − Lose opportunity to provide service to community in the form of store and possible jobs
   B. Grant the loan
      + Gain interest income on loan
      + Get future business: another loan; commercial checking account
      + Encourage future business from other people who hear from Smith where he received the loan
      + Provide shopping convenience to the community
      − Smith fails as owner and defaults
      − Smith's hometown is too small to support a shoe store; bank loses money
   C. Delay making decision (the "do-nothing" option)
      + Permits determination of reason Smith was refused loan at age 22
      + Avoids risk
      − Smith might go to a different bank

VII. Recommendation
   Bank loan officer should give the loan to Bob Smith
   A. He has six years' experience in the shoe-store business, as salesperson and assistant manager.
   B. He shows a consistent work record from childhood.
   C. He is familiar with his hometown and has the opportunity to succeed there because people know him.

Comments about the written case analysis

The most important issue for the teacher dealing with a student's written analysis is the realization that there is *no one correct version* of an analysis. A language teacher leading a case discussion class for the first time should beware of the tendency to judge students' efforts in comparison to a preconceived analysis.

Instead, the instructor should view a student's analysis with the following five concerns: sense, understanding and control, format, quality of recommendation, and creativity. Does the analysis under consideration make sense? Is it possible to follow the student's reasoning and is there logical development? Next, does the student understand what has been read and demonstrate control of where the case material fits into the analysis? Third, is the student using the format for a case analysis effectively, with headings for each component and an outline format to organize the material that pertains to each section of the analysis? If so, the student benefits from greater ease in dealing with the mass of material and the instructor from a greater understanding of what the student is trying to do.

The recommendation is the most beneficial segment for a language teacher to emphasize and analyze, since it is viewed as most important by case leaders. Is the recommendation relevant? Does it relate to the problem in the case and accommodate some of the issues that played a part in provoking the problem? Does it reflect a careful and realistic appraisal of the possible options with their advantages and disadvantages? Does it include a detailed action plan or a step-by-step process for carrying out the recommendation decided upon? When students first begin doing analyses, the nature of the case itself will usually require only a simple recommendation. However, with more experience and with cases of more complexity, a recommendation with a specific, detailed plan of action should become a routine step for students, especially those planning to attend business school.

The final consideration in evaluating an analysis is *creativity*. The teacher looks for some ingenuity in what the student has recommended. After reading from ten to forty analyses of the same case with greatly varying degrees of grammar control and clarity, the teacher will immediately recognize – with gratitude – a recommendation and action plan that demonstrate creativity. A good action plan will be useful as a sample in class discussions about writing an analysis. This will not only benefit students having difficulty in grasping the essentials of an analysis, but may even help to improve the quality of the teacher's own analysis.

The foreign-language component

Aside from handling the case itself, the student must also deal with difficulties that fall directly within the expertise of the foreign-language teacher. These involve the nature of a case analysis and such components as the summary or the problem statement, which must be not only relevant but direct and brief in expression. Writing is a difficult task for most people in their native language, but to require that students write in a foreign language in a mode that is noted for its straightforward and pithy style is an awesome demand. The teacher should expect students to have writing problems, not only with the format itself but also with organization of ideas, grammar, and style. With sufficient practice and motivation, students will learn how to write an analysis, but the task is more easily accomplished if the instructor sets goals for student improvement in each section. The first goal for students is to master the format; then comes organization, and after that style and grammar. Evaluative feedback should focus in stages on each of these goals, progressing from comments on format to those on material organization as the student displays more dexterity with practice. Finally, within the context of time and resources available, the more analyses the student writes, the more the student progresses in clarity, precision, and confidence.

The case discussion class

As the case class begins, the teacher calls upon a student to "lead off," or introduce the case. Students should not know in advance who is going to be called on, and each student should have this opportunity as the course progresses. Using his or her analysis, the student begins with the summary, going on to the cast of characters, the issues, options, and plan of action. The teacher interrupts only to clarify vague points or to rectify any significant omissions. Quite often, mistakes or omissions provide a basis for discussion, and the case takes off on its own. Ideally, the student leading off should be given the opportunity to defend his or her analysis and be permitted to continue the presentation after these discussions. This prepares students for business schools, which usually begin their cases this way, and provides excellent speaking practice. Using the case analysis as a launching point for the presentation repays the effort expended by the student in writing it up before class.

The role played by the teacher is that of facilitator, guiding the case class from its beginning, superintending the ensuing discussion, encouraging wide student participation, curbing excesses or digressions, and, from time to time, summarizing points made by students in order to bring the case back into focus. Restating a student's contribution so that all can understand provides correct language models. Asking questions furthers group thinking and provides the opportunity to elucidate cultural problems. The teacher should close the discussion with a recapitulation of major points raised as they relate to the recommendation and action plan and share with students the actual outcome of the case, if that information is available.

Initially, students may have difficulty *learning to operate within the discipline of the analysis format.* In addition to lacking the necessary speaking skills, they may be unaccustomed to the give-and-take of discussion, and may overcompensate for their insecurity by trying to force their decisions on the class rather than discussing them. The results are often disputatious, redundant, and emotional. Some students become very aggressive and even personal in pushing their solutions; others refuse to listen to anyone else because they have prior experience and already know the answer; and finally, some students, appalled at the emotionally charged arguments, withdraw from participating in any discussion at all.

The teacher's summaries can tactfully bestow praise where it is due or cut short the more rampageous outcries of the voluble. Comments about style and finesse, coupled with quiet professionalism, will calm students down and give them greater self-confidence as they become more comfortable with the discussion parameters of this method. Extensive role playing and team presentations encourage students to work together and build tolerance for diversity of opinion.

Participation in case discussion requires *specific speaking skills*, which the teacher will want to help students develop. Chief among these skills is getting to the point and expressing it briefly. American business schools often have up to ninety students in a case discussion class. Since all students are required to participate, a high premium is placed on the succinct and relevant comment. Students from cultures where consensus-building or hierarchical direction-taking are the common means of conducting meetings will require some encouragement to take risks and give their opinions in a forthright manner. In addition, speaking skills can be enhanced by active instruction and practice in using opening gambits, ways of indicating agreement, and other common speaking strategies.

SPEAKING SKILLS AND STRATEGIES

(This information can be recast in an evaluation form format for feedback to students.)

Case Presentation Skills
Organization
1. Attention-getting leadoff, connector, or answer
2. Main points
3. Supporting details
4. Connection of main points and details
5. Logical ordering of main points and details

Physical presentation
1. Clear, strong voice
2. Eye contact with teacher and students
3. Appropriate speed
4. Use of body language

Interactive Speaking Skills
1. Agreeing
2. Disagreeing
3. Asking for opinions
4. Giving opinions
5. Asking for clarification
6. Giving clarification
7. Attacking
8. Answering an attack
9. Suggesting courses of action
10. Suggesting alternative courses of action
11. Reinforcing suggestions
12. Asking for more exact information
13. Giving more exact information

Speaking Strategies
1. Controlling the floor
2. Presenting positions
3. Pressing positions
4. Responding
5. Checking for understanding
6. Releasing the floor
7. Miscellaneous strategies
   a. criticizing
   b. bandwagoning
   c. echoing
   d. giving exceptions
   e. examining in detail
   f. ridicule
   g. getting to the basics

Use of videotape

Videotaping of the class can be of great assistance, especially at the start. Anyone who has ever seen students watching themselves on TV knows what a powerful focus it provides for attention to feedback concerning their verbal and nonverbal performance. It is important to show the tape right after taping in order to take full advantage of its immediacy.

Letting students see themselves while filming may also lead to monitoring and self-correction of overuse of hands and nervous mannerisms. Having students critique themselves can be very useful because they will see things the teacher might miss or hesitate to call attention to. Students have a tendency to be far too critical of themselves and others, so teachers may need to establish balance by emphasizing positive points.

Team teaching is ideal for the videotaping session, with one instructor guiding the case discussion while another records counter numbers at which problems of communication occur for subsequent discussion. Helping at such sessions provides a useful apprenticeship in the case method. (If no technician is available, the second teacher may also operate the camera.) If no video equipment is available, the observer's notes may form the basis for the "post mortem" session.

Supplemental interaction with the community

An additional note of realism can be added by the inclusion in the curriculum of guest speakers from the business community and field trips into the business world. These are particularly valuable in the foreign-language setting, where the teacher is all too often the only native or near-native model to which students are exposed. The care and planning necessary to make such additions successful should not be underestimated. Guest speakers must not only be carefully selected, but helped to organize and, if necessary, simplify their communication in order to be understood by the students. The sites must be carefully selected and can be made more meaningful if they are integrated into the curriculum – for example, by having students read the company's annual report as if it were a case. The day after the trip students can report their recommendations for the improvement of company performance as though they were consultants.

Student and teacher resistance to the case method

Certain features of the case method make it particularly difficult for students from other cultures. Principal among these are the teacher's indirect role, the lack of a single correct answer, the need for cooperation with the group while asserting individual positions forcefully, and the shared responsibility for the success of the class. In traditional educational systems, the teacher is an authority figure whose role is to tell students the correct answer. In the case method there is no one correct answer, but options with resultant advantages and disadvantages that may differ so slightly that there is no readily apparent decision. Faced with ambiguity, students may press the teacher to lecture. Bearing in mind that not all cultures place a high premium on risk-taking, the instructor must help students to think independently in the context of a democratic classroom and assert themselves in the presence of a teacher and classmates who may be older or possess more expertise. Developing the confidence necessary to succeed in such a classroom is valuable preparation for both the North American university classroom and the business world.

Similarly, teachers – even those who have already exchanged the role of lecturer for that of facilitator – may be tempted to retreat to the security of traditional classroom roles when threatened by their lack of expertise in a professional area. This seeming handicap may actually prove an advantage, however, if the teacher can overcome insecurity and share with students the excitement of learning. As language expert, the teacher may then act as a "consultant" to the "client" (student), observing and analyzing strengths and weaknesses on which to base a jointly planned program for improvement (Piotrowski 1982: 232–3). Such a "management-by-objectives" approach is kinder to the egos of both the professional student and the teacher.

What kinds of cases work best?

Over five thousand cases are available from the Harvard Business School. The shortest are from three to four pages long, although the normal range is from eight to twenty pages, and some are even twenty to forty pages long.

The following five types of case studies have proved most useful for the purpose of language teaching:

1. *Organizational behavior* cases are excellent to begin with because they are general rather than technical. Since they revolve around issues of communication in the workplace, often complicated by sociological dimensions like power position, age, sex, or race, they lend themselves particularly well to role play, which can be video-taped for feedback purposes.[2]
2. *Marketing* cases deal with ways to increase sales. It is best to select those which, like organizational behavior cases, require the application of good common sense rather than technical expertise.
3. *Control* cases are pure number problems of the production-line va-

2 We use, for instance, "Road to Hell," a case about a white Caribbean executive grooming a Caribbean black and the problems each has giving and receiving feedback, respectively. In interracial groups, students are often asked to play the reverse of their real-life situation. The same goes for sexes, and it is effective.

riety. They are best avoided by teachers who suffer from math anxiety, but they provide an opportunity for certain students to shine if the teacher is secure enough to let them come to the board and teach.

4. *Production* cases involve issues of managing groups of people in a manufacturing setting. Those requiring a strong theoretical background should be avoided.
5. *Finance* cases cater to the entrepreneurs in the group, since they concern investment decisions.

Having studied several examples, teachers can make up their own cases, preferably basing them on available information from local businesses but changing names and locations.

Can the case method be used outside the professional context?

Since language is best acquired by putting it to work, *what* is studied is not nearly so important as *how* it is studied – interactively and with enthusiasm! Consequently, the case approach can be transferred with advantage to a general language course. The following ideas for cases are of general applicability:

- You must decide whether to buy an expensive plane ticket and be assured of a scheduled seat or travel more cheaply on a standby basis. (Issues to consider: the value of one's time, the importance of arriving on time, and so on.)
- You have been placed at the wrong level in a language program, but the term is half over. Is it better to stick it out or transfer?
- A surgeon must decide between two recipients for an available organ transplant.
- You have been accepted by the college of your second choice, but must accept or decline the offer before you have heard from the one you really want to attend.
- A child robs a bank. What should the judge do with the child?
- You discover that your younger brother smokes marijuana. Should you smoke with him? lecture him? turn him in to the police? do nothing?
- Your daughter has stolen library books. Should you help her smuggle them back onto the shelves? make her return them? report her? do nothing?
- You must decide whether to take on two jobs. (Issues to consider: affordable life style; impact on family, health; importance to you of leisure activities, and so on.)

Other ideas for cases may be developed from news items about cases before the courts, people's problems, or political scandals. Letters to the editor and advice columns are also fruitful sources.

Let's act on it

1. Go through a business newspaper in the target language looking for articles that easily provide the basis for cases. Especially useful for English classes are *The Wall Street Journal* and the business section of *The New York Times*.
2. Visit or write to international companies for copies of annual reports. Students can read them to identify problems the company is facing and make recommendations. (Better suited for students with advanced language proficiency or business experience, since the style of these reports is difficult.)
3. Write a sample case that would be useful with a multicultural class because of the particularly North American cultural assumptions underlying it.
4. Using the model of Bob Smith, write a nonbusiness case based on an issue facing your students in their own lives. Give sufficient data to permit discussion and alternative solutions. *Example*: Should a family with limited resources spend a lot of money to prepare their children for exams that determine admission to highly selective universities?

Annotated reading list

Byrd, Donald R. H., and Cabelas, Iris C. 1980. *React Interact: Situations for Communication*. New York: Regents. Explanatory paragraphs and details in chart form make this speaking exercise book particularly good for the case method.

Gragg, Charles I. 1951. *Because Wisdom Can't Be Told*. Case No. 9–451–005. Boston: Harvard Business School. A classic examination of the effects the case system has upon students.

Harvard Business School. 1986. *Directory of Course Material*. Boston: Harvard Business School Case Services. An expansive annotated catalogue of 5,000 cases (1,500 restricted for Harvard use) listed by type. Descriptions may be inadequate for assessing ESL potential, so obtain a case copy for examination. Teachers' notes containing actual decisions require special authorization.

Keller, Eric, and Warner, Sylvia T. 1979. *Gambits 1: Openers; Gambits 2: Links; Gambits 3: Responders, Closers and Inventory*. Hull, P.Q., Canada: Public Service Commission of Canada. Pioneer handbooks on the "glue" of English interaction.

Piotrowski, Maryann W. 1982. "Business as Usual: Using the Case Method to Teach ESL to Executives." *TQ* 16: 229–39. Argues persuasively for the case method.

Rooks, George. 1981. *The Non-Stop Discussion Workbook: Problems for Intermediate and Advanced Students*. Rowley, Mass.: Newbury House. The situations in this speaking text work fairly well, but often contain more elements than the teaching points justify.

Sadow, Stephen A. 1982. *Idea Bank: Creative Activities for the Language Class.* Rowley, Mass.: Newbury House. Provides an array of brief problems for students to solve.

Sevareid, Eric. *Enterprise.* New York: McGraw-Hill. A text related to Enterprise videocassettes (25 programs; 30 minutes each) obtainable from Learning Corporation of America, 1350 Avenue of the Americas, New York, NY 10019 USA. Cases such as "The Levi Strauss Co." presented in video offer a nice change of medium for case presentation.

Woods, Ralph L. 1982. *Dilemmas.* Baltimore, Md.: Avalon Hill Publishers. A game of over 150 unusual situations usable as case material.

Bibliography

Allen, H. B., and Campbell, R. N., eds. 1972. *Teaching English as a Second Language: A Book of Readings*. 2d ed. New York: McGraw-Hill.

Allen, V. G. 1983. *Techniques in Teaching Vocabulary*. Oxford: Oxford University Press.

Allwright, R. L. 1980. "Turns, Topics, and Tasks: Patterns of Participation in Language Learning and Teaching," in Larsen-Freeman, ed. (1980), pp. 165–87.

1984. "Why Don't Learners Learn What Teachers Teach? – The Interaction Hypothesis." In *Language Learning in Formal and Informal Contexts*, ed. D. M. Singleton and D. G. Little. Dublin: Irish Association of Applied Linguistics.

Applegate, J. L., and Delia, J. G. 1980. "Person-Centered Speech, Psychological Development, and the Context of Language Usage," in St. Clair and Giles, eds. (1980), pp. 245–82.

Ariew, R. 1984. "Computer-Assisted Foreign Language Materials: Advantages and Limitations." *CALICO Journal* 2: 43–7.

Asher, J. J. 1966. "The Learning Strategy of the Total Physical Response: A Review." *MLJ* 50: 79–84.

Berger, P. L., and Luckman, T. 1966. *The Social Construction of Reality*. Garden City, N.Y.: Doubleday.

Birckbichler, D. W. 1982. *Creative Activities for the Second Language Classroom*. Washington, D.C.: Center for Applied Linguistics.

Bolinger, D. L. 1983. "Intonation and Gesture." *American Speech* 58: 156–74.

Born, W. C., ed. 1979. *The Foreign Language Learner in Today's Classroom Environment*. Middlebury Vt.: NEC.

Bourdieu, P. 1982. *Ce que parler veut dire. L'Economie des échanges linguistiques*. Paris: Fayard.

Brandt, R. C., and Knapp, B. H. 1982. "Interactive Videodisc's Authoring Concepts," in De Bloois (1982), pp. 89–100.

Breen, M., and Candlin, C. N. 1980. "The Essentials of a Communicative Curriculum in Language Teaching." *AL* 1: 89–112.

Brown, G. 1977. *Listening to Spoken English*. London: Longman.

Brown, G., and Yule, G. 1983. *Teaching the Spoken Language*. Cambridge: Cambridge University Press.

Brown, P., and Levinson, S. 1978. "Universals in Language Usage: Politeness Phenomena," in Goody, ed. (1978), pp. 56–289.

Brophy, J. E., and Evertson, C. 1976. *Learning from Teaching: A Developmental Perspective*. Boston: Allyn and Bacon.

Brumfit, C. J., ed. 1983. *Applications of Video in Language Teaching*. Oxford: Pergamon Press.

211

Bibliography

Brumfit, C. J. 1984. *Communicative Methodology in Language Teaching: The Roles of Accuracy and Fluency*. Cambridge: Cambridge University Press.

Byrd, D. R. H., and Cabelas, I. C. 1980. *React Interact: Situations for Communication*. New York: Regents.

Canale, M., and Swain, M. 1980. "Theoretical Bases of Communicative Approaches to Second Language Teaching and Testing." *AL* 1, 1: 1–48.

Carrell, P. L. 1983. "Some Issues in Studying the Role of Schemata, or Background Knowledge, in Second Language Comprehension." *Reading in a Foreign Language* 1, 2: 81–92.

Carroll, J. M.; Tanenhaus, M. K.; and Bever, T. G. 1978. "The perception of relations: the interaction of structural, functional, and contextual factors in the segmentation of sentences." In *Studies in the Perception of Language*, ed. W. J. M. Levelt and G. B. Flores d'Arcais, pp. 187–218. New York: Wiley.

Chambers, J. A., and Sprecher, J. W. 1983. *Computer-Assisted Instruction*. Englewood Cliffs, N.J.: Prentice-Hall.

Chastain, K. 1976. *Developing Second-Language Skills: Theory to Practice*. 2d ed. Chicago: Rand McNally.

Cicourel, A. V. 1972. "Basic and Normative Rules in the Negotiation of Status and Role," in Sudnow, ed. (1972), pp. 229–58.

Clark, J. L. 1983. "Language Testing: Past and Current Status – Directions for the Future." *MLJ* 67: 431–43.

Clarke, M. A., and Handscombe, J., eds. 1983. *On TESOL '82: Pacific Perspectives on Language Learning and Teaching*. Washington, D.C.: TESOL.

Cohen, S. A. 1969. *Teach Them All to Read*. New York: Random House.

Curran, C. A. 1976. *Counseling-Learning in Second Languages*. Apple River, Ill.: Apple River Press.

Cziko, G. A. 1978. "Differences in First- and Second-Language Reading: The Use of Syntactic, Semantic and Discourse Constraints." *CMLR* 34: 472–89.

Davies, N. F. 1985. "Getting Started with Microcomputers – A Practical Beginner's Guide." *System* 13, 2: 119–32.

De Bloois, M., ed. 1982. *Videodisc/Microcomputer Courseware Design*. Englewood Cliffs, N.J.: Educational Technology Publications.

Di Pietro, R. J. 1982. "The Open-Ended Scenario: A New Approach to Conversation." *TQ* 16: 15–20.

Dixon, C. N., and Nessel, D. 1983. *Language Experience Approach to Reading (and Writing): LEA for ESL*. Hayward, Cal.: Alemany Press.

Duff, A. 1981. *The Third Language: Recurrent Problems of Translation into English*. Oxford: Pergamon Press.

Edmondson, W., and House, J. 1981. *Let's Talk and Talk About It: A Pedagogic Interactional Grammar of English*. Munich: Urban and Schwarzenberg.

Fanselow, J. F. 1977. "Beyond RASHOMON – Conceptualizing and Describing the Teaching Act." *TQ* 11: 17–39.

Fanselow, J. F., and Crymes, R. H., eds. 1976. *On TESOL '76*. Washington, D.C.: TESOL.

Fillmore, L. Wong. 1979. "Individual Differences in Second Language Acquisition." In *Individual Differences in Language Ability and Language Be-*

havior, ed. C. Fillmore, D. Templer, and W. Wang. New York: Academic Press.

Finocchiaro, M., and Brumfit, C. 1983. *The Functional-Notional Approach: From Theory to Practice.* New York: Oxford University Press.

Gaies, S. J. 1985. *Peer Involvement in Language Learning.* Language in Education: Theory and Practice No. 60. CAL/ERIC. Orlando, Fla.: Harcourt Brace Jovanovich.

Gallwey, W. T. 1974. *The Inner Game of Tennis.* New York: Random House.

Gareth, R. 1984. "Computers and Second Language Learning," in Terry, ed. (1984), pp. 147–56.

Gattegno, C. 1972. *Teaching Foreign Languages in Schools: The Silent Way.* New York: Educational Solutions.

Gaudiani, C. 1981. *Teaching Writing in the FL Curriculum.* Washington, D.C.: Center for Applied Linguistics.

Girard, C.; Huot, D.; and Lussier-Chasles, D. 1984. "L'Evaluation de la compétence de communication en classe de langue seconde." *ELA 56*: 77–87.

Goffman, E. 1959. *The Presentation of Self in Everyday Life.* Garden City, N.Y.: Doubleday.

1967. *Interaction Ritual: Essays on Face-to-Face Behavior.* Garden City, N.Y.: Doubleday.

Goody, E. N., ed. 1978. *Questions and Politeness: Strategies in Social Interaction.* Cambridge: Cambridge University Press.

Gragg, C. I. 1951. *Because Wisdom Can't Be Told.* Case No. 9-451-005. Boston: Harvard Business School.

Grellet, F. 1981. *Developing Reading Skills: A Practical Guide to Reading Comprehension Exercises.* Cambridge: Cambridge University Press.

Guiora, A. Z., and Acton, W. 1979. "Personality and Language Behavior." *LL* 29: 193–204.

Guiora, A. Z.; Beit-Hallahmi, B.; Brannon, R.; Dull, C.; and Scovel, T. 1972. "The Effects of Experimentally Induced Changes in Ego States on Pronunciation Ability in a Second Language: An Exploratory Study." *Comprehensive Psychiatry* 13: 421–28.

Guiora, A. Z.; Brannon, R.; and Dull, C. 1972. "Empathy and Second Language Learning." *LL* 22: 111–31.

Gumperz, J.; Jupp, I.; and Robert, E. 1979. *Crosstalk: A Study of Crosscultural Communication.* Long, England: National Centre for Industrial Language Training.

Hakuta, K. 1986. *Mirror of Language: The Debate on Bilingualism.* New York: Basic Books.

Hall, E. T. 1959. *The Silent Language.* Garden City, N.Y.: Doubleday.

1966. *The Hidden Dimension.* Garden City, N.Y.: Doubleday/Anchor Books.

1976. *Beyond Culture.* New York: Anchor Press.

Hapgood, E. R., ed. and trans. 1963. *An Actor's Handbook: Alphabetical Arrangement of Concise Statements of Aspects of Acting by Constantin Stanislavski.* New York: Theatre Arts Books.

Harper, D. O., and Stewart, J. H., eds. 1983. *RUN: Computer Education.* California: Brooks/Cole.

Hartley, J. R. 1984. "An Appraisal of Computer-Assisted Learning in the United Kingdom," in Rushby, ed. (1984), pp. 30–43.

Harvard Business School. 1984. *Directory of Course Material*. Boston: Harvard Business School Case Services.

Higgins, J., and Johns, T. 1984. *Computers in Language Learning*. Reading, Mass.: Addison-Wesley.

Holmes, G. 1984. "Of Computers and Other Technologies," in Jarvis, ed. (1984), pp. 93–106.

Hosenfeld, C. 1979. "Cindy: A Learner in Today's Foreign Language Classroom," in Born, ed. (1979), pp. 53–75.

Illich, I. 1973. *Tools for Conviviality*. New York: Harper and Row.

Jarvis, G. A., ed. 1984. *The Challenge for Excellence in Foreign-Language Education*. Middlebury, Vt.:NEC.

Jones, K. 1982. *Simulations in Language Learning*. Cambridge: Cambridge University Press.

Kasper, Gabriele. 1979. "Errors in Speech Act Realization and Use of Gambits." *CMLR* 35: 395–406.

Keller, E., and Warner, S. Taba. 1979. *Gambits 1: Openers; Gambits 2: Links; Gambits 3: Responders, Closers and Inventory*. Hull, P.Q., Canada: Public Service Commission of Canada.

Kramsch, C. J. 1981a. *Discourse Analysis and Second Language Teaching*. Language in Education, Vol. 37. Washington, D.C.: Center for Applied Linguistics.

1981b. "Teaching Discussion Skills: A Pragmatic Approach." *FLA* 14: 93–104.

1983. "Interaction in the Classroom: Learning How to Negotiate Roles and Meaning." *Unterrichtspraxis* 2: 175–90.

1984. *Interaction et discours dans la classe de langue*. Paris: Hatier-CREDIF.

Krashen, S. D. 1981. *Second Language Acquisition and Second Language Learning*. Oxford: Pergamon Press.

Krashen, S. D., and Terrell, T. D. 1983. *The Natural Approach: Language Acquisition in the Classroom*. Oxford: Pergamon Press; and Hayward, Cal.: Alemany Press.

Larsen-Freeman, D., ed. 1980. *Discourse Analysis in Second Language Research*. Rowley, Mass.: Newbury House.

Laver, J., and Hutcheson, S., eds. 1972. *Communication in Face to Face Interaction*. Harmondsworth, Middlesex: Penguin.

Lee, W. R. 1979. *Language Teaching Games and Contests*. Oxford: Oxford University Press.

Lewis R. 1958. *Method or Madness*. New York: Samuel French.

Lonergan, J. 1984. *Video in Language Teaching: A Practical Handbook for Teachers*. Cambridge: Cambridge University Press.

Long, M. H.; Adams, L.; McLean, M.; and Castanos, F. 1976. "Doing Things with Words – Verbal Interaction in Lockstep and Small Group Classroom Situations," in Fanselow and Crymes, eds. (1976), pp. 137–53.

Lozanov, G. 1978. *Suggestology and Outlines of Suggestopedy*. New York: Gordon and Breach.

Maley, A., and Duff, A. 1982. *Drama Techniques in Language Learning.* 2d ed. Cambridge: Cambridge University Press.

Mehan, H. 1979. *Learning Lessons: Social Organization in the Classroom.* Cambridge: Cambridge University Press.

Meléndez, G. S. 1980. "Interactive Instruction in Spanish Interfacing the Microcomputer and the Videodisc." *MICRO* 1: 11–12.

Molinsky, S. J., and Bliss, B. 1983. *Side by Side: English Grammar Through Guided Conversations.* Englewood Cliffs, N.J.: Prentice-Hall.

Moore, S. 1960. *The Stanislavski System.* New York: Penguin.

Morris, D.; Collett, P.; Marsh, P.; and O'Shaughnessy, M. 1979. *Gestures.* New York: Stein and Day.

Moskowitz, G. 1978. *Caring and Sharing in the Foreign Language Class.* Rowley, Mass.: Newbury House.

Olsen, S., ed. 1985. *CAI and the Humanities.* New York: Modern Language Association.

Omaggio, A. C. 1981. "Priorities in Classroom Testing for the 1980's," in D. L. Lange, ed., *Proceedings of the National Conference on Professional Priorities, November 1980, Boston, Massachusetts,* pp. 47–53. Hastings-on-Hudson, New York: ACTFL Materials Center.

1983. "Methodology in Transition: The New Focus on Proficiency." *MLJ* 67: 330–41.

1986. *Teaching Language in Context: Proficiency-Oriented Instruction.* Boston, Mass.: Heinle and Heinle.

Paulston, C. B. 1970. "Structural Pattern Drills: A Classification." *FLA* 4: 187–93.

Phillips, J. K. 1984. "Practical Implications of Recent Research in Reading." *FLA* 17: 285–96.

Pifer, G., and Mutoh, N. W. 1977. *Points of View.* Rowley, Mass.: Newbury House.

Piotrowski, M. W. 1982. "Business as Usual: Using the Case Method to Teach ESL to Executives." *TQ* 16: 229–239.

Porter, P. 1983. "How Learners Talk to Each Other: Input and Interaction in Task-Centered Discussions." Unpublished paper presented at TESOL 1983 in Toronto, Canada.

Raimes, A. 1983. *Techniques in Teaching Writing.* New York: Oxford University Press.

Ramírez, A. G., ed. 1985. *Teaching Languages in College: Communicative Proficiency and Cross-cultural Issues.* Albany: Center for Languages, Literacy and Cultures Education, School of Education, State University of New York at Albany.

Richards, J. C. 1983. "Listening Comprehension: Approach, Design, Procedure." *TQ* 17: 219–40.

1985. *The Context of Language Teaching.* Cambridge: Cambridge University Press.

Richards, J. C., and Rodgers, T. S. 1986. *Approaches and Methods in Language Teaching: A Description and Analysis.* New York: Cambridge University Press.

Bibliography

Richards, J. C., and Sukwiwat, M. 1985. "Cross-cultural Aspects of Conversational Competence," in Richards (1985), pp. 129–43.

Rivers, Wilga M. 1981. *Teaching Foreign-Language Skills.* 2d ed. Chicago: University of Chicago Press.

   1983a. *Communicating Naturally in a Second Language: Theory and Practice in Language Teaching.* New York: Cambridge University Press.

   1983b. *Speaking in Many Tongues: Essays in Foreign-Language Teaching.* 3d ed. New York: Cambridge University Press.

   1988. *A Practical Guide to the Teaching of French.* 2d ed. Lincolnwood, Ill.: National Textbook.

Rivers, W. M.; Azevedo, M.; and Heflin, W. H., Jr. 1988. *A Practical Guide to the Teaching of Spanish.* 2d ed. Lincolnwood, Ill.: National Textbook.

Rivers, W. M.; Dell'Orto, K.; and Dell'Orto, V. 1988. *A Practical Guide to the Teaching of German.* 2d ed. Lincolnwood, Ill.: National Textbook.

Rivers, W. M., and Nahir, M. In press. *A Practical Guide to the Teaching of Hebrew.* Tel Aviv: University Publishing Projects.

Rivers, W. M., and Temperley, M. S. 1978. *A Practical Guide to the Teaching of English as a Second or Foreign Language.* New York: Oxford University Press.

Robinson, G. L. N. 1978. "The Magic-Carpet-Ride-to-Another-Culture Syndrome: An International Perspective." *FLA* 11: 135–46.

   1981. *Issues in Second Language and Crosscultural Education: The Forest Through the Trees.* Boston: Heinle and Heinle.

   1985: *Crosscultural Understanding: Processes and Approaches for FL, ESL, and Bilingual Educators.* Oxford: Pergamon Press.

Robinson, G. L. N.; Underwood, J.; Rivers, W. M.; Hernandez, J.; Rudesill, C.; and Ensenat, C. 1985. *Computer-Assisted-Instruction in Foreign Language Education: A Comparison of the Effectiveness of Different Methodologies and Different Forms of Error Correction.* Final Report. Washington, D.C.: U.S. Dept. of Education, International Research and Studies Division.

Rooks, G. 1981. *The Nonstop Discussion Workbook: Problems for Intermediate and Advanced Students.* Rowley, Mass.: Newbury House.

Rushby, N., ed. 1984. *Selected Readings in Computer-Based Learning.* New York: Nichols Publishing Co.

Russo, G. M. 1983. *Expanding Communication: Teaching Modern Languages at the College Level.* New York: Harcourt Brace Jovanovich.

Sadow, S. A. 1982. *Idea Bank: Creative Activities for the Language Class.* Rowley, Mass.: Newbury House.

St. Clair, R. N., and Giles, H., eds. 1980. *The Social and Psychological Contexts of Language.* Hillsdale, N. J.: Lawrence Erlbaum Associates.

Savignon, S. J. 1972. *Communicative Competence in Foreign Language Teaching.* Philadelphia: Center for Curriculum Development.

   1983. *Communicative Competence: Theory and Classroom Practice. Texts and Contexts in Second Language Learning.* Reading, Mass.: Addison-Wesley.

Scarcella, R. C. 1978. "Socio-drama for Social Interaction." *TQ* 12: 41–6.

Schlesinger, I. M. 1977. *Production and Comprehension of Utterances.* Hillsdale, N.J.: Lawrence Erlbaum Associates.

Schneider, E. W., and Bennion, J. 1981. *Videodiscs.* Englewood Cliffs, N.J.: Educational Technology Publications.

Schneider, E. W., and Bennion, J. 1983. "Veni, Vidi, Vici Via Videodisc: A Simulation for Instructional Conversations." *System* 11: 44–6.

Schulz, R. A. 1977. "Discrete-Point Versus Simulated Communication Testing in Foreign Languages." *MLJ* 61: 94–101.

Selinker, L. 1972. "Interlanguage." *IRAL* 10: 219–31.

Sevareid, E. 1983. *Enterprise.* New York: McGraw-Hill.

Smith, F. 1971. *Understanding Reading: A Psycholinguistic Analysis of Reading and Learning to Read.* New York: Holt, Rinehart and Winston.

Smith, L. 1983. "The Five Senses of Teaching/Learning English as an International Language." *Pasaa Journal* (June). Bangkok: Chulalongkorn University Language Institute.

Smith, S. M. 1984. *The Theater Arts and the Teaching of Second Languages.* Reading, Mass.: Addison-Wesley.

Spencer, D. D. 1979. *Computer Dictionary for Everyone.* New York: Scribner's.

Spolin, V. 1963. *Improvisation for the Theatre.* Evanston, Ill.: Northwestern University Press.

Stern, H. H. 1983. *Fundamental Concepts of Language Teaching.* Oxford: Oxford University Press.

Stevick, E. W. 1982. *Teaching and Learning Languages.* New York: Cambridge University Press.

1986. *Images and Options in the Language Classroom.* New York: Cambridge University Press.

Straight, H. S. 1985. "Communicative Proficiency Through Comprehension," in Ramírez, ed. (1985), pp. 19–43.

Sudnow, D., ed. 1972. *Studies in Social Interaction.* New York: Free Press.

Terry, C., ed. 1984. *Using Micro-computers in Schools.* New York: Nichols Publishing Co.

Treichler, P., and Kramarae, C. 1983. "Women's Talk in the Ivory Tower." *Communication Quarterly* 31, 2: 118–132.

Trevarthen, C. 1974. "Conversations with a Two-Month-Old." *New Scientist* (May 2): 230–5.

Ur, P. 1981. *Discussions that Work: Task-Centred Fluency Practice.* Cambridge: Cambridge University Press.

1984. *Teaching Listening Comprehension.* Cambridge: Cambridge University Press.

Utz, P. 1982. *The Video User's Handbook.* 2d ed. Englewood Cliffs, N.J.: Prentice-Hall.

Valdes, J. M., ed. 1986. *Culture Bound: Bridging the Cultural Gap in Language Teaching.* New York: Cambridge University Press.

Valdman, A., and Moody, M. 1979. "Testing Communicative Ability." *FR* 52: 553–61.

Via, R. A. 1976. *English in Three Acts.* Honolulu: University Press of Hawaii.

Vygotsky, L. S. 1978. *Mind in Society: The Development of Higher Psychological Processes.* Cambridge, Mass.: Harvard University Press.

Bibliography

Wells, G., et al. 1981. *Learning Through Interaction: The Study of Language Development*. Cambridge: Cambridge University Press.
Wessels, M. G. 1983. *Cognitive Psychology*. New York: Harper and Row.
West, M. 1960. *Teaching English in Difficult Circumstances*. London: Longman.
Widdowson, H. G. 1983. "Competence and Capacity in Language Learning," in Clarke and Handscombe, eds. (1983), pp. 97–106.
Woods, R. L. 1982. *Dilemmas*. Baltimore, Md.: Avalon Hill Publishers.
Wright, A.; Betteridge, D.; and Buckby, M. 1984. *Games for Language Learning*. 2d ed. Cambridge: Cambridge University Press.
Wyatt, D. H. 1983. "Computer-Assisted Language Instruction: Present State and Future Prospects." *System* 11: 3–11.
Wylie, L. 1985. "Language Learning and Communication." *FR* 6: 777–85.

Index

accuracy, *see* errors, correction of
ACTFL proficiency guidelines, 126, 126 n5
Acton, W., 12
advanced level
  creative activities at, 41–3
  materials for, 47–8, 50, 54–6, 68
  problem solving at, 36
  in reading, 39, 76–7, 78, 82
  speaking at, 209–10
  testing at, 129–30, 132, 135
  in writing, 84
advertisements, 36, 46, 47, 134
affective element, *xiv*, 9–10, 12–13, 42, 43, 58, 110–12, 122
  anxiety as, 25, 53
  in testing, 128, 131, 132
  see also face-saving; humanistic approach; social distance
Allwright, R.L., 18, 19, 29
ambiguity, in case study method, 207
anxiety, *see* affective element, anxiety as
Applegate, J.L., 18
approach, *xii–xiii*, 5–6, 16
  see also Natural Approach
audio- and videotapes, 10–11, 46, 49, 51–2, 160, 162, 166
  for business case studies, 205–6
  in the classroom, 168
  computer with, 166–7, 186
  equipment for, 162–4, 169
  interviews on, 46, 48–9
  sources for, 164, 168
  student-created, 160–1
  in testing, 129–31, 133, 135
  training films on, 175
  videotape recorders for (VTRs), 155

see also satellite reception; video-discs and audiodiscs
audiolingualism, *xii–xiii*
auditory discrimination, 148
authentic materials, *xii*, 10, 44, 107, 109, 129
  with audio and video, 51–2
  in the classroom, 46–9, 50–1
  collection of, 49–50, 170–1, 175
  for comprehension, 52–4
  for culture, 45–6
  on film, 160
  poetry as, 107
  for speaking, 54
  from television, 166
  see also interviews

Bacon, P.A., 100
Barkman, B., 82
beginning classes, *see* elementary level
Bell, M., 102
Benigni, C., 61
Bennion, J. 186
Berger, P.L., 17
Betteridge, D., 69
Bever, T.G., 7
bilingualism, 15
  see also multicultural classes
Birckbichler, D.W., 43
Bliss, B., 63
Bolinger, D.L., 12
Bork, A., 190
Bourdieu, P., 19
brain, 5
Brandt, R.C., 187
Brannon, R., 12
Breen, M., 18, 29
Brown, G., 19, 25, 29, 93, 94, 109
Brown, P., 19
Brumfit, C.J., 24, 29

House, J., 21
humanistic approach, *xiii*, 35, 43, 113
  see also self-concept
Humboldt, W. von, 8
Huot, D., 131, 136
Hutcheson, S., 142
hypothesis-testing, 24
  in reading, 73

Illich, I., 18, 28
imagination and creativity in language learning, 14–15, 33–42, 62–3, 66–8, 87, 91, 105, 114
  see also creative use of language
individualization of learning, *see* computer-assisted language learning (CALL), individualization by
inductive learning, 8, 195
inference, 7, 8–9, 26, 81
  in reading, 72–3, 76
information gap, 22
interaction, *xiii–xiv*, 4–5, 9, 17, 29–30, 54, 209
  activities for, 10–16, 25–8, 33–43, 48, 147–53
  by computer, 188
  continuum of, 17–18
  diversity in, 141, 154
  exercises as, 57
  forms of, 24
  inside classroom, 17, 19–20, 23
  instructor-to-student, 65–8, 95
  language in, 94
  outside classroom, 171
  process of, 18–19
  strategies for multicultural, 146–53
  student-to-student, 58–68, 95
  style of, 18, 28
  with text, 52–3, 70–82, 81
  in writing, 91
  see also communication; computer-assisted language learning (CALL); discourse; interactive activities
interactive activities, 194, 208–10

in case study course, 195
in the community, 174
on computer, 181, 182–3
in reading, 73–4, 77–80, 180
with poems, 94–8
videotaped, 161, 180
  see also community, use of; testing, interactive; simulations
interference, 131
interlanguage, *xii* n4
intermediate level, 36, 39–40, 43–4
  in reading, 78
  speaking at, 209–10
  testing at, 130, 135
interviews, 48, 58, 64, 89–90, 96, 151, 160–1, 170
  as tests, 133
  see also audio- and videotapes, interviews on
intonation, *see* pronunciation

jazz chants, 102–3
Johns, T., 185, 187, 190
Jones, K., 41, 43
Jordan, R.R., 82

Kasper, G., 17
Keller, E., 43, 209
Knapp, B.H., 187
Kramarae, C., 20
Kramsch, C.J., 24, 30, 43, 187 n3
Krashen, S.D., 4 n2, 6, 145

Lamoureux, N.J., 63
Larsen-Freeman, D., 29
language experience approach, 92
language learning laboratory, 52, 111
  disadvantages of, 178
  see also testing, in language laboratory
Laver, J., 142
Lee, W.R., 68
level of language, 7
  in reading, 74
Levinson, S., 19
listening, *xii–xiv*, 29, 46, 109, 147–9, 151, 168–9